GOOD ROCKIN' TONIGHT

GOOD ROCKIN' TONIGHT

Sun Records and the Birth of Rock 'n' Roll

Colin Escott

with

Martin Hawkins

St. Martin's Press

New York

The Sun Records logo is a registered trademark of
Sun Entertainment Corporation, 3106 Belmont
Blvd., Nashville, Tennessee 37212.

For information on photographs and other visual
material, address Showtime Archive, 191 Concord
Ave., Toronto, Ont., Canada M6H 2P2.

Design by Richard Oriolo

Library of Congress Cataloging-in-Publication Data

Escott, Colin.
    Good rockin' tonight : Sun Records and the
birth of rock 'n' roll / Colin Escott with Martin
Hawkins ; foreword by Peter Guralnick.
        p.   cm.
    Includes index.
    ISBN 0-312-05439-4
    1. Sun Records—History. 2. Rock music
—United States—To 1969—History and criti-
cism. I. Hawkins, Martins.   II. Title.
ML424.S85E83   1991
781.66'0973—dc20   90-48351
                                               CIP

First Edition: April 1991

10 9 8 7 6 5 4 3 2 1

Contents

Sam Phillips
at the console

Foreword

by Peter Guralnick

If **t h e** story of Sun Records were merely the story of the discovery, and emergence, of a single performer, Elvis Presley, it would be astonishing enough. But it is not. The story of Sun Records, as it is presented in this book, is a tale of almost epic dimension virtually unparalleled within the context of American popular culture. It delineates the roots of a revolution in popular taste, sketches in uniquely idiosyncratic figures like Charlie Rich, Jerry Lee Lewis, B. B. King, and Howlin' Wolf, and, in Sam Phillips, suggests a combination of visionary hero and mythic prophet who lived to see his vision realized. And it all happened in Memphis.

The book is clearly a labor of love—and then some. Colin Escott and Martin Hawkins have been collaborating on *Good Rockin' Tonight* and a score of associated book and record projects for over fifteen years now, and while I have no doubt that the present edition will prove to be definitive, Colin and Martin would be the first to admit that it will by no means be the end of the story. Their seemingly indefatigable research has turned up more detail than even the original participants could have imagined and has fleshed out a world that, for those of us who were merely fans of the music, was at one time little more than an exotic dream. At the same time their work has sent us back to the music.

It is a music of almost unparalleled richness and diversity. Sam Phillips, in scarcely a decade of full-scale involvement in the record business—and for most of that decade functioning largely as a one-man operation—created a legacy comparable to no other, really, provided the stylistic bedrock not just for rock 'n' roll but for much of modern blues as well. And, as Escott and Hawkins make plain, it was no accident of spontaneous generation but, rather, the culmination of a social and historical vision.

Elvis Presley, as Memphis legend and Nashville producer Jack Clement has frequently said, was a star—but Sam Phillips was a superstar. Nearly everyone who has dealt with Phillips at one time or another, in his varied career in radio and record-making, would probably agree. Escott and Hawkins document not just Sun's beginnings but Sam's; they underscore that the Sun label was as much a statement of social philosophy, a declaration of independence and freedom, as it was a commercial enterprise. For seldom in the history of the so-called "record business" has greater faith in the possibilities of the human spirit been expressed. It was Sam Phillips' mission to free whatever creative spark might exist within each individual who stepped in front of the microphone of his tiny studio at 706 Union Avenue; it was his mission to find the unlocking key, "to open up an area of freedom within the artist himself." And while in some recent stabs at revisionist history I have noticed a tendency to quantify this achievement (Jerry Lee Lewis had only so many Top 10 singles; Carl Perkins was a "one-hit artist"), nothing could be further from the greater truth. Just listen to the music. Read this book.

The music that Sam Phillips recorded reflected, as he has so frequently said, a kind of spirituality. The motivation behind the music was self-expression, that and an implicit belief in both the richness of the African-American tradition and the possibilities of cultural integration. Sometimes the process worked, and sometimes it didn't, but the aim was constant and the music, no matter how varied it may have been in its particulars, was all part of a broad continuum, a self-styled heritage of American individuation. People have often quoted with some disbelief Sam Phillips' statement that he never regretted selling Elvis Presley's contract to RCA, but if you read this book you will understand why it is true, not only from a business but from a philosophical point of view.

As Phillips said of the music of the Howlin' Wolf, the bluesman whom he regards as the single greatest performer he ever recorded, "When I heard him, I said, 'This is for me. This is where the soul of man never dies.' " This is what Sun Records was about. As Escott and Hawkins write of the prodigious scope of Jerry Lee Lewis's musical achievement, "The simple truth is that Lewis could never have made those recordings for a major label. Phillips' willingness to keep the tape running while Lewis plundered his memory was crucial to Jerry's development as an artist and performer. . . . Phillips knew his artist. 'The conditions had to be right. You had to have a good song, of course, but atmosphere is nearly everything else.' " It was atmosphere, and atmosphere alone, that characterized the Sun studio. And it was in the Sun studio that rock 'n' roll was born.

Good Rockin' Tonight tells the story in sometimes astonishing detail, but with a clarity of vision and no-nonsense manner that makes every detail count and frequently leaves you wanting more. The text is filled with descriptive insights bred of nearly two decades' immersion in the subject. *Good Rockin' Tonight* could be regarded as an ever-evolving source book, I suppose, one in which Colin Escott and Martin Hawkins, and numerous acknowledged colleagues, generously share their research and observations and invite the rest of us to participate. It's an open invitation—you need no special qualifications to join. All you have to do is to set aside preconceptions, forget about categories of fashion and taste, and put a Sun record on the turntable. Then you, too, will become part of the Sun legacy.

technology. I would also like to thank Hank Davis, who contributed a portion of the research and scrutinized some early drafts. Additionally, thanks are due to Roland Janes, who worked almost daily in the Sun studio during the golden era, and was among the least egocentric people to walk through its doors. His recollections have been especially insightful, balanced, and detailed.

Writing about Sun Records has become something of a growth industry recently, and we have drawn upon some of what we have read to supplement and cross-check our own work. Virtually all of those who recorded at Sun (with the notable exception of Elvis Presley) have contributed their reflections to us or to others, and we would like to thank those whose work we have used and all others who contributed their time, opinions, and research.

Finally, I'd like to offer a special acknowledgement to our editor, Cal Morgan, who brought the sensibilities of a fan to his job and persuaded St. Martin's Press that they needed this book, and to Peter Guralnick, who took time out from his mammoth work in progress to write the Foreword.

As always, apologies to anyone we missed.

COLIN ESCOTT
April 1990
Showtime Music, Toronto

*B*eale Street
in the 1950s.
At center is Lansky
Bros. Mens Shop,
"Just Around the Corner
From High Prices"

Chapter One

"THAT MUDDY OLD RIVER..."

"**It was** back in 1939. I was 16 years old, and I went to Memphis with some friends in a big old Dodge. We drove down Beale Street in the middle of the night and it was *rockin'!* The street was *busy*. It was so active —musically, socially. God, I loved it!"

That was Samuel Cornelius Phillips' first experience of Memphis. He was a country boy from the northwest corner of Alabama, where the state borders Mississippi and Tennessee. A half-century later, Sam Phillips is an uncontested legend in his adopted hometown. He came to the city where there was, as he put it, "a meeting of musics," and in a tiny storefront studio he recorded music that would change the face of popular culture. He also ensured that not even the most cursory history of American popular music could be written without reference to Memphis or Sam C. Phillips.

Phillips is responsible for two of the most enduring images in American iconography: Elvis Presley, barely twenty-one years old, shaking his butt and singing the blues on network television, and Jerry Lee Lewis staring at those same cameras with wild-eyed fury, kicking his piano stool back behind him across the soundstage. Together those images defined a revolution.

It wasn't just that these were white kids singing black music; after all, that had been done before. The white folk group the Weavers, for example, had sung the black folk song "Goodnight Irene" on television a few years before. But when Elvis Presley and Jerry Lee Lewis performed on the same shows, they did more than borrow the form of black music: they borrowed its fervor. What they were offering was not a blatant copy—something new had been forged, and Sam Phillips was responsible.

Phillips was not the first person to open a studio in Memphis. He was not the first to start a record label there, nor the first to experiment with white kids singing what was essentially the blues. In fact, much of what Phillips did others had done before, but he did it with a consistent artistic conception of the way music should sound. He recognized the primacy of the blues and looked for the raw blues feel in virtually all of the artists he recorded.

Phillips also sensed that he was in the right place at the right time, and he had the tenacity to hold fast through six largely desolate years to see his vision pay off.

The notion that a record label of national importance could emerge from Memphis would have been—in fact, was—laughed at in 1950. Even Nashville was seen only as a convenient recording outpost for the major labels, which were located in either New York or Los Angeles. Memphis may have been associated with the blues in much the same romantic way that New Orleans was associated with jazz, but it was tantamount to lunacy to suggest that a record label with national aspirations should base itself there. It was even more unlikely that such a company could hope to achieve national success by recording a strange hybrid music that flouted all conventional barriers.

In beginning the story of Sun Records, it is worth looking at the musical and cultural scene in Memphis when Sam Phillips hung his neon "Memphis Recording Service" sign in the window and announced to the few who cared that he was open for business.

The Talking Machine Comes to Memphis

There is an old adage that Nashville is the capital of Tennessee and Memphis is the capital of Mississippi. Geographically isolated from most of the state, Memphis has always looked south toward the Delta, rather than east toward Nashville, for the commerce that sustained it.

As in life, so in music. By the mid-1920s record companies had started to bring portable recording equipment into the South, usually setting up shop in a hotel, staying for a few days, then moving on. When Ralph Peer, representing the Victor Talking Machine Company, set up makeshift studios in Tennessee in 1927, he captured entirely different musical traditions at the two extremes of the state. In the far northwest corner, the city of Bristol yielded Appalachian folk ballads grounded in the Anglo-Celtic traditions. In Memphis,

Early morning on
Beale Street,
c. 1930

(Hooks Bros./Escott)

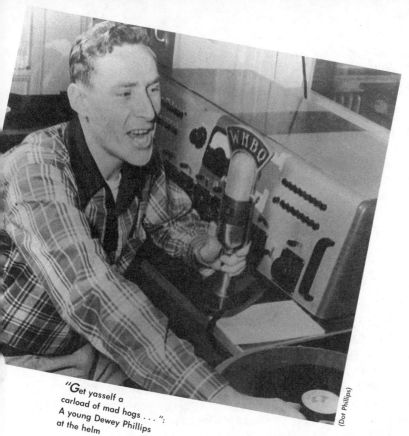

"*Get* yasself a carload of mad hogs . . .": A young Dewey Phillips at the helm

(Dot Phillips)

(Dot Phillips)

Rock 'n' Roll Dewey, mid-'50s

The year 1948 also marked the radio debut of Dewey Phillips, whose radio style virtually defied categorization. He was a white disc jockey from rural Tennessee who hosted a show called "Red Hot and Blue" on WHBQ. Randy Haspel, who would later record for Sun as part of Randy and the Radiants, has written a luminous description of Dewey hosting his show: "His style was pure country. He was an irreverent squawker with a stream of consciousness speed rap that never quit—even while the record was playing. From the midst of trained, deep and resonant voices that filled the airwaves, came this countrified rapid fire drawl with an indefinable vocabulary."

During its first year on the air, the show was expanded from fifteen minutes to three hours daily. Dewey programmed an eclectic mix of blues, hillbilly, and pop that would become an institution in Memphis, and his importance to the cross-cultural miscegenation that became rock 'n' roll is incalculable. Among the few who followed in his immediate wake was Sam Phillips, who soon began programming a comparably freewheeling show on WREC on Saturday afternoons. Sam and Dewey Phillips weren't related by blood ties, but it's not going too far to say they shared a relationship that ran much deeper.

Just as the formation of BMI had increased the number of stations programming black music, those stations, and the DJs like Dewey Phillips who manned them, were vital to the exposure and promotion of new records. In fact, the proliferation of black radio was a major factor in the astonishing growth of the number of independent record companies aiming their product at the R&B market in the postwar years.

The Age of the Indie

A shortage of shellac, a key component in the manufacture of 78-rpm records, contributed to the slumping fortunes of the record business through the war years. The problems were exacerbated by a recording ban called by the American Federation of Musicians (AFM) in 1942. After the war, however, with the shellac shortage easing, the economy booming, and the music industry's grudging acceptance of the AFM's new recording rates, the record business grew in quantum leaps.

The major record labels (Decca, Capitol, Victor, and Columbia) concentrated on the most lucrative sector of the market: pop music. Pop accounted for over 50 percent of the market and was firmly controlled by the majors. The small independent labels, known as "indies," sensibly decided to look elsewhere. "Some indies," reported *Billboard* in April 1946, "frankly admit they are going to stay out of fields in which the majors push heavily and concentrate on items where the majors do more or less of a token job."

It was in the field of black music, then dubbed "sepia" or "race" music, that the majors fell conspicuously short. Their A&R (artists and repertoire) men didn't understand the music, and their salesmen didn't know how to promote or sell it. The result was a market share reported to be less than 5 percent of the total pie. It was hardly surprising that the indies would gravitate toward such an open market. The prospect of recording the music was made even more attractive because the sessions were cheap to produce. The groups were comparatively small, and the AFM's presence was marginal at best. "The major labels used to laugh at [the indies]," recalled Sam Phillips in 1981. "Atlantic, Aladdin, Sun, Dot. They figured these damn people would go away—and what percentage of the market are they gonna get anyway? One or two percent? So while their eyes were closed to us who were hungry and knew what we were doing, and weren't shackled by corporate routine, we grew beyond what they expected."

Although most country music and blues emanated from the South, very few labels of appreciable size were headquartered there. Nashville spawned the Bullet label in 1945, which had one of the biggest hits of 1947 with Francis Craig's "Near You," but that was the only hit the label ever saw. Virtually every southern city had a small record company, but none made a steady national impact until Randy Wood founded Dot in Gallatin, Tennessee, in 1950. Like Wood, Phillips never envisioned his label servicing just the local market. He was convinced that he could buck the odds and launch a national label from a storefront in Memphis.

The Memphis Scene

The Memphis music scene, such as it was, was a mixed bag of different, sometimes opposing, forces. The successful country artists based in Memphis, such as Eddie Hill, the Delmore Brothers, and the Louvin Brothers, were snapped up by out-of-town record companies. Those artists and countless others worked daily on local radio and nightly at the honky-tonks, most of which were outside the city limits. News of their activities rarely if ever reached the newspapers.

The focus of activity for polite society was the Skyway ballroom at the Peabody Hotel. The cream of the touring big bands played at the Skyway, and their music was fed nightly into the CBS network via WREC. Sam Phillips was one of the technical staff working the Skyway. His first job was as a "spotter," staying on the phone, relaying information to the engineer at WREC's control room, telling him which musician was about to take a solo and into which microphone he was going to play.

The opulence of the Skyway and the accommodations provided for band members at the Peabody contrasted starkly with the touring conditions for black bands. Under the alliterative headline "Bible Belt Heads Back to Banjo Bands and Blackfaces: Beat Bandsmen with Bats," *Billboard* in November 1946 described the facilities for black bands in the mid-South: "As a rule, Southern club operators are hostile toward labor and are kept in their best cooperative spirits when the word 'Union' is not spoken aloud in their presence. They regard the AFM as a force of banditry. Negro bands often have to choose between vermin-infested hotels or the band bus. All of this in addition to filthy cafés, poor or no valet service, long jumps on tar-graveled roads, crippled pianos and buzzing PA systems make the South the least attractive hinterland to musicians."

Juke joint in Memphis, early '50s

(E. C. Withers/Escott)

downbeat magazine conducted a random survey in May 1947 and found that most renowned black bands chose to ignore the South. With hipper-than-thou obliqueness, Nat "King" Cole told the magazine, "I try my best to keep my kicks along Route 66—and there's no place I know of where that route dips down south."

Conditions in Memphis were a little better than in the Deep South, and the city drew some top black bands to play the regular Midnight Rambles at the black night spots, accommodating them in comparative luxury at the Mitchell Hotel. Local black artists had steady work as supporting acts in the clubs, at black baseball parks, on the radio, and at juke joints, but the dearth of local recording companies ensured that few got onto disc. The truth was that the South, which had given birth to rhythm and blues, was regarded as a pest hole by those who played it for a living.

It is also true that the cultural cross-pollination Sam Phillips has often pointed out undoubtedly took place. White kids listened to R&B and blacks listened to country music long before rock 'n' roll; but the mixing of the musics took place in a social climate that was rigidly segregated.

Record producer Jim Dickinson (who later worked at Sun as part of the Jesters) is one of many who believes that segregation was one of the factors that gave a distinct edge to Memphis music. "I started noticing as a producer," he asserts, "that Spooner Oldham, the keyboard player, played drastically differently in different places. His best playing was done in Memphis. I wondered if the same was true of me, so I got out my own tapes, and by God it's true. I may not play better in Memphis, but I certainly play differently, and if I stay away too long I start to play funny. Memphis music is about racial collision

DOWN BEAT

Memphis Gestapo Smashes Records Eyes Radio-Flicks

downbeat,
February 25, 1948

(Showtime Archive)

in both directions. The rednecks who are playing blues still feel funny about it because they're playing black music."

Later, after rock 'n' roll exploded, black and white kids from coast to coast and overseas began playing "southern" music, but they were drawing on a culture that they had only experienced vicariously, and the result was that they tried too hard to emulate it. They were *too* frantic. In fact, singers like Elvis Presley, Carl Perkins, and Jerry Lee Lewis rarely rasped and screamed the way their many imitators usually did. In general, those from outside the southern culture built a style around exaggerations of southern music, and missed the lonesome hillbilly and blues feel that was its core. In the quest for abandon, they also failed to understand that southern music is lazy music—at any tempo.

As bandleader and producer Willie Mitchell has observed, "Jazz players here could play really fast, but they still played behind the beat just a little bit. That lazy quality is something the jazz and R&B players in Memphis have always had in common. Even the Bill Black Combo and Otis Redding, they'd be playing behind the tempo just a little bit, and all of a sudden everyone would start to sway. Even the lazy horns. They'd be half a beat behind, so it sounded like they were going to miss it altogether, and they'd sway like that and be right up on the beat. I could hear that quality in Memphis blues when I was coming up and could hear it right through into Al Green."

It was into this climate that Sam Phillips came from Florence, Alabama, via Nashville.

Memphis, 150 Miles

Sam Phillips was born on January 5, 1923, the youngest of eight children. He was raised on a three-hundred-acre tenant farm on the Tennessee River, just outside Florence, Alabama. At first, Philips grew up in comparative comfort. "Then came the Crash of 1929. One day my father had money. The next thing he knew, it was gone. A few hundred dollars left maybe. All gone. That kind of thing could break you, but my father had courage and determination and refused to give up."

Phillips cites his father as his first inspiration and credits him for much of his inner strength. "I was often a sick child. Other kids around me were rough and self-sufficient, and I learned from what I saw that you have to believe in yourself and what you can do."

In 1941 Phillips was forced to leave high school to help make ends meet at home. His father had died just after Pearl Harbor, and Phillips had to help support his mother and deaf-mute aunt. He worked at a grocery store and later a funeral parlor. With the proximity of bereavement, Phillips learned interpersonal skills that would become more useful than he could ever have imagined. "I was very sensitive to the things I heard, saw, and felt around me. You see, back then most people died at home in the country areas and often without a lot of warning. Those times working with the country mortician made me very aware of how to handle people and their problems later on."

Phillips' first goal had been to study law, but grim economic reality forced him to forsake it in favor of radio. He either attended or took correspondence courses from the Alabama Polytechnical Institute in Auburn, specializing in engineering, including audio engineering for radio. He had first broken into radio in 1940 when he conducted and emceed the band for a college concert. Impressed with his performance, Jim Connally, station manager at WLAY in Muscle Shoals, hired him.

"Once I got into radio," Phillips recalls, "my interest in music resurfaced. I was not interested in becoming a musician, but back in the 1930s all the music of the country people—black blues, hillbilly, and spirituals—all influenced me, and in radio I saw a medium where I could do something with the music I loved. I'm an artistic person emotionally. I played music from the sixth to the eleventh grade in school, but I never was a very good musician. I was a good conductor. I could always see the people that did have talent and get it out of them. And they would *know* that I was getting it out of them."

"After I got into radio, I worked hard at becoming an announcer—there were no DJs as such then—but I really wasn't a talented announcer in the strictest terms, although I had to be good just to hold my job in those days. I looked on it as a serious job through the later part of the 1940s, because I had to make enough money to live and raise a family."

Formal music aside, Phillips also learned to love the music of hardship. "There were two types of downtrodden people back then. There were the black field hands and the white sharecroppers. It was impossible in those days not to hear and grow to love all the music of oppression and the music that uplifted people—blues, country, gospel, all of it—either in the fields, or the black women doing their chores, or on a weekend. One man in particular, Uncle Silas Payne, an old black man, taught music to me. Not musical notes or reading, you understand, but real intuitive music."

Phillips married Rebecca (or Becky) Burns from Sheffield in 1942, and they began a journey that would take them to WMSL in Decatur, Alabama, for three years and then to WLAC in Nashville for a few months before settling in Memphis during June 1945 to take up a position with WREC. Phillips' entrée to WREC was probably his brother Jud, who had been established at the station for some time as a member of the Jollyboys Quartet, singing on the air every morning.

At WREC Phillips hosted the "Songs of the West" show under the pseudonym of Pardner at 4:00 P.M. daily. He also honed his engineering skills in support of the transcription manager, Milton Brame. In the days before tape, many programs were prerecorded, or transcribed, onto sixteen-inch acetate discs, which were often duplicated and circulated to other stations. This meant that local radio engineers were also recording engineers, and Phillips was able to develop his recording skills in a way that is uncommon today. He also looked after the station's sound effects and ventured out in search of records for the

Sam Phillips
at WREC

station's library. "One of my first jobs," he recalls, "was to go to the Home of the Blues record store and buy up any records that WREC weren't getting shipped to them. This went on through the mid to late '40s. I would listen to a lot of what was current, and I would also go play a lot of the older records they had accumulated."

Phillips used his knowledge to host a show on WREC called the "Saturday Afternoon Tea Dance." Local journalist Edwin Howard recalls that "Phillips played what he liked on that show and talked about the records very knowledgeably. He played jazz, blues, and pop, and that was where many people in Memphis first heard his name."

In 1949 Phillips decided to apply his engineering expertise and his catholic taste in music to the operation of a recording studio, which he would run in addition to his other jobs. As well as providing extra income, the studio would give him an outlet for his creativity that was unavailable at WREC. Unable to sing or play, Phillips would now be able to "create" music, the art form that had become paramount in his life.

Recommended Listening

Memphis Blues, 1928–1930, 2 LPs (RCA [France] NL 89276), provides a general overview of the earlier styles of Memphis blues recorded by RCA. For comparison, *The Bristol Sessions, 1927* (CMF [USA] 011L) carries a selection of the repertoire recorded in northeast Tennessee at approximately the same time.

(Escott)

The Memphis Recording Service,
706 Union Ave.,
Memphis, Tennessee

Chapter Two

BLUES BEFORE SUNRISE

When Sam Phillips opened the doors of his Memphis Recording Service in January 1950, he was taking a chance on an area of business that remained unproven in Memphis. Just about the only similar venture anyone could remember was a short-lived company called Royal Recording, which had been founded in 1948 to record private functions and the like, only to become defunct a year later. "It was because of the closure of the Royal studio downtown that my bosses at WREC warned me against trying to start my own recording business," Phillips would recall years later.

At first, Phillips had little local expertise to draw on, other than that of local radio engineers. In addition to doing transcription work, radio studios occasionally doubled as commercial recording studios of last resort. In fact, Phillips would cut a hit in just that way for bandleader Art Mooney, who was playing in town and wanted to cover a fast-breaking tune called "Oh!" Phillips arranged to record the band in the studios of WMC (presumably the Memphis Recording Service studio, at 20 by 35 feet, was too small), and even conjured up some primitive echo from the stairwell. That was 1953.

There was, however, one outpost of the record business that was thriving in Memphis. In January 1946 Robert E. "Buster" Williams and Clarence Camp had launched a record distributorship in Memphis and New Orleans called Music Sales. The major labels largely controlled their own distribution, but small distributors handled the indies. Music Sales distributed most of the R&B labels, such as Atlantic and Chess.

In 1949 Williams started a pressing plant, Plastic Products, on Chelsea Avenue in Memphis. His intention was to press some product for the labels he distributed, thereby taking advantage of the shipping location of Memphis, in the center of the country. Williams found the major plants unwilling to share their technology, though, and, in a display of rugged individualism, he designed his own presses and compound (the shellac-based amalgam from which records were made). Williams and Phillips became fast friends, and Williams supplied the manufacturing credit and local distribution that Phillips came to need after he started Sun, as well as supplying a warehousing and shipping point.

Sam Phillips at the
dawn of his career

(M. Keisker/Escott)

MODERN STUDIOS

MEMPHIS *Recording* SERVICE

706 UNION AT MARSHALL

TELEPHONE 37-7197

"WE RECORD ANYTHING—ANYWHERE—ANYTIME"

DISC

TAPE

In October 1949 Phillips signed the lease on a small storefront property at the junction of Union and Marshall Avenues, near the heart of downtown Memphis. The rent at 706 Union was $150 a month. He installed his recording and transcription equipment with the help of a two-year loan from Buck Turner, a regular performer on WREC. Working with the slogan "We Record Anything—Anywhere—Anytime," Phillips opened the doors of the Memphis Recording Service in January 1950. Becky Phillips took a photo of her husband standing outside the studio and pasted it into the scrapbook with the caption, "A Man's Dream Fulfilled—What Next?"

The Hardware

Forty years later, it is difficult to comprehend the changes that have overtaken the industry since Phillips started the Memphis Recording Service. Today, music can be recorded using computer scans of any audio signal. Over fifty different inputs can be stored separately on digital tape, and entire tracks can be based on a single note sampled digitally and manipulated electronically. Every aspect of recording is now a sophisticated specialty, often requiring formal training.

Contrast that with the equipment Sam Phillips had available to him: "I had a little Presto five-input mixer board. It was portable and it sat on a hall table. The mixer had four microphone ports, and the fifth port had a multiselector switch where you could flip it one way and get a mike and flip it another to play your recordings back. That was my console." The first tape machines were just as primitive: "I had a Presto portable tape recorder, a PT 900, companion

Presto ads, late '40s

(Bruce Leslie)

piece to the mixer. Before that I had a Crestwood tape recorder, a little amateur thing. The second one I got at the same time was a Bell recorder. The Bell was in a red case and the Crestwood was in a beige case. I'll never forget them. I was real proud to get the Presto. Man, that was big-time for me!"

With his equipment in the trunk of his car, Phillips would lug the machines to any social event and religious gathering he could book. He recorded weddings, funerals—all the same gigs that Royal Recording had tried to subsist on a few years earlier.

Suspicious of the quality and durability of tape, then an unproven medium, Phillips did most of his early commercial recording (i.e., for airplay or release) onto acetate discs. "In the very beginning I recorded a lot onto those sixteen-inch discs, which I cut at 78 rpm," he recalled. "Normally you wouldn't do that. You recorded at 33 rpm on transcriptions, but in order to improve the sound, I recorded at 78 rpm and would make an acetate master from there. For making acetates I had the Presto 6-N lathe, which was connected to a Presto turntable. That's how I cut most of my early music."

By 1954 Phillips had upgraded his equipment and installed two Ampex 350 recorders: one console model and another mounted on a rack behind his head for the tape delay echo, or "slapback," for which Sun became famous. By "bouncing" the signal from one machine to another, with a split-second lag between the two, he created his characteristic echo effect. By the mid-'50s he

MARION

Until November 1955 Phillips' only assistant was Marion Keisker. There was little in her background to qualify her for the role: She was born in Memphis on September 23, 1917, and attended Southwestern College. After her marriage in 1939, she moved to Peoria, Illinois, returning to Memphis after her divorce in 1943. She began work as a secretary to a businessman named Chambers, who had offices in the Peabody Hotel. The Peabody also housed WREC, and Marion joined the station in 1946, a year after Phillips.

When Phillips opened his own recording studio she came along as his office manager, although she continued to work part-time at the station until 1955—she needed the radio station paycheck because the Memphis Recording Service barely did more than meet its own rent. Even after Phillips launched Sun Records in 1952, the picture didn't improve. Marion recalled that she would sometimes place her own money into petty cash in order to disguise the company's desperate financial picture from Phillips, who suffered from frequent depression because of his inability to sustain a living from the studio and the label.

Despite a background in light classical music, Marion developed a genuine taste for the blues during her early years at Sun. She came to share Phillips' musical vision, and to cherish the unsophistication that he sought. She had especially fond memories of Howlin' Wolf, and even retrieved the rejected acetate masters of his sessions with Phillips from the garbage for her own collection.

She was the one who called in the musicians, paid them, and logged events in a notebook that is the prime source for Phillips' activities during those early years. Without Marion's notebook, Sun archaeology would be a barren field. Phillips' documentation skills barely ran beyond sticking a paper marker in a tape before his preferred cut. Marion also handled much

WHER—1000 Beautiful Watts. Marion is second from left, Sam's wife Becky at right in front.

(Mississippi Valley Collection)

of the day-to-day contact with distributors and pressing plants, which accounted for her distaste at later being tagged Sam Phillips' "secretary." Together with Sam and his brother Jud, she nurtured the distribution network and radio contacts that would serve as a launching pad for Sun Records. In her courtly southern manner she dealt with some of the most rapacious individuals in the cutthroat R&B business.

After Marion quit WREC in 1955 she worked with Phillips to launch WHER, an "all-girl" radio station (with all-male shareholders). The parting of the ways eventually came in September 1957, when Marion left to join the Air Force. The rapidly growing success of Sun Records had destroyed the personal and professional relationship between Marion Keisker and Sam Phillips that seemed to have flourished in leaner times.

After she left the Air Force in a flurry of litigation in 1969, Marion returned to Memphis to begin a new career in theater. On her return, she discovered that the era of instant history was awaiting her. There was a steady procession of music historians waiting to interview her about her involvement in Sun Records. Her assertion to Jerry Hopkins that she recorded the first Presley acetate brought her into conflict with Phillips, a conflict that—like a Middle Eastern border war—would flare up intermittently over the next two decades.

After an operation for cancer in August 1989 and subsequent hospitalizations, Marion Keisker died on December 29, 1989. Sam Phillips would probably have accomplished what he did without her, but Marion's organizational skills and support eased the pain. Though she never sought to deflect attention from Phillips' artistic achievement, for six largely barren years she underpinned his maverick operation.

At her desk, 1956

(Escott)

Sam and his
sons in the studio,
early '50s

(Escott)

had also ditched his Presto board in favor of the RCA 76-D radio console. Inputs and outputs were all coupled through transformers, giving a distinct warm coloration (often dubbed the "tube" sound) to anything passing through them. Phillips recorded his most important music with that simple configuration.

For years after Phillips made the switch from acetate discs to magnetic tape in late 1951, the relatively high price of tape ensured that, watching every penny, he reused every spare inch—including hours of Elvis Presley outtakes and rejected masters. Not until 1956, with the financial picture much improved and the price of tape lowered, did he finally feel able to let the tapes roll freely. From then on, much of the activity within the Sun studio was captured on tape and preserved for posterity.

Southern Juke Coin

"I opened the Memphis Recording Service," recalls Phillips, "with the intention of recording singers and musicians from Memphis and the locality who I felt had something that people should be able to hear. I'm talking about blues—both the country style and the rhythm style—and also about gospel or spiritual music and about white country music. I always felt that the people who played this type of music had not been given the opportunity to reach an audience. I feel strongly that a lot of the blues was a real true story. Unadulterated life as it was.

"My aim was to try and record the blues and other music I liked and to prove whether I was right or wrong about this music. I knew, or I *felt* I knew, that there was a bigger audience for blues than just the black man of the mid-South. There were city markets to be reached, and I knew that whites listened to blues surreptitiously." But for all his commercial sensibilities, there was also an element of the folklorist in Phillips, a streak of the musical archaeologist who wanted to capture sounds he knew might be lost: "With the jet age coming on, with cotton-picking machines as big as a building going down the road, with society changing, I knew that this music wasn't going to be available in a pure sense forever."

Buck Turner, who had lent Phillips some of the up-front cash he needed to install his studio hardware, also gave him his first paying gig—recording transcriptions of Turner's band for the Arkansas Rural Electrification Program. The transcriptions were distributed to fifteen or twenty stations throughout the mid-South. "Remember," says Phillips, "that I still had a day job at WREC until the middle of 1951, and I was presenting the big bands at the Peabody at night. After I got off from the station at 3:30 in the afternoon, I went down to the studio, and everything had to be fitted in at that time of day."

It was probably five or six months before Phillips started to record artists with a view to selling or leasing the masters. "When I opened the studio I had already talked to record labels, but I didn't have any deals lined up. I felt I had to please myself first with the music and then go out and sell it. As I began to record, the word gradually got around that I might have something. The first deal I made was with Bill McCall and Don Pierce at 4-Star and Gilt Edge Records."

Bill McCall had purchased 4-Star, one of the first postwar indies based on the West Coast. He had been astonishingly successful with a primitive boogie pianist, Cecil Gant (a World War II veteran billed as "Private Cecil"), and a large country catalog. "I had known Bill for some time," said Phillips, "and I contacted him and told him what I was trying to do with blues. The first music they took was by John Hunter, who was a blind man from South Memphis. He was a pianist with a lot of potential. Then they took some country items by the Slim Rhodes band."

Phillips' assessment of "Lost" John Hunter was perhaps overly charitable. Indeed, McCall's enthusiasm may have stemmed from the passing musical resemblance that Lost John bore to Private Cecil. But *Billboard*, reviewing his 4-Star record "Boogie for Me Baby," seemed to pick up on the energy Phillips must have found in the piano player: "A crude boogie blues," they called it, "that could pick up some southern juke coin."

The Hottest Thing
in the Country

The relationship with 4-Star seemed unlikely to lead anywhere, so Phillips and his friend Dewey Phillips took the brave step of launching their own record label. For Sam Phillips, his own label meant an end to the frustration of finding

The Phillips—Dewey and Sam

(Knox Phillips)

The Pep-Ti-Kon Boy
on WDIA

"I went to KWEM and asked if I could sing on the radio, and that's how I came to know Sonny Boy. It happened that he had two jobs one night and he arranged for me to fill one of them. So I went out to the Sixteenth Street Grill. The lady's name was Miss Annie. She paid me twelve dollars that night, which was more than I had ever had in my life. Miss Annie said she would hire me six days a week if I got a radio spot where I could advertise her place. So I went over to WDIA and got a job there. I played ten to fifteen minutes live every day." King went back to Mississippi, collected his wife, Martha, together with their few belongings, and moved to Memphis.

WDIA gave King a gig hustling a patent cure-all, Pep-ti-Kon. "If you feel run down, tired, achy, painy, can't sleep, are nervous, can't eat, have indigestion and bloating gas, you are guaranteed satisfaction," he would call over the air. "Get Pep-ti-Kon today and see if you don't say, 'Man, I'm really living.' " He also persuaded his bosses at WDIA to help him get on record. At that time, Bullet Records in Nashville was the closest label, and WDIA pulled a few strings to get their budding star two releases in July and November 1949.

By that point, Riley King had acquired his nickname, B.B., which has always been thought to stand for Blues Boy. Yet an article in the local black newspaper, *The Tri State Defender*, dated March 29, 1952, suggests a more probable derivation in a synopsis of his story: "Riley King, whose public had christened him 'Singing Black Boy,' was producing a popular radio show of his own. His public donated nickname was shortened to 'B. B.' King and under this title the slim guitar strummer from Itta Bena realized his ambition to cut original platters."

As one of the most popular performers on WDIA, it was inevitable that King would come to Phillips' attention. Phillips recorded King for approximately a year—from mid-1950 until June 1951. The Biharis drew five singles from the repertoire that Phillips supplied to them, making King one of the first artists on their new RPM subsidiary.

At the dawn of his long career, King's sound was not nearly as distinctive as it later became. His voice—like his figure—was thinner, and his guitar playing had yet to take on the stinging tone and dramatic flourishes that would become his trademarks. Yet the promise in those early sides was undeniable. As he later would with Elvis Presley, Phillips kept King to an established formula, coupling an uptempo boogie with a slow number. On some of the faster songs Phillips indulged his budding taste for overamplification to produce a primitive fuzz effect.

One song in particular, "She's Dynamite," was a showcase for Phillips' flair for experimentation, as he encouraged the bass, piano, and guitar to play a boogie riff in unison. It was a bottom-heavy sound that challenged established precepts of how recordings should be balanced. A comparison of B.B. King's version of the song with Tampa Red's original, recorded earlier the same year, illustrates Phillips' evolving production philosophy: there is an explosiveness and barely contained energy in King's version that overwhelms the mannered restraint of Tampa Red's. It was that blistering energy and the willingness to experiment that pointed unerringly into the future.

Unfortunately, Phillips' involvement with King ended after a session on June 18, 1951, the casualty of a dispute between the Biharis and Phillips over "Rocket 88," a song that Phillips had placed with Chess Records. After that point Saul Bihari came to Memphis and recorded King on a portable Magnecord at the YMCA or Tuff Green's house. It was in 1952, during one of those makeshift sessions, that King cut "3 O'Clock Blues," the song that established him in the R&B market and got him out of Memphis.

The Be-Bop Boy

After the Phillips label disappeared back into the obscurity from which it had barely arisen, Phillips finally placed Joe Hill Louis with RPM/Modern. Although both Louis and B. B. King were part of the staple diet on WDIA, Louis's music was a far cry from King's: it was primitive, countrified, and inscrutable. He sang with the harmonica in front of his face, usually rendering his vocals muddy, and there was little room for virtuosity on any of the three instruments he routinely played at once. Louis's performances had a dense texture and a compelling drive that compensated for the lack of pure technique. His lyrics were laced with threats and a dark sense of humor: "I sent my baby a brand new ten-dollar bill," he sang, "If that don't get her back, you know my shotgun will."

Louis was an enigmatic character, about whom little would be known if not for the research of musicologist Stephen LaVere. He was born Lester or Leslie Hill on September 23, 1921, in Whitehaven, Tennessee. At age fourteen he ran away from home, and was hired as a houseboy by the Canales, a white family who controlled much of Memphis's soda pop and vending industry. The Canales dubbed him Joe Hill Louis, with a nod to the boxer Joe Louis, after he won a fight with a local bully.

(Escott)

Louis played first Jew's harp and then harmonica, before finally adding guitar, drums, and hi-hat to his act. Dubbing himself the Be Bop Boy, he played in the local parks and at black ball games. After WDIA became a black-oriented station, Louis was hired as the first Pep-ti-Kon Boy. He made his first records for Columbia in Nashville under circumstances that are far from clear. Columbia had almost no penetration into the market that Louis serviced, and the records sold so poorly that Phillips had no problem in obtaining his release when he wanted to record Louis in 1950.

After falling out with the Biharis, Phillips succeeded in placing Louis with Chess, for whom he recorded an electrifying atmospheric blues, "When I Am Gone," that transcended form and meter in the manner of John Lee Hooker. Another record by Louis relaunched the Sun label in 1953, earning him the distinction of having his recordings issued on every label with which Phillips had been affiliated during his three years in the record business (except 4-Star). After the Sun record failed to sell, Louis and Phillips finally parted ways, and Louis recorded for a few other labels before succumbing to tetanus on August 5, 1957.

It is a testament to Phillips' love of primitive, even obscure, country blues that he persevered in recording Louis. The path toward commercial salvation had become clear as far back as March 1951: One look at the *Billboard* R&B charts made it obvious that country blues were already considered passé by the black record-buying audience. It was the R&B bands, with their fuller instrumentation, that were selling. And one of them had already arrived unexpectedly on Phillips' doorstep.

Rocket 88

March 5, 1951, was the night it all came together for Sam Phillips. Ike Turner, a DJ on WROX in Clarksdale, Mississippi, had driven up to Memphis with a band featuring his underage cousin Jackie Brenston. A feature in the Memphis *Commercial Appeal* in June 1951 reported that "B. B. King of Memphis, one of the race artists Sam has been recording, passed the word along to Ike Turner, a negro bandleader of Clarksdale, Mississippi, that the market was open." Ike, Jackie, and the band had worked up a rollicking R&B number—called "Rocket 88," after the hot Oldsmobile coupe—and they decided to audition it for Phillips.

But during the drive from Clarksdale, guitarist Willie Kizart's amp fell off the top of the car, breaking the speaker cone. "We had no way of getting it fixed," Phillips told Robert Palmer, "so we started playing around with the damn thing, stuffed a little paper in there and it sounded good. It sounded like a saxophone."

Rather than submerge the distorted sound of Kizart's guitar, Phillips took a chance and overamplified it, making it the centerpiece of the rhythm track. Kizart played a simple boogie riff in unison with Ike Turner's piano. Raymond

FIRST TIME IN MEMPHIS!
W.C. HANDY THEATRE
2 DAYS ONLY - SAT. & SUN. APRIL 7-8
ON STAGE! ----- IN PERSON

JACKIE BRENSTON
THE TERRIFIC ROCKET "88" SENSATION
WITH IKE TURNER
"THE KING OF THE PIANO"
AND "HIS KING OF RHYTHM"
JACKIE IS GONNA TEAR THE HOUSE DOWN

Jackie Brenston

Hill contributed two screeching tenor sax solos, and Brenston rode over the top with a hugely confident vocal that belied his tender years. Phillips later characterized "Rocket 88" as the first rock 'n' roll record. Its raucous, unbridled energy certainly foreshadowed much that was to follow, although arguably it owed a greater debt to what had come before.

After the session, Phillips ran off dubs and sent them to the Chess brothers in Chicago the same night. It is unclear why the dubs went to Chess rather than to RPM. Leonard Chess was a frequent visitor to Memphis, where Buster Williams handled some of his pressing and distributed Chess locally via Music Sales. It is possible that Williams had turned Chess onto Phillips and that Chess had promised Phillips a better royalty or front money. With the naïveté that colored his early years in the business, Phillips probably thought he could supply repertoire to both Chess and Modern without conflict, and hoped to impress Chess with a strong initial cut. Chess snapped up "Rocket 88" together with an undistinguished blues single from Ike Turner. They were released in April 1951. "Rocket 88" reached the charts in May, hit number 1 in June, and eventually became the second-biggest R&B record of the year (the Dominoes' "Sixty Minute Man" was the biggest).

Phillips had been vindicated; as he declared later, " 'Rocket 88' was the record that really kicked it off for me as far as broadening the base of music and opening up wider markets for our local music." As with most successes, though, it brought as many problems as rewards. "I was still recording weddings and funerals," recalls Phillips, "taking care of the PA system at the Hotel Peabody, and I was doing the Skyway broadcast every night at ten-thirty and

(Escott)

then back at work at seven-thirty the following morning. I was an eighteen-to-twenty-hours-a-day person. Then I went home and told my wife, 'Becky, I can't stand it.' I'd already had a nervous breakdown and this was so emotionally and mentally exhausting. I told her, 'I've just got to make a decision. I've worked awfully hard to get where I am in radio. I like it but it's not what I want to do.' She said, 'Whatever you want to do, we'll be there.' June of 1951 is when I resigned. I had no income, my kids were growing up and going to school, and there was a lot at stake. It had been a big decision to quit WREC, and if it all fell through then I would have had to start a lot further down back in radio." Nevertheless, on the day he resigned, Phillips knew that "Rocket 88" was sitting atop the R&B charts. As incentives go, it was better than most.

The feature on "Rocket 88" in the *Commercial Appeal* gives a little of the flavor of Phillips' business: Phillips "has agreements with two recording companies to locate and record hillbilly and race music. Race numbers are those tailored for the negro trade. Sam auditions musicians with original songs. When he finds something he's sure will sell, he gets it on acetate and sends it to one of the companies. He doesn't charge the musicians anything. Like them, he gets his [*sic*] from the companies. Sam may branch out one day . . . so he says if anyone wants to bring him a pop song, he'll be glad to look it over."

Brenston's success on Chess ensured that Phillips now had only one record company to whom he could pitch product; the Biharis were understandably incensed. The record's success also caused dissent in the ranks of the band. Phillips explains: "Ike Turner wanted a record out real badly. I said, 'Ike, man, you're a hell of a piano player, you play guitar real good, but you just can't sing. Now Jackie here has this vocal that we can really go somewhere with.' Well, this did not please Ike, and it created a little problem. I tried to handle

(Escott)

Juiced! Roscoe Gordon and Billy "Red" Love (center, right and left) with friends

it right and explain the way it was, but I guess I can understand how Ike felt—that Jackie's success was really *his* success. Anyway, Ike took Jackie's band away from us and we had a problem. At that time, Chess was screaming for more top-notch product, so I recorded Billy Love singing 'Juiced.' We used that as the follow-up and issued it under Jackie's name. I bought it off Billy for Jackie." Love was a local singer and pianist who sounded convincing in a number of styles; little is known of him except that he had a proclivity for the bottle. Phillips later leased several recordings by Love to Chess, one of which, "Drop Top," was modeled closely after "Rocket 88."

Ike Turner defected to the Biharis, for whom he assumed Phillips' role, cutting sessions in Memphis and the vicinity. Meanwhile, Brenston recruited a new set of Delta Cats, featuring Phineas Newborn, Jr. But Brenston's flirtation

Howlin' Wolf and the Houserockers—Chicago, mid-'50s

Lest Get
Booted
Rosco Gordon
Jr.

Roscoe Gordon

(Chess Records/ Showtime Archive)

with fame was short-lived. The follow-ups failed, and Brenston later reunited with Turner and took refuge in drink.

Phillips, having cut himself loose from the Biharis and WREC, was now free—and obligated—to serve but one master: Chess Records. With Brenston and Turner gone and the need to find new talent ever pressing, he turned to a precocious young piano player named Roscoe Gordon, who had first come to see him in February 1951. Phillips had succeeded in placing him with the Biharis, and now he moved him to Chess after the fallout from "Rocket 88." For the first Chess session Phillips secured a sloppy-drunk song called "Booted," which he encouraged Gordon to deliver with slurred diction and an appropriately booting tenor sax solo. The record was underpinned by a primitive, loping shuffle that Phillips later dubbed "Roscoe's rhythm." Released on Chess at the end of 1951, "Booted" rose quickly up the R&B charts and eventually captured the top slot. The only problem was that the Biharis considered Gordon to be still under their contract. Ike Turner, in his new role as the Biharis' A&R representative in Memphis, hastily rerecorded Gordon singing "Booted" for RPM.

The complexities mounted when Phillips signed another artist to Chess whom the Biharis considered theirs—a singer who was perhaps the greatest of Phillips' discoveries during the years he recorded rhythm and blues.

The Wolf Is at the Door

Like most of the true greats Sam Phillips recorded, Chester Burnett, a.k.a. Howlin' Wolf, brought to the studio a style that he neither cared to alter nor could possibly improve. Dressed in his field overalls, with holes cut in his oversize shoes to accommodate his corns, Wolf made his recording debut in the summer of 1951. Leaving his small group to find their way as best they could, he began to sing his unearthly tales of darkness and pain.

Chester Burnett had been a farmer, blues singer, and soldier by the time he first recorded. His adopted nickname, though far from original, fitted him with made-to-measure precision. Born near Aberdeen, Mississippi, on June 10, 1910, Burnett developed a fondness for the music of the primordial Delta bluesman Charley Patton, who lived near the Burnett family after they moved to Ruleville, Mississippi. After four years in the service, between 1941 and 1945, Burnett returned to farming near Penton, Mississippi, before deciding to move to West Memphis, Arkansas.

Soon after coming to West Memphis, Wolf secured steady work playing whorehouses, black baseball parks, and other spots that catered to country folk in search of a little diversion. The feral energy with which he sang added a new dimension to the traditional Delta blues upon which he based his style. Wolf landed a spot on KWEM in 1950. Monday through Saturday, he appeared between 4:45 and 5:00 P.M., lacing his blues with pitches for grain and fertilizer. In his fortieth year, he became a hot item among the rural blacks around Memphis.

"A disc jockey from West Memphis told me about Wolf's show," recalled Sam Phillips to Robert Palmer. "When I heard him, I said, 'This is for me. This is where the soul of man never dies.' Then the Wolf came to the studio and he was about six foot six, with the biggest feet I've ever seen on a human being. Big Foot Chester is one name they used to call him. He would sit there with those feet planted wide apart, playing nothing but the french harp and I tell you, the greatest sight you could see today would be Chester Burnett doing one of those sessions in my studio. God, what it would be worth to see the fervor in that man's face when he sang. His eyes would light up, you'd see the veins on his neck and, buddy, there was *nothing* on his mind but that song. He sang with his damn soul!"

The first demo session was in the spring of 1951, probably in May. Framed by the small group he had assembled in West Memphis, led by the aggressive, distorted guitar of Willie Johnson, Wolf recorded "How Many More Years" and "Baby Ride with Me." Phillips sent the dubs to RPM/Modern, and may have sent them to Chess. RPM almost certainly agreed to sign Wolf, but by that point—June 1951—they were falling out with Phillips over "Rocket 88." Phillips sold Wolf's recording contract to Chess and rerecorded "How Many More Years" and another title, "Moanin' at Midnight," which together formed the first single. As he had with Roscoe Gordon, however, Ike Turner simultaneously recorded Wolf for RPM. "Moanin' at Midnight" was surreally recast as "Morning at Midnight," and the RPM recording entered the national R&B charts in September 1951.

In February 1952 Chess and the Biharis resolved their conflict in an agreement by which Chess kept Wolf and the Biharis kept Roscoe Gordon. Chess released their second Wolf single immediately after the deal was struck. Nevertheless, both Wolf and Roscoe would have to wait a number of years to recapture their initial success.

Howlin' Wolf's last known appearance in Phillips' studio was in October 1952. Phillips' log book noted that Wolf was to return and cut some more titles to fulfill his obligation, but there is no indication that he ever did. There may have been some discussion over whether Wolf was to remain with Chess or join other Chess acts that Phillips recorded, Joe Hill Louis, Rufus Thomas, and Walter Horton on the new Sun label, but the Chess brothers seemed to place the matter beyond doubt by spiriting him off to Chicago. "Leonard Chess kept worryin' me to come to Chicago," Wolf recalled to David Booth. "They talked me the notion [sic] to give up my business and come. I turned my farming business over to my brother-in-law, my grandfather's farm that he left me. I moved to Chicago in 1952 or 1953. I had a four-thousand-dollar car and $3,900 in my pocket. I'm the onliest one drove out of the South like a gentleman."

Once Howlin' Wolf was in Chicago, the Chess brothers tried to recreate the sound that Phillips formulated, even to the point of rerecording some of the unissued titles from Wolf's Memphis sessions. After a few missed cues, Wolf evolved a slightly modified sound in Chicago and eventually brought Willie Johnson up to join him. He became one of the seminal figures in postwar blues, which ensured that he spent his last years touring college campuses, where he looked strangely out of place amid a sea of freshly scrubbed, young white faces. After his death in January 1976, he received a tribute from Sam Phillips: "He had no voice in the sense of a pretty voice but he had command of every word he spoke. When the beat got going in the studio he would sit there and sing, hypnotizing himself. Wolf was one of those raw people. Dedicated. Natural."

Phillips never found a bluesman to equal Howlin' Wolf. He has said that he would never have given up on him, that he would have recorded him until the day he died. Phillips has even rated Wolf—above Elvis and all others—as his greatest discovery. And even without the private video that Phillips can play in his mind of Wolf performing in his little studio, his enthusiasm is easy to understand. The bizarre, haunting images that populated Wolf's songs, the quality of his voice, and his frightening energy were the marks of a true original. His music ran the gamut, from purest evil to heartbreaking tenderness. There was an emotional greatness to Howlin' Wolf, a greatness that Phillips was the first to capture.

Blues Before Sunrise

The success of Jackie Brenston, Howlin' Wolf, and Roscoe Gordon kept the arrangement between Chess and Phillips healthy into 1952. But their relationship eventually became strained, as Phillips' later offerings failed to live up to their predecessors' sales. There were the inevitable squabbles about money. "Confusion arose between Leonard Chess and me about what I was supposed to be paid," he recalls. "I made some wrong moves with RPM and Chess. If I'd had my way, I'd rather have done only the creative end and left the business to other people, but once you set up in business you have to carry it through. I grew up on a handshake deal, which I guess is not a good thing to rely upon in business. Len and Phil [Chess] were not being honest with me. I have to say that. I was not being greedy. I'd have stayed with them, but I was working my ass off and I couldn't afford not to get what was due to me."

There was another factor in the equation by early 1952. Where just a few years ago it had been empty, the Memphis recording scene was suddenly becoming rather crowded. Ike Turner was still scouting and recording for RPM/Modern; meanwhile, a fourth Bihari, Lester, had recently returned to Memphis, intending to start a label that would attract the local talent—although he had a head start with a stash of RPM/Modern masters from Chicago. In addition, David James Mattis, production manager at WDIA, started Duke Records at around the same time in partnership with Bill Fitzgerald from Music Sales.

With these factors weighing heavily upon him, Phillips decided early in 1952 that he would start his own label, despite his personal preference for the creative side of the business. "I truly did not want to open a record label," he contends, "but I was forced into it by those labels either coming to Memphis to record or taking my artists elsewhere. What people did not realize was the importance of producing records with the potential to be hits. Hit sounds. Good music. A guarantee of money to the Wolf or the others looked fine, but it was not the answer. It only raised everyone's expectations, and let everyone down on both sides when they didn't deliver."

With the dismal experience of the Phillips label now two years distant, and with three national R&B hits under his belt, Phillips once again decided to start his own label. "Sun Records was forced on me," he says, "but at the same time, it presented the opportunity to do exactly as I wanted."

Recommended Listening

A selection of Phillips' pre-Sun and Sun blues recordings, including cuts by Howlin' Wolf, B. B. King, Joe Hill Louis, and Jackie Brenston, can be found on *Blue Flames: A Sun Blues Collection* (Rhino [USA] R2 70962).

Transcriptions of Dewey Phillips on the air are included on *Red Hot and Blue* (Zu-Zazz [UK] Z 2012).

B. B. King's Memphis sessions are largely contained on *The Memphis Masters* (Ace [UK] CH 50) and *The Best of B. B. King* (Ace [UK] CH 30). Other recordings from the same period are on *One Niter Blues* (Ace [UK] CHD 201) and *Across the Tracks* (Ace [UK] CHD 230).

Joe Hill Louis's recordings for the Phillips, Chess, and Sun labels are gathered on *The Be-Bop Boy* (Bear Family [Germany] BCD 15524).

Roscoe Gordon's pre-Sun recordings are chronicled on *Roscoe Gordon, Vol. 1 and 2* (Ace [UK] CH 26, 51).

Howlin' Wolf's early recordings for Phillips are issued complete on *Memphis Days, Vols. 1 and 2* (Bear Family [Germany] BCD 15460, 15500). A good sampling appears on *Cadillac Daddy* (Rounder [USA] CD/SS 28). The RPM recordings are on *Ridin' in the Moonlight* (Ace [UK] CH 52).

Elvis with Junior Parker (center) and Bobby Bland

Chapter Three

SELLIN' MY STUFF

"**T**he *sun* to me—even as a kid back on the farm—was a universal kind of thing. A new day, a new opportunity," said Sam Phillips, reflecting on the confluence of events that had brought him to the formation of his own label. "I chose the name Sun right at the beginning of 1952, when I had determined to try to start issuing my own recordings. It was a frightening experience for me. I had a heavy workload already, and now here I was with lack of time, lack of know-how, and lack of liquidity."

At the same time, having Sun Records meant that Phillips would have to answer only to himself for a record's success or failure. He could release music that others had deemed unworthy, he could hand-carry sample discs to every station within a five-hundred-mile radius, and he could exert pressure on his distributors. Then, if the record succeeded, he would reap the rewards. He was no longer forced to second-guess Chess Records' accountings, or to fret that others had won the acclaim for his productions. By the same token, if one of his records bombed, there was only one scapegoat.

"My first step," he continues, "was to sketch out a label design and take it to Memphis Engraving on North Second Street. A man named Parker I had known and played with in the high school band was there. He drew several designs from my sketch and I decided on the one with the sun rays and the rooster. I honestly feel I can say that I know what it's like to have a baby. That's what Sun Records was to me."

Drivin' Slow

On February 25, 1952, Phillips recorded the duo of harmonica player Walter Horton and jug band veteran Jack Kelly, who together had worked up two tunes, "Blues in My Condition" and "Sellin' My Stuff." On March 5 Phillips sent dubs (acetates run off the master tape) of the tunes to Chess, inquiring whether they would be interested in releasing them. Chess said they would not. On March 8 Phillips made up a new set of dubs of "Blues in My Condition"

and sent one to Memphis station WHHM, asking that it be aired as the introduction to the Sun label. The response was good enough to persuade him to
ship the masters for processing. "Sellin' My Stuff" was retitled "Sellin' My
Whiskey" in anticipation of release, and the duo was dubbed Jackie Boy and
Little Walter. By the time the stampers (the metal parts used in the manufacture
of records) were shipped back from Shaw Processing, however, Phillips had
decided that Chess had been correct: the record wasn't strong enough for
release. The first Sun record, number 174, was never issued.

The record that finally got Sun off the ground was cut a week after the
Horton and Kelly session, by a sixteen-year-old alto saxophonist named Johnny
London. He recorded two tunes on the afternoon of March 1, 1952; the better
was an original instrumental, "Drivin' Slow." Phillips ran dubs for Dewey
Phillips, who aired them on WHBQ the same night to test the reaction. Four
days later, Phillips sent dubs to Chess—which rejected them. On March 8 he
brought London back into the studio to recut "Drivin' Slow" and sent out
another set of dubs to local DJs to test out his hunch that Chess was wrong.
Obviously encouraged, Phillips shipped the masters for processing two days
later, together with the Jackie Boy and Little Walter cuts. By the time the
stampers arrived back, he had decided to place all his energy behind "Drivin'
Slow." The first records were pressed on March 27, 1952, and the Sun label
made its low-key debut that day.

Even on this first release, all the hallmarks of a Sam Phillips Sun record
were in place: the raw sound, the experimental origin, the dark texture, even
the trademark echo. Phillips and London created the illusion of a sax heard
down a long hallway on a humid night by rigging something like a telephone
booth over London's head while he played. The record's appeal had more to

Johnny London

(Escott)

do with feeling than virtuosity—in short, it offered everything music buyers could expect from Sun for the remainder of the decade. A copy of "Drivin' Slow," Sun #175, was mounted on the studio wall near the door after its release, where it remained until the old studio was closed.

Blues and Trouble
Everywhere

London's haunting and almost themeless improvisation made it onto some local charts, but the rewards for Phillips were meager. He released a mediocre blues record by Forrest City, Arkansas, DJ Walter Bradford at the same time, and then temporarily folded the Sun label to contend with a new set of problems.

The first concerned the company's name. Another Sun label had been founded in Albuquerque, New Mexico, at about the same time, and there was a dispute over the right to the name. "Sun" had been used before—by a Yiddish record company in New York during the 1940s, and by a Detroit label that had come and gone in 1947—but the Albuquerque label posed a more direct problem. The trade magazines never reported the outcome of the dispute, but it's safe to assume that Phillips won, by default if nothing else.

A bigger problem was posed by Mattis and Fitzgerald's Duke label, which looked set to steal much of Phillips' thunder. They began by recording Roscoe Gordon, who was still under contract to the Biharis. Then Mattis signed a local pianist, John Alexander, whom he dubbed Johnny Ace. His first record, "My Song," became a number 1 R&B hit, comfortably outselling every record that had emerged from Memphis since "Rocket 88." In the wake of Ace's success, Mattis signed Bobby Bland, whom Phillips had recorded briefly for Chess, and Duke seemed poised to become a big factor in the R&B market. But, again, success brought more problems than rewards. In July 1952, unable to collect on their shipments of Johnny Ace records, Mattis and Fitzgerald were forced to sell most of their interests in the label to Don Robey at Peacock Records in Houston.

As a Memphis-based entity, Duke Records had come and gone in a matter of months. Lester Bihari's Meteor label, on the other hand, was better equipped to survive. It had the Biharis' expertise and distribution network behind it, although it was technically separate from RPM/Modern. Launched during the last days of 1952, Meteor began on a higher note than Sun: its first release, "I Believe" by Elmore James, cracked the national R&B charts in February 1953.

Phillips knew that he must infuse Sun with both capital and instant expertise if he was to relaunch the label with success comparable to that of Duke and Meteor while avoiding the problems that had beset Duke Records. Fortunately, he was able to solicit instant expertise from Nashville in the form of Jim Bulleit (pronounced "Bu-lay" by Bulleit himself but "Bullet" by everyone else). Bulleit had been a pioneer in the independent record business in Nashville, recording a variety of music for the Bullet label, which he co-owned. That label had scored one of the biggest hits of 1947 with Francis Craig's "Near You," shortly before Bulleit was forced out.

"Jim'd had hits that were real door-openers for independent labels," recalled Phillips. "He really helped me an awful lot as much as understanding what the problems were and could be, and he gave me most of the early insight into what I was confronted with—and that was frightening." Bulleit, who operated his J-B label concurrently with his involvement in Sun, also handled Phillips' music publishing. With his help, Sun was relaunched in January 1953 with three singles by local musicians, followed closely by the first classic recording on the Sun label.

Easy

Walter Horton, born just south of Memphis in Horn Lake, Mississippi, in 1918, had picked up the harmonica early on; from the age of nine he was playing for pennies on the street. He later shuttled back and forth between Chicago and Memphis, although at the time Phillips recorded him, Horton had a fairly steady Memphis day job hauling ice. Phillips first saw him playing in Handy Park. As Horton told the story, a few days later he was walking past the studio when Sam Phillips saw him pass and tapped on the window, inviting him in to record.

Phillips first recorded Horton for RPM/Modern. A single he later pitched to Chess was accepted but subsequently withdrawn because Chess had decided to concentrate on another harmonica player, Little Walter Jacobs, whose recording of "Juke" was just starting to break. (Ironically, Horton was also known in those days as "Little Walter"; later, he would become "Big Walter".) Phillips then decided to record Horton for Sun. The first planned release, with Jack Kelly, was scrapped, but Horton returned a few months later with something stunning.

On February 25, 1953, Horton arrived at Sun with guitarist Jimmy DeBerry and drummer Houston Stokes. Horton was fronted one dollar to buy a harmonica and was paid another three dollars for the session; DeBerry was given two dollars, Stokes five together with another seventy-five cents to haul his drums home in a cab. The group cut three numbers, including an instrumental from Horton that they titled "Easy"—actually a thinly-veiled version of Ivory Joe Hunter's 1950 hit "I Almost Lost My Mind." The following day Phillips sent masters off for processing, and two weeks later "Easy" was released.

With the minimal and often shaky support of DeBerry, Horton played the same theme five times, with mounting intensity. By the fourth chorus, he was playing with such ferocity that his harmonica sounded like a tenor saxophone. Phillips' virtuosity with tape delay echo was rarely used to better advantage;

he made three instruments sound as full as an orchestra. Any other instrument would have been redundant.

By the time "Easy" was released, Horton had returned to Chicago to replace Little Water in Muddy Waters' band. His record sold negligibly, and, on his last visit to Sun in April 1954, Horton received his final royalty check in the amount of $5.00. He stayed in Chicago, eventually becoming a fixture of the local blues scene until his death in 1981.

Phillips also saw promise in Horton's guitarist, Jimmy DeBerry, who had done some recording before the War. "Before Long," the flipside of "Easy," was DeBerry's feature. It showcased his laconic delivery and barely proficient playing. Like Jimmy Reed, however, who never rose above bare proficiency, DeBerry had an ear for haunting couplets and an elemental charm that transcended his technical limitations. Some of this glimmered through on "Before Long": "Woman I love dead and in her grave / Woman I hate, I see her every day."

Phillips brought DeBerry back into the studio in May to cut a solo single. The standout cut, "Take a Little Chance," was a primitive twelve-bar blues, lifted from a 1941 Robert Lockwood recording, that Phillips characterizes as "one of the real classic recordings of the blues. It was so basic, yet it had such feel to it." Phillips felt that it should have been a hit, although he probably underestimated the sophistication of the R&B market in 1953. Yet again one understands his point; the compelling drive of the recording more than compensates for the obvious technical deficiencies, including a wobbly beat and some asthmatic wheezing during the guitar break.

Walter Horton

(Brian Smith)

The stark primitivism of "Easy" and DeBerry's work reflected Phillips' personal taste as much as anything. "When I was leasing to other labels," he said, "those labels wanted me to compromise. They wanted a fuller blues sound than I did. They were selling excitement. I was recording the *feel* I found in the blues. I wanted to get that gut feel onto record. I realized that it was going to be much more difficult to merchandise than what Atlantic or Specialty, for example, were doing, but I was willing to go with it."

Faced with mounting expenses and little financial return from such ventures, though, Phillips found he wasn't above a stab at pure commercialism, and the success he found with it provided a serious incentive to abandon the unsophisticated Delta blues in favor of slightly slicker territory.

Bear Cat

The elemental twelve-bar blues "Hound Dog" has been the subject of an inordinate number of lawsuits since Jerry Leiber and Mike Stoller copyrighted it in early 1953. It was written for Big Mama Thornton (who also claimed to have written it while in the company of her favorite relative, Old Grandad). The latter-day interest, of course, results from the fact that Elvis Presley would make it into one of the most lucrative copyrights in popular music.

But back in March 1953 Elvis was sitting on the side of his bed trying to learn the song, while Sam Phillips was sitting in the studio rewriting it as "Bear Cat." On March 8, only a few weeks after Thornton's version had been released, Phillips called local DJ Rufus Thomas into the studio to cut the song. It entered the national R&B charts on April 18, only two weeks after Thornton's original version, sparking *Billboard* to call it "the fastest answer song to hit the market." It eventually climbed all the way to number 3 on the R&B charts, becoming Sun Records' first hit.

A lawsuit from Don Robey at Peacock Records/Lion Music, correctly charging copyright infringement, followed in short order. Phillips didn't have a leg to stand on when the case came to trial in July, and he was forced to surrender two cents a song to Lion along with court costs. "I should have known better," Phillips later remarked to Robert Palmer. "The melody was exactly the same as theirs."

The artist, Rufus Thomas, had seen a long career on the periphery of the Memphis music scene before he finally broke through with "Bear Cat." Born in Cayce, Mississippi, on March 26, 1917, Thomas was raised in Memphis and began his career in minstrelsy and vaudeville. In 1935 he started a regular gig at the Palace Theater as a comic with Nat D. Williams, a local high school teacher, as his straight man. Thomas also began singing with the Bill Fort Orchestra, although he has sensibly never made great claims about his singing. "I'm not a singer, I'm an entertainer," he told David Booth. "I've taught a lot of people how to get a song across and project a song, but as a singer myself—no dice."

Rufus Thomas (center) in a WDIA promotional gag

(Escott)

(Robert Pruter)

Stars of Radio

A.C. "Moohah" Williams

RUFUS THOMAS

WILLA MONROE

FORD NELSON

NAT WILLIAMS

FOR REPRINTS OF THE ABOVE PHOTOGRAPHS WRITE TO...
WDIA
MEMPHIS, TENNESSEE.

WDIA

WDIA
50,000 Watts of Goodwill

In 1948 Nat Williams became the first black on-air personality in Memphis, hosting a show called "Brown America Speaks," the success of which prompted WDIA to change format. "Nat got me my job at WDIA," recalled Thomas. "In those days they wouldn't let us twist the knobs. We'd pull the records, give them to the engineer, and give him a sign when we were ready to play another one."

In addition to his daily gig on WDIA, Thomas had worked a day job since January 1941 with an industrial uniform manufacturer. "I was making twenty-five cents an hour," he recounted to Booth. "I'd finish at two-thirty, run home, go to the station, and be on the air at three o'clock. I did that for years and years and years. I also did weekend live shows, and often I'd get home at four o'clock on Monday morning and be punching that clock at six-thirty. It took all of that to make a living."

Thomas made his recording debut in 1950 or 1951 for the Star Talent company from Dallas. In June 1951 he made his first recordings for Sam Phillips, who leased three singles to Chess.

Just under a year after his last session for Chess, Phillips called Thomas back to the studio to cut "Bear Cat." After the record broke, Thomas formed his own group, the Bear Cats, and started touring on weekends. His follow-up, "Tiger Man," written by Sam Phillips and Joe Hill Louis, was another novelty number that should have done comparably well, but didn't. Thomas was not asked to record for Sun again, a fact that galls him to this day. "I sold a hundred thousand records for him," he told David Booth, "and all the time he was looking for a white boy. Sam never mentions that I was the first to make money for Sun Records either."

Thomas recorded one single for Meteor Records; his recording career then went into abeyance for a few years. In 1959 he and his daughter, Carla, went to the newly formed Satellite label. Their debut, "'Cause I Love You," was a small hit and was followed by Carla's smash, "Gee Whiz" (recorded in 1961 at Phillips' studio in Nashville). By that point, Satellite had been renamed Stax Records, and Rufus went back in 1963 with a dance number called "The Dog." It became a modest R&B hit and led the way for his biggest hits, "Walkin' the Dog" and the "Funky Chicken." It was the success of "The Dog" that gave Thomas the impetus to finally quit his day job, although he maintained his shows at WDIA until changing times forced him out.

Yet Rufus Thomas, with his first Sun release, had given the label its first national hit—a record tainted with illegitimacy, but, even so, displaying both Phillips' musical values and his business acumen.

Feelin' Good

Almost as successful on the commercial level—and far more so artistically— was a record Phillips produced in the early summer of 1953 by another waiting-to-break local artist, Little Junior Parker.

Parker had hosted his own show on KWEM in West Memphis, and it was there that Ike Turner recorded him for the Biharis in 1951 or 1952. By that point, Parker had assembled his own band, in which the linchpin was guitarist Floyd Murphy. The brother of another accomplished blues guitarist, Matt "Guitar" Murphy, Floyd was as technically adroit as any picker who ever set up his amp in Phillips' studio. "He had this tremendous ability to make the guitar sound like two guitars," Phillips remembers—an ability that was showcased on Parker's Sun debut.

Parker, with Murphy and the band in tow, had auditioned for Phillips at some point in 1953, playing their brand of slick, uptown R&B. But Phillips wanted to hear something a little rougher, so the group worked up a tune called "Feelin' Good," with a nod to the king of the one-chord boogies, John Lee Hooker. Parker himself apparently despised that simplistic style of music, but Phillips was convinced he heard something marketable in the record; he released it in July 1953. On October 3 it entered the national R&B charts, to Parker's surprise, peaking at number 5 during its six-week stay.

Called back for another session, Parker brought a moody, elegiac blues called "Mystery Train"—a phrase that appears nowhere in the song but well characterizes the aura Parker and Phillips created in the studio. It is a slow, atmospheric piece in which a loping, syncopated beat, slap bass, and gently moaning tenor sax coalesce to produce a ghostly performance. But at the time, its poise, understatement, and lack of an obvious "hook" were sure predictors of commercial oblivion. Almost as remarkable was the flip side, "Love My Baby," whose pronounced hillbilly flavor might just qualify it as the first black rockabilly record. Released in November, the record failed to sustain the momentum of "Feelin' Good," and Parker began to get itchy feet.

Parker had joined Johnny Ace and Bobby Bland on the Blues Consolidated tours booked by Don Robey at Duke/Peacock Records. Parker was induced to

(Showtime Archive)

Blues Vocal
2:20

Memphis Music
U-89 BMI

MYSTERY TRAIN
(Parker)
LITTLE JUNIOR'S
BLUE FLAMES
192

SUN RECORD COMPANY

MEMPHIS, TENNESSEE.

Little Junior Parker

sign with Duke, prompting Phillips to file a suit against Robey. When the case came to trial, Phillips won a $17,500 settlement—which must have carried some personal gratification after the loss on "Bear Cat." Phillips also seems to have acquired 50 percent of "Mystery Train" at approximately the same time; when Elvis Presley's version appeared as his final Sun single almost two years later, it was published by Phillips' Hi-Lo Music, with Phillips' name appended to the composer credit.

Continuing to record for Robey, Parker worked as part of the Blues Consolidated Revue until Ace killed himself backstage in Houston on Christmas Eve 1954. Parker and Bland continued to work together, touring the black lounges and night spots. Parker scored fairly consistent hits in the R&B market for some years; ironically, after leaving Duke, his music edged closer to the primitive blues feel he had disavowed in Memphis. He died during brain surgery in Chicago on November 18, 1971.

A Prisoner's Prayer

Parker's group may have gone to Texas, but Phillips had another group under contract who weren't traveling anywhere except under armed guard. As part of the arrangement with Jim Bulleit, Sun acquired a black vocal group from Tennessee State Penitentiary in Nashville—five inmates who called themselves the Prisonaires.

The group had been introduced to Bulleit by Red Wortham, a Nashville music publisher. At that time, the pen was seen as a fertile source of new songs, and many of the Grand Ole Opry stars paid regular visits to buy material from both black and white inmates. Wortham was on a similar quest when he heard about the Prisonaires. Formed by lead singer Johnny Bragg shortly after he went inside in 1943, the group already had a steady gig on two local stations, WSOK and WSIX, and was part of warden James Edwards' rehabilitation program.

Wortham gave Bulleit a rough demo tape of Bragg and the Prisonaires singing four songs (recorded over an early performance by Pat Boone on WSIX). Bulleit forwarded the tape to Phillips. One of the songs, "Just Walkin' in the Rain," had been written by Bragg and another inmate, Robert Riley. They had been walking in the rain to the prison laundry wondering, as Bragg put it, "what the little girls are doing right about now." Although Phillips had no love for their close-harmony, Ink Spots-inspired style, he saw the potential novelty slant, and, after some tortuous negotiations, the Prisonaires, escorted by an armed guard and a trusty, arrived in Memphis on June 1, 1953. On the way, Bragg remarked, "Gee, look at that funny cemetery." He was seeing a drive-in movie lot for the first time.

Over the course of a session that lasted from 10:30 A.M. to 8:30 P.M., the Prisonaires honed "Just Walkin' in the Rain" to perfection. Phillips released it two weeks later. It started to get action almost immediately, no doubt due

(Escott)

The Prisonaires and a captive audience

in part to the novelty appeal of the group, but also to the beauty of the song and the stilling quality of Bragg's lead vocal. Against a wordless background vocal and a simple strummed guitar, he sang:

Just walking in the rain
Getting soaking wet
Torturing my heart
By trying to forget . . .

After a meeting in Nashville with Jim Bulleit at the end of July, Jud Phillips went out to see the group in the pen. They told him they were already getting ten to twenty-five fan letters a day. "They plan to bring all of them to you when they come over," wrote Jud. "They make me think of a bunch of baby birds. They are fine boys all of them. I get a great joy out of helping people like that and think they really appreciate it." In November 1953 *Ebony* magazine reported that the record had sold 225,000 copies, although 50,000 was probably nearer the mark.

The strictly segregated penitentiary where the Prisonaires were doing time had been dubbed Swafford's Graveyard after a notorious previous warden. Despite its rough reputation, the prison's new warden, Edwards, encouraged rehabilitation and allowed the group out on day passes to perform on radio, and subsequently at live concerts. They even played some of the plusher white hotels in Nashville. Held up as examples of rehabilitation at work, they were introduced to Tennessee governor Frank Clement, who regularly brought the group to the gubernatorial mansion for performances—thereby eliciting the unissued paean "What About Frank Clement (A Mighty Mighty Man)," a song that had *parole, please!* written all over it.

Phillips and the Prisonaires blew their momentum by following "Just Walkin' in the Rain" with a gospel record, "Softly and Tenderly," backed with "My God Is Real," featuring Ike Turner in the unaccustomed role of church pianist. A hokey and hastily contrived third single, "A Prisoner's Prayer," was rushed onto the market, but the appeal of the group was fading fast. The last single was issued in July 1954. Just one year after the brouhaha surrounding their debut, the group was forgotten again.

Some of the Prisonaires were paroled in 1954 and 1955. Bragg remained inside and formed a group called the Marigolds. He was released in 1959, but soon found himself back in trouble, facing two counts of assaulting white women "with intent to ravish, murder, and rob." Jailed again in 1960, he was visited by Elvis Presley, who asked him repeatedly if he needed a lawyer or any help. Needing help so badly he could taste it, Bragg nevertheless declined. He was eventually released in 1967.

Bragg had emerged from the pen in better financial shape than most ex-convicts. He had half the proceeds from "Just Walkin' in the Rain" awaiting him. The publishing on the song was purchased by Gene Autry in May 1954, and Autry himself recorded it soon afterward, to small success. But Columbia's head of country A&R, Don Law, had faith in the song. One day, walking through

The Prisonaires, with Johnny Bragg (second from left)

(Escott)

These little girls of mine: Johnny Bragg and Ray Charles

(Escott)

the head office in New York, he met Mitch Miller, who was scouting material for a Johnnie Ray session. Law suggested "Just Walkin' in the Rain," and Ray took it to number 2 on the pop charts during the fall of 1956. The first writer's check Bragg received was for fourteen hundred dollars. Bragg, who had never seen such a sum on a check or anywhere, mistook it for fourteen dollars and asked the warden to deposit it in the commissary cash register so he could get some cigarettes and candy.

The Prisonaires' talent far transcended their novelty appeal. Bragg's breathtakingly pure lead tenor could have put the group in the front rank of vocal groups. But they were drawing on traditions that were alien to Phillips, who recorded little else in the close-harmony style, either sacred or secular. He would later say he regretted that he had not done more in the gospel field. He recorded one gospel single by the Brewsteraires for Chess, and released another by the Jones Brothers on the Sun label, but sales were poor. "It certainly wasn't intentional neglect," he said in 1984, "but you have to compromise. There's no telling what I should and could have done in gospel music from the Memphis area. I'm ashamed to say I barely touched the surface. It was a whole different area to merchandise, and you run out of time after working eighteen hours a day."

A more concerted effort to break into the black gospel field was made by Sam's brother Jud, who started the Sun Spot label in Hattiesburg, Mississippi. Some of the releases by the Sun Spot Quartet carried a spoken introduction from Jud and were almost certainly recorded by Sam in Memphis. Marion Keisker recalled that the label was launched at the time Elvis Presley came into Sun to record his first personal disc, which would place it in 1953. There

were at least four releases on Sun Spot, and it may have been seen as a companion label to Sun; but little more is known of the venture than the music contained on those records.

The Law of Increasing Returns

By the fall of 1953, even though Sam Phillips was again riding the kind of wave he had enjoyed with "Rocket 88" two summers earlier, he had not found the prosperity he had doubtless anticipated. Phillips' margin per single was small; his profit was tied up in repressings, and with slow-paying distributors.

After "Bear Cat" broke, Sam's first move had been to bring Jud into the picture. Jud had the knack for promotion that Sam had for production. He was gregarious, flamboyant, and, given half an opportunity, extravagant. By the time he joined Sam, Jud had worked as a singer, a gospel promoter, a front man for Roy Acuff's tent show, and a production assistant to Jimmy Durante.

In November 1953 Jud was on the road by himself, where he learned that some of the deals Bulleit had cut were not necessarily in Sun's best interest. From Richmond, Virginia, Jud wrote, "I've found the same thing here that I've found in several other places. Jim has promised them [distributors] free Sun records to compensate for the bad stock they were caught with on his other labels such as J-B. They were very fed up with the way Jim had given them the runaround since he had been with Sun."

By the end of 1953, Sam and Jud Phillips were pressuring Bulleit to sell his share of Sun Records. In February 1954 Jud borrowed the money to buy him out. The amount, Bulleit later recalled, was "twelve hundred dollars—but it really wasn't worth any more than that." During that same month Sam and Jud got a license from BMI to form their own publishing company, Hi-Lo Music, so they wouldn't have to place their copyrights through Bulleit.

The infrastructure that Sam and Jud had created—reliable distributors, accommodating DJs, and so on—was built on the assumption that the hits would keep on coming. As it happened, they didn't. Junior Parker left for greener pastures in Houston, Rufus Thomas could not recapture the novelty appeal of "Bear Cat," and the Prisonaires, unable to support their records with many personal appearances, found their popularity hard to sustain. The new artists that Phillips recorded did not have the allure of those faded or departed hitmakers. The most prolific artists during the demise of the blues era at Sun were Little Milton and Billy "The Kid" Emerson.

Little Milton

(Escott)

Milton

While once he traveled through Mississippi in a jalopy, hustling gigs where he could, Little Milton Campbell now travels North America in a converted Scenicruiser. Chart success has been elusive for some time, but Milton continues to keep a full engagement book. Some of his appearances today may seem half-hearted, the inevitable product of unpacking his guitar and walking out on stage ahead of the Miltonettes a few times too many. At his best, though, Little Milton can still recapture the fire of his youth, and make one believe he is walking the streets crying.

"Big" Milton was Milton's father, although his parents never married. Milton grew up with his mother and stepfather near Leland, Mississippi, and developed an early fascination for the guitar. "We lived on the outskirts of Leland," he told *Living Blues* magazine. "The town would close up by . . . 11:00 at night, and most of the black people who could do so would have suppers or juke joints out in the country—even if it was just outside the city limits where we lived. . . . My mom would put the kitchen table across the door and sell sandwiches, lemonade, corn liquor. My stepfather would have a dice game going and they would hire a guitar player. I'd be tucked in bed but the minute that the guy would hit the guitar, they'd look around and I'd be standing there, little long drawers on."

Like many rural blacks, Milton's family listened to the Grand Ole Opry as regularly as any other radio program, and Milton still cites such country

Little Milton
at the opening of Sunbeam
Mitchell's Club Paradise

Greeting a fan
after the show

musicians as Ernest Tubb and Roy Acuff among his favorites. At the age of eleven he got his first guitar from a mail order catalog, eventually parlaying his $14.52 Roy Rogers guitar into a career.

Married at fourteen and single again at fifteen, he started sitting in with the Eddie Cusic (or Kusic) band in Leland. "My older brother took me to this club in Leland. Eddie was playing there. I picked up his guitar, which was an electric model and sounded much better than my little thing, and I said, 'I'm really gonna get into this.' I'd come into town every weekend and sit in. Finally, the lady who owned the club (who was B. B. King's mother-in-law), she started throwing me a few bucks. Then Eddie hired me for $1.50 a night."

Milton made his studio debut as a sideman for Willie Love, who recorded for the Trumpet label in Jackson, Mississippi. But it was the ubiquitous Ike Turner who landed Milton his deal with Sun. "Ike lived seventy-five miles north of me in Clarksdale," recalled Milton to David Booth. "We were all playing up and down the Delta; I'd meet him here and there. I'd get into a car on Monday and travel to maybe three towns to set up my gigs, try and get a deposit, you know. Ike was always a smooth operator. He had a lot of ingenuity. He'd act as a talent scout for record companies, and he was solely responsible for getting me onto Sun Records."

Milton suffered from two problems during his tenure at Sun. The first was

(Joe Fritz/Norbert Hess)

Bobby Bland, Junior Parker (second from left), and Pat Hare (far right)

Cotton left town shortly after his second single was released. He joined the Muddy Waters revue and relocated to Chicago, where he remained. Hare also left town at roughly the same time, joining Junior Parker in the Blues Consolidated package that worked out of Houston.

Hare never realized his full potential. Born in Cherry Valley, Arkansas, in 1930, he had played at country suppers and fish fries as a teenage one-man band before moving to West Memphis in 1947. His first paying gig was with Howlin' Wolf, serenading the johns in a whorehouse. On Christmas Day 1949, five days after his nineteenth birthday, Hare married a 13-year-old girl and set up house in West Memphis.

He first appeared at the Sun studio in 1952 in the company of Walter Bradford, and surviving tapes from that session show that Hare had already developed a distinctive sound. Hare "had a Fender amp and a pretty good guitar," Phillips told Robert Palmer. "His pickup was powerful, and I think he had a mismatch of impedance. It was a little more than his amp could stand, but it felt good." From 1952 until he left town with Junior Parker in 1954, Hare became a fairly regular fixture at the studio, and his trademark sound —coarse, distorted, marked by aggressive fills and a fondness for playing them under vocal lines—became something of an early Sun trademark as well.

In 1956 Hare left Blues Consolidated and his wife and kids, moved to Chicago, and joined James Cotton in the Muddy Waters band. Sober, the man was self-effacing to the point of meekness, but drunk Hare became violent and aggressive. Shortly after playing the 1960 Newport festival with Waters, he was fired for being drunk once too often. Hare moved to Minneapolis to work with Mojo Buford. It was there that he committed one of his last acts as a free man: he shot his girlfriend (or her husband, according to some reports) and an arresting police officer, a crime chillingly presaged in "I'm Gonna Murder My Baby." He was sentenced to ninety-nine years and shipped to the Minnesota Correctional Facility in Stillwater in February 1962, where he died in September 1980.

The Boogie Disease

The blues releases on Sun tapered off during 1954. There were two singles (and reels and reels of unissued cuts) from the eccentric Dr. Ross, who epitomized all that Phillips loved about the blues. His approach was rhythmic, propulsive, and countrified. Ross had worked as a one-man band, but Phillips usually brought in some backup musicians when he recorded at Sun. By 1953 Phillips had perfected his use of slapback echo and used it to give a depth and resonance to the primitive drive of Ross's music; yet even a superficial comparison of that music with the R&B hits of 1953 and 1954 shows how anachronistic Ross had become—a fact Ross may have recognized before Phillips. He soon left Memphis for Flint, Michigan, where he started work in the auto plants.

The only other blues artist to record consistently into the Presley era was W. R. "Billy the Kid" Emerson. He saw five singles hit the market, each to diminishing acclaim. Emerson was a fine writer, though, and his material would assume a greater importance in Phillips' publishing catalog than it ever had in the record catalog.

Emerson, a fairly proficient pianist from Tarpon Springs, Florida, played with the Billy Battle band before being seconded into one of the countless incarnations of Ike Turner's Kings of Rhythm. It was Turner who brought Emerson to Phillips in January 1954. The first single they cut, "No Teasin' Around," got only limited attention, but Emerson returned to the studio three months later with an old nursery rhyme, "The Woodchuck." It was neither identifiably black nor white music; in Emerson's hands, it was a hybrid that intrigued Phillips in the same way that Elvis Presley would intrigue him eight weeks later when he struck up "That's All Right."

Doctor Ross—
and family

(Jim Dickinson)

After "The Woodchuck" got some healthy airplay, Emerson formed his own band and started working out of Cairo, Illinois. In October 1954 he returned to the Sun studio with an unorthodox blues he'd written, "When It Rains, It Really Pours." "That song," says Emerson, "was nearly a monster seller. Sam Phillips loved it, but he didn't concentrate on it, he didn't push on it." Emerson was one of the first Sun artists to feel Sam's ear turning to rock 'n' roll; "He wanted Elvis to cut it," he remembers.

By that point, Phillips was riding Presley's first hit and was desperately searching for copyrights that he owned in order to increase his margin on Presley singles. He did try to get Presley to record "When It Rains," first in 1955 and again during the Million Dollar Quartet session in December 1956. But the notion that Phillips deliberately failed to push Emerson's record in the R&B market so that Presley could record it for the country market is somewhat farfetched. The truth is probably that Presley was already stretching Sam's slender promotional resources as far as they could go, leaving little room for Emerson or anyone else.

Emerson grew to like Presley, despite the fact that he was cornering most of Phillips' attention. "Elvis was a real sweet kid," he recalls. "The white guys didn't talk to us colored guys too much back then, but Elvis was different— until they poisoned his mind. I remember one time we took him out to see Pee Wee Crayton at the Flamingo Club."

When Emerson returned to the studio in May 1955, it was with yet another group and an even stronger piece of material. "Red Hot" had been adapted from a high school cheerleader chant, "Our team is red hot . . ." In Emerson's hands it became "My gal is red hot," followed by the deathless retort: "Your gal ain't doodley squat." Eighteen months later, after Emerson had quit the label, rockabilly singer Billy Riley cut a speeded-up and stripped-down version that secured the song's place as a seminal rock 'n' roll tune. Bob Luman covered Riley's version, Sam the Sham revived it in 1966, and Robert Gordon turned in a sizzling rendition a decade later.

Emerson's last Sun single was released in January 1956. By that point Emerson had relocated to Chicago, and Phillips had other sounds in his head. Emerson and Phillips came into conflict in 1966 when Emerson claimed the publishing on "Red Hot" after Sam the Sham recorded it. Otherwise, his Sun recordings were firmly consigned to the past until, years later, he was called to Europe to revive them.

Roscoe's Rhythm: Reprise

With Emerson's departure, there was only one black artist left on the Sun label. After three years away from Phillips' studio, Roscoe Gordon had returned to sign a three-year deal with Sun in June 1955.

By the following year, the national music scene had changed broadly enough that black music could potentially cross over into the pop market, if it was

Roscoe Gordon and
Sam Phillips, 1956

(Photo by E. C. Withers, © Stephen C. LaVere 1991)

oriented to white radio. Roscoe's first calculated shot at the Top 40 came with a medium-tempo shuffle, "Shoobie Oobie," that stood a fair chance at following in Fats Domino's oversized footsteps. The flip side was a strange novelty tune, "Cheese and Crackers." The lyrics had been left on the studio piano by a white rockabilly, Hayden Thompson, who could do little with them. When Gordon appeared a few days later he found the lyrics, put his patented shuffle behind them, and came up with something truly bizarre. It was hailed by *Billboard* as the "weirdest record of the week," but neither side cracked the charts.

The end of Gordon's affiliation with Sun is harder to piece together. He returned in 1957 to record the ersatz rockabilly tune "Sally Jo," which stands with some recordings by Ray Sharp, Tarheel Slim, and Roy Brown among the few examples of black rockabilly. Its appearance must have upturned a few eyebrows among Roscoe's diehard constituency; but if Gordon can be said to have "sold out," he did it with style and boundless enthusiasm: "Sally Jo" was delightfully at variance with everything else he recorded.

Gordon's last visit to the Sun studio, in August 1958, resulted in a truly abysmal revival of the old Perez Prado hit "Cherry Pink and Apple Blossom White" that deservedly remained unissued. The following year Gordon signed with Vee-Jay Records and resuscitated his career with "Just a Little Bit" (his only pop hit) and a reprise of "No More Doggin.' "

By 1958 all of Roscoe's associates from the early days of the Memphis Recording Service and Sun Records had been firmly consigned to the past. The surviving tapes had been tied together with elastic bands and stored away as mementos of less prosperous days. The blues singers who remained in Memphis did not have the marketability of those who had departed, and Phillips' head had been turned around by the gold he found in an unexpected quarter. Still, his success with rock 'n' roll should not obscure the insight that Phillips brought to recording the blues. He worked hard to get the best from his artists. He usually knew when they were trying to play something to please the white guy behind the glass. He wouldn't yell at them if they arrived late, and when other labels might do one or two takes and call it a night, Phillips would sit behind his tape deck until sunup if he thought the musicians on the studio floor might capture the sound that he heard in his head.

Despite his perfectionism, the hits he had enjoyed in 1953 showed Phillips that the demographic base he was servicing was simply too narrow. "Keep in mind there were a number of very good R&B labels," he said in 1982. "The base wasn't broad enough because of racial prejudice. It wasn't broad enough to get the amount of commercial play and general acceptance overall—not just in the South. When you're on the road—sixty-five or seventy thousand miles a year—as I was in those days, you get a lot of input from the ground. On Mondays and Wednesdays, when the jukebox operators would come by the distributor for their weekly supply of records, and on Tuesdays and Thursdays, when the smaller retail outlets would come by, I'd be there. They'd tell me, 'These people [the blacks] are ruining our children.' Now these were basically good people, but conceptually they did not understand the kinship between the black and white people in the South. So I knew what I had to do to broaden the base of acceptance."

The path toward commercial salvation was made clear by the success of one young singer who, like Phillips, intuitively understood black music and quickly synthesized both a musical style and an image that would enable Phillips to take yellow Sun records into places where they had never been before.

Recommended Listening

A selection of Phillips' pre-Sun and Sun blues recordings can be found on *Blue Flames* (Rhino [USA] R2 70962).

Sun Records Harmonica Classics (Rounder [USA] CD/SS 29) features key performances from Walter Horton, Dr. Ross, Hot Shot Love, Sammy Lewis and Willie Johnson, and Joe Hill Louis.

The Prisonaires' recordings for Sun can be found on *Just Walkin' in the Rain* (Bear Family [Germany] BCD 15523).

Mystery Train (Rounder [USA] CD/SS 38) comprises the Sun recordings of Junior Parker, James Cotton, and Pat Hare.

A selection of Little Milton's Sun recordings are on *Hittin' the Boogie* (Zu-Zazz [UK] Z 2007) and *The Sun Masters* (Rounder [USA] CD/SS 35).

WKH
Louisiana
Be Happy
Go Lucky!
LUCKY STRIKE
CIGARETTES
L.S./M.F.T.

ELVIS PRESLEY: SUN #209

The story of Elvis Presley's association with Sun Records is essentially the story of three rapid transformations. A painfully shy nineteen-year-old kid was transformed into a twenty-year-old strutting peacock. A singer with barely enough confidence to sing on the front porch was transformed into a performer who was being sought by virtually every major record label in the United States. And a country singer was transformed into an artist with the potential to cross the rigid demarcation lines separating pop, country and western, and rhythm and blues.

It was an eventful seventeen months that Presley spent at Sun, and much of what happened has been taken for granted. For as long as most can remember, Elvis Presley has represented the benchmark of success in popular music. Every other performer of epic stature is measured against him. It is hard to appreciate today that when Presley walked into Sun Records for the first time, he was a household name only in his own household. Now that his achievement in blending pop, country, and R&B into a new hybrid has become a commonplace of American popular culture, it is difficult to understand how alien his music was in 1954. It is even harder to view the course of Presley's early career through the correct end of the telescope, or to imagine a time when a record salesman would go into a store and encounter the riposte, "Elvis who?"

How did the shrinking violet of July 1954 become the self-proclaimed Hillbilly Cat of November 1955? And why was virtually every major record label in the United States coming to Sam Phillips with checkbook in hand, willing to sign an artist whose appeal was largely untested outside the South? It all happened very quickly, in a short period that deserves another look. Though it may be a cliché to say that Elvis Presley blended hillbilly music with R&B and pop, it has never been fully explained just how the music he created became so hot so quickly.

A rare early shot of Elvis on the Louisiana Hayride, c. 1954

"Potent New Chanter..."

Popular wisdom, which has now taken on the power of a classical myth, has it that the first the world ever heard from Elvis Presley was in the summer of 1953, when Elvis walked into the Sun studio to record a personal disc for his mother's birthday.

As some have pointed out, it is more likely, considering that Gladys Presley's birthday was in the spring, that Presley made the first record for himself, to hear how he sounded. That first disc soon ended up in the hands of Presley's schoolmate Ed Leek. They shared a homeroom in the twelfth grade at Humes High and hung out together for a year or two. By Leek's own account, he hung on to the disc, which coupled "My Happiness" with "That's When Your Heartaches Begin," because his grandparents owned a record player and the Presley family didn't.

Either Sam Phillips or Marion Keisker noted that Presley had a good feel for ballads and that he should be invited back. The personal disc was cut in the summer of 1953; the invitation to audition for Sun came in May or June 1954. It seems inconceivable that there was no contact between Presley and Sun in the interim. Presley probably cut a second personal disc before Phillips was impressed enough to ask him to record for Sun. Presley probably followed up, opportunistically, with some appearances at the studio. At one time, Phillips recalled seeing him quite frequently, and remembered saying, "Here's ol' Elvis coming to see what kind of star we can make of him today."

One serious challenge to that scenario, though, comes from Johnny Bragg, the lead singer of the Prisonaires, who suggests that Presley's face was a familiar sight at Sun as early as June 1953. Bragg clearly recalled that Presley was present during the all-day session on June 1 that resulted in "Just Walkin' in the Rain." "I was having problems phrasing some of the words," said Bragg. "Sam was ready to give up on it, and here come this guy out of nowhere, wearing raggedy blue jeans. He said, 'I believe I can help him pronounce the words.' Sam got mad. He said, 'Didn't I tell you to stay outta here? These men are prisoners. We're likely to be sued.' I said, 'If he thinks he can help me phrase this thing, give him a chance.' I was getting disgusted because Sam didn't like 'Just Walkin' in the Rain,' and I knew it could amount to something. Eventually, Sam said, 'OK, let him try,' so we took a break, and Elvis worked with me on my diction. He didn't know too much about what he was doing, but he worked with me on it, and when we went back, we got it on the first cut."

Bragg may have telescoped the time frame, confusing the first Prisonaires session with a later one; certainly, there is no mention of Presley in the article about the session that appeared in the Memphis *Press Scimitar* the following day. Still, it's fairly clear that Presley met Bragg at some point in 1953 or early 1954 when the Prisonaires were recording for Sun. The last Prisonaires session logged at Sun was in February 1954, although they returned for another

(Escott)

Elvis in 1953 or '54

unlogged session, when Phillips recorded them over outtakes of Presley's "Good Rockin' Tonight." Presley remembered Bragg and went to the Tennessee State Penitentiary in 1960 to visit him—"He has known Bragg from back when he was starting out," said the accompanying report.

The one indisputable fact is that at some point in May or June 1954 the Presley family, residing at 462 Alabama Street, took a phone call from Sun Records. At Sam Phillips' behest, Marion Keisker had called, wondering if Elvis would care to come down and try out a new song that Phillips had picked up in Nashville.

Phillips remembers that the song was called "Without You," and that he had acquired it from Peer-Southern Music in Nashville. That seems plausible, though unlikely: Peer does indeed have a song called "Without You" on file, but that song is an English adaptation of a Spanish song called "Tres Palabras" that had been kicking around since 1942. Another, more credible, scenario is that Phillips had picked up an unpublished song called "Without You" from one of the musicians at the Nashville State Penitentiary, which he visited on May 8, 1954, when he was recording the Prisonaires.

In any event, Presley ran down Alabama Street to Manassas Avenue, down Manassas to Union Avenue, and then half a block west to the Memphis Recording Service. He arrived, as Marion Keisker told the story, "before I had hardly put the phone down." The thoughts in Presley's head as he raced that half-mile to Sun can only be guessed at. Like the black hopefuls who had gone through that door before him, he knew that this was his one shot at escaping a bleakly predictable future.

Leaving aside the unresolvable question of how many appearances Presley had made at the studio, there is also some dispute over how much performing experience he had acquired when he arrived that afternoon. Sam Phillips told Peter Guralnick, "He didn't play with bands. He didn't go to this little club and pick and grin. All he did was set [sic] with his guitar on the side of his bed at home. I don't think he even played on the front porch."

Of course, Phillips would have had no reason to assume that Presley was anything other than the painfully shy, introverted kid who looked down at the floor when he spoke and could barely manage anything other than "yessir" and "nossir" without tripping over himself. Phillips is also careful to emphasize his role in bringing Presley's peculiar genius to fruition—and that role cannot be questioned. Perhaps no one else would have had the insight or patience even to embark on such an undertaking. Nevertheless, the few facts we have today do suggest, whatever Phillips thought at the time (or decided later), that young Elvis Presley was more of a gadabout than had been thought.

That early personal disc, finally released in 1990 by RCA on their collection *Great Performances*, betrays a musical confidence that had been nurtured in more places than his bedroom. One of those who remembered seeing Elvis playing around town before "That's All Right" was Paul Burlison, who would have good reason to remember Presley because he worked with him at Crown Electric. Burlison later played guitar with Johnny Burnette and the Rock 'n' Roll Trio, but in 1954 he was in Shelby Follin's hillbilly band.

(J. L. Denson)

"Over at KWEM [in West Memphis]," recalled Burlison, "they'd have a Saturday afternoon matinee. They'd have bands playing for thirty minutes in sponsored segments. Our sponsor was Airways Motors. One day we broadcast right off the car lot, and Elvis come up and sung with us. Shelby announced over the radio that if anyone wanted to sing or play an instrument that they should come on out and join in. I already knew Elvis could sing because every Saturday afternoon Elvis, Johnny Black [Bill Black's brother], and Lee Denson would play at the Girls' Club at Lauderdale Courts, and I'd already seen him there 'cause I lived right around the corner. There was a chaperoned hop every Saturday night and Elvis, Johnny, and Lee would get down there on Saturday afternoon, sit out on the lawn, and sing before the hop. Then I saw him standing by the stage when we were broadcasting and I said to Shelby, 'Get that fella up here. He sings.' "

According to Burlison, Presley sang a tune called "Keep Your Hands Off of It (Birthday Cake)," a country blues laden with double entendre that Jerry Lee Lewis would record for Sun in 1960. If that's true, his choice of material alone bespeaks an early desire to test the limits.

Memphis record producer and musician Jim Dickinson also remembers seeing Elvis play at small clubs and hops around town before "That's All Right." Presley would play quite regularly at basement parties in the Hotel Chisca. One of those who dropped in from time to time was Dewey Phillips, who worked upstairs at WHBQ. In fact, Dickinson surmises that one of the reasons that Dewey latched onto Presley's first record was that he already knew him and had an inkling of his potential. In an interview with Memphis writer and broadcaster Charles Raiteri, local DJ George Klein (who had gone to school with Presley and was one of Dewey Phillips' gofers in 1954) recalled that Dewey had told him that he had a new record in his hands by one of Klein's school buddies. Klein said that he knew it must be Presley, because he was the only one who sang.

The Denson family connection that Burlison mentioned in passing offers another intriguing glimpse into Presley's early years. Jesse Lee Denson's parents ran the Poplar Street Mission, where, according to Denson's brother,

Jimmy Lee, the Presleys obtained most of their household possessions. Jesse Lee was a gregarious kid, which, by all accounts, Elvis was not; he appears to have taught Elvis some rudiments of the guitar and brought him to the basement jam sessions and Girls' Club gigs at Lauderdale Courts. Jimmy Lee remembers Presley as a wallflower, in awe of bad-ass kids like Jesse Lee and Dorsey Burnette, who had served time together at state reform school in Nashville.

Jimmy Lee Denson's portrait of Elvis is that of an incorrigibly wimpy and terminally withdrawn kid for whom complete sentences were a problem. That may be, but it's clear that a transformation began to occur at some point in 1953 or early 1954—a transformation that Denson wouldn't have witnessed, as he left town to sell automobiles in Houston in 1953. Jesse Lee remained in Memphis and eventually recorded for Vik, the RCA subsidiary, in 1957, apparently without Presley's intercession.

The picture begins to sharpen after Marion Keisker's phone call. Phillips paired Presley with guitarist Scotty Moore and bassist Bill Black, whom he had seconded from Doug Poindexter's Starlite Wranglers, and told them to work up some material. "Bill reported back that he didn't see much in Elvis," Phillips told Robert Palmer. "They were in the studio four or five different times. I'd listen to what they were doing and they'd go back and work some more. It was an informal thing, with no promises to anybody." Phillips recalled that they were in and out of the studio over a three- to six-month period, although that seems unlikely. On the other hand, Scotty Moore telescopes the time period considerably, contending to Peter Guralnick that they recorded "That's All Right" within days of getting together, which seems just as improbable.

With his cheap guitar and the grudging support of Black and Moore, Presley tried to sing "Without You." If Phillips ever got as far as committing any cuts to tape, they must have sounded as woeful as Presley's attempt at "Harbor Lights" recorded a little later in the sessions. Trying to croon, Presley could only manage an insecure whine—not a good astringent nasal howl like Hank Williams', but the immature sound of a voice that has yet to find itself.

Still working on his crooning, Presley tried "I Love You Because," which moved Phillips to hit the RECORD button on his Ampex. Then, apparently, the little group took a break for coffee and Cokes. "All of a sudden," recalled Scotty Moore, "Elvis started singing a song, jumping around, acting the fool, and then Bill picked up his bass and started acting the fool too, and I started playing with 'em. Sam had the door to the control booth open . . . he was either editing some tape or something, and he stuck his head out and said, 'What're you doing?' We said, 'We don't know.' 'Well, back up,' he said, 'try to find a place to start and do it again.' "

The song that Presley was fooling around with was "That's All Right (Mama)," a song that had been on his mind for possibly seven years. It had been that long since Arthur "Big Boy" Crudup had recorded a version for RCA Victor every bit as primitive and energized as Presley's own. Elvis made one telling change in the lyrics: the line, "The life you're living, son, women be the death of you," became, "Son, that gal you're fooling with, she ain't no good for you." The truly surprising thing, though, is how perfectly Presley, Moore, and Black retained the loose-jointed swing of the original. This was the unmistakable black feel to which Phillips responded when he stuck his head around the door.

Phillips has often been quoted as having said something to the effect of, "If I could only find a white boy who could sing like a negro I could make me a million dollars." Although it remains the quote most often associated with him, Phillips knew better than most that a white boy imitating black blues singers would be ludicrous. A generation of British blues singers strangling their voices trying to sound like Elmore James would prove that point with finality. Phillips was looking for a white artist who could bring the feel of black music to white kids who were too hidebound by racial intolerance to accept the genuine article. Marion Keisker remembered his mentioning that on innumerable occasions. As he stuck his head into the studio that day in 1954, he heard what he had sought.

With "That's All Right" on tape, Phillips needed a B side for his debut Elvis Presley single, and looked back to 1947's "Blue Moon of Kentucky," Bill Monroe's stately bluegrass waltz. Presley changed the meter and the tempo, bringing Arthur Crudup's sparse, freewheeling approach to the country song. A fascinating bit of rehearsal tape from the session was found in the early '70s; the song started out slower, more countrified, not yet removed an entire dimension beyond its origin, as it became. Those who discovered the tape couldn't identify the artist until the snippet was played to Jim Dickinson, who declared, "What you have there is what it sounded like ten minutes before rock 'n' roll was invented." Phillips' eureka— "Hell, that's fine!" he cries, "that's different! That's a pop song now!"—was captured on the tape. He is clearly electrified by what he has just heard.

With both sides of the single wrapped up, Sam Phillips ran off a few preproduction acetates to test out his hunch. He circulated them to some key local DJs in Memphis. "Sleepy-Eyed" John Lepley at WHHM and Bob Neal at WMPS got them. So did Dewey Phillips at WHBQ.

"Get yasself a wheelbarrow load of mad hogs, run 'em through the front door, and tell 'em Phillips sentcha," screamed Dewey, wired from his usual combination of uppers and corn liquor. "This is Red Hot and Blue comin' atcha from the magazine floor of the Hotel Chisca. And now we got somethin' new gonna cut lost, DEE-GAWWWW! cut LOOSE! Good people, this is Elvis Presley . . ."

Dewey Phillips created some local demand for Presley's debut, and it was Dewey who conducted his first on-air interview. Telling the story to Memphis writer Stanley Booth, Phillips asserted that he had "played the record thirty times, fifteen times each side. When the phone calls started to come in I got hold of Elvis's daddy Vernon. He said Elvis was at a movie down at Suzore's #2 theater. 'Get him over here,' I said. Before long Elvis came running in. 'Sit down, I'm gone interview you,' I said. He said, 'Mr. Phillips, I don't know nuthin' about being interviewed.' 'Just don't say nuthin' dirty,' I told him.

(Robert J. Dye)

Elvis and
Dewey Phillips

"He sat down and I told him I'd let him know when I was ready to start. I had a couple of records cued up and while they played we talked. I asked him where he went to high school and he said, 'Humes.' I wanted to get that out because a lot of people listening thought he was colored. Finally, I said, 'Alright Elvis, thank you very much.' 'Aren't you gone interview me?' he asked. 'I already have,' I said, 'the mike's been open the whole time.' He broke out into a cold sweat."

According to Sam Phillips' production log, "That's All Right," backed with "Blue Moon of Kentucky," was released as Sun #209 on July 19, 1954. He sent a review copy to *Billboard* magazine. To their credit, Bob Rolontz and the review staff at *Billboard* picked up on Presley immediately. In the issue dated August 7, reviewing Presley among the new country releases, they said, "Presley is a potent new chanter who can sock over a tune for either country or R&B markets. . . . A strong new talent."

Despite the favorable reaction to the record, Phillips knew that he needed to get Presley some exposure. A Slim Whitman package show was coming to town, and Phillips managed to secure a spot for Presley as a warm-up attraction. Just before the show, on July 28, 1954, Presley received his first mention in the local papers. Edwin Howard worked across the street from Sun Records at the Memphis *Press Scimitar*, where he held the title of Amusements Editor. "Marion Keisker was a friend of mine," recalls Howard, "and she called me one day and asked if I would interview a young man whom they considered very promising. I said I'd be happy to. She brought Presley in and I did a very minimal interview. He was absolutely inarticulate and limited himself to 'Yessir' and 'Nossir.' Marion filled in everything else." Presley was then dispatched to a staff photographer who snapped the first publicity shot of Elvis Presley—looking wholly ill at ease with a brush cut and bow tie.

The story goes that Presley appeared on the afternoon show of July 30 and did poorly, limiting himself to ballads, which seems strange considering he had been placed on the show to plug his new record. During the evening show, Presley apparently sang up-tempo songs, and either from nervousness or in emulation of flamboyant R&B singers like Wynonie Harris, he began to shake his legs. The Slim Whitman fans were being treated to something stranger than they could possibly have conceived; we can only imagine their shock. But there must have been a younger crowd present that night; perhaps more than a few had even come to see Presley, wondering what the singer of "That's All Right" looked like. Marion Keisker sat among the crowd, and sensed the electricity that spread like fear through an antelope herd.

Even Presley was surprised as he stepped backstage. "Everyone was screaming and everything," he recalled in 1956, "and my manager told me they was hollering because I was wiggling." The Presley legend had its uncertain birth during that evening concert on July 30, 1954, when the musical and visual elements came together for the first time.

Less than a month after the release of his debut record, Presley's momentum was growing. Scotty Moore, who had signed him to a management contract just days after the first record was released, had secured him a few gigs around

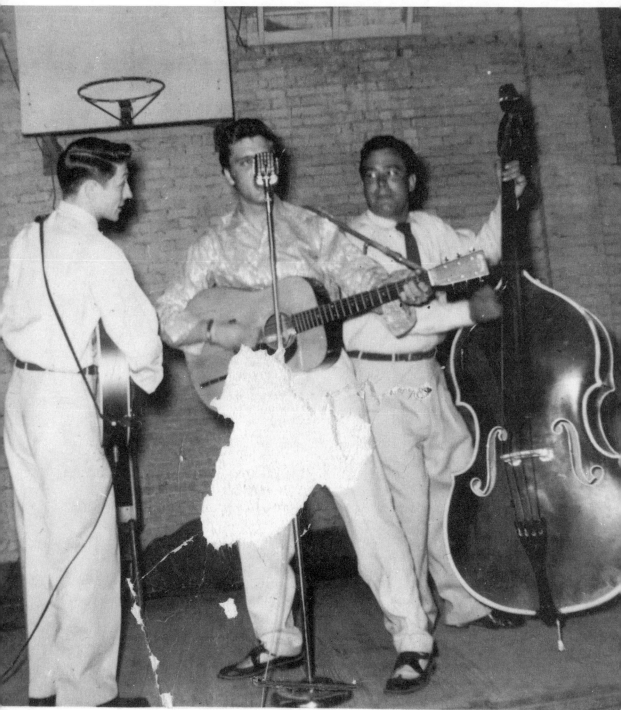

The earliest-known photo of Elvis on stage: with Scotty and Bill, 1954

(Escott)

Memphis. Some stations in the Dallas area had also picked up on the record, and Alta Hayes, who ran the one-stop operation of the local branch of Big State Record Distributors, pushed his records to her jukebox customers and became an important booster in that key market. Sam Phillips, Scotty Moore, Dewey Phillips, Marion Keisker, and a few others such as Alta Hayes now believed in Presley—possibly before Presley believed in himself.

Tears at the Grand Ole Opry

The days and nights between August and October of 1954 are still obscure from our distant perspective. For his part, Sam Phillips was trying to break Presley outside Memphis. In a conversation with Charles Raiteri, Phillips elaborated on how difficult it was to get Presley's music on air: "He was an immediate hit in Memphis but on the road it drug my ass out. I remember talking to T. Tommy Cutrer at KCIJ in Shreveport, who's one of the greatest guys in the world. One thing I never did was try to overpower somebody with my conviction of what I had in my little black bag. 'If you can give me some play on it, I'd appreciate it. If you can't, I understand.' T. Tommy told me, 'Sam, I would but if I put this on, they'll run me out of town.' I said, 'Tommy, I can't believe that "Blue Moon of Kentucky" . . .' He said, 'Man, Sam. I know . . .' "

Just down the street from KCIJ, Fats Washington played R&B on KENT. "Fats played my R&B records," asserted Phillips. "All of them. But when I went to play him 'That's All Right' he played it for me but he said on the air, 'I just want to tell all my listeners I got Sam Phillips in the studio with me and he thinks this is gonna be a hit record. I'm tellin' him that this man should not be played after the sun comes up in the morning. It's so country.' I'll never forget that statement, but at least he was honest about it."

Presley continued to work as a gofer at Crown Electric and played local hillbilly nightspots like the Eagle's Nest, where he was an intermission attraction for Sleepy-Eyed John's western swing band. He also worked at KWEM in West Memphis with Doug Poindexter, and played with Scotty and Bill as an intermission attraction on Poindexter's personal appearances.

It had been during the sessions that produced Poindexter's sole Sun record that Phillips first became aware of Bill Black's bass playing and Scotty Moore's picking. "Scotty and Bill really evolved that rockabilly sound through discussions we had right there in the studio," recalls Phillips. "I credit Scotty with being one of the easiest persons to work with and for having a real desire to be innovative. His mind was always open and that was an awful lot of help to me. He had a lot of patience, too. He had been around the studio for a while, hoping that there was some way I could use him. He was sympathetic to what I was trying to do—come up with something a little different. One thing I did

(Escott)

Doug Poindexter
and his Starlite Wranglers,
with Bill Black (left)
and Scotty Moore (right)

not like was that Scotty was a great fan of Chet Atkins, because I didn't have that kind of playing in mind. But, like I say, he was willing to try something else and was real keen to succeed."

Of Bill Black, Phillips recalls that he "just caught my ear as a real good rhythmic bass player. He had a stand-up bass that had an unusual sound. It was a slap beat and a tonal beat at one and the same time. It was important back then that we worked a rhythm into the bass patterns, since I didn't use drums much in 1954."

The studio's tape delay echo and Phillips' miking techniques enabled Elvis, Scotty, and Bill to create a rich texture from three pieces. The bass slapping fulfilled two roles: the click of the strings hitting the neck created a percussive effect, while the pitch and resonance filled out the bottom end. The echo "fattened" the sound, giving some of the faster numbers a compelling syncopation. The group ran into problems, however, when they tried to recreate that sound on the road using their primitive PA equipment. Their thin sound was just one of the problems they encountered when they got an unexpected invitation to play a guest shot on the Grand Ole Opry.

That Elvis Presley was invited to appear on the Opry in 1954 is remarkable and not easy to explain. In the business only a shade over twelve weeks, he was not yet a professional singer. True, his first single was sitting atop the country chart in Memphis, but it hadn't made much of an impact elsewhere. It was unprecedented for an artist to appear on the Opry at such an early stage in his career.

Despite having a second single on the market, Presley performed "Blue Moon of Kentucky" on the 10:15–10:30 segment of the Opry on October 2, 1954. He was worried that he might offend Opry veteran Bill Monroe with his goosed-up version of the song, but Monroe apparently told him that it was fine for his style of music and the way he sang. Those may just have been the most charitable words Presley heard that night. Irascible Opry manager Jim Denny made it clear that he would not exercise a month-long option on Elvis's services. He was upset at not getting the "full band," and was especially concerned that Presley was not singing country music. It was Denny's lack of enthusiasm that may have accounted for the story, perpetuated by Presley, that he was told that night to "go back to driving a truck."

It was probably Bill Monroe, the stern, unsmiling apostle of pure country music, who knew that he had heard something special that night. Two decades earlier, Monroe had forged his style by mixing a heavy dose of the blues with his mountain music, and his high, keening vocals would later influence a generation of rockabillies with their passion and drive. A month before Presley appeared on the Opry, Monroe made a date with his A&R manager to go to the studio and record just one song: "Blue Moon of Kentucky." He sang the first verse and the bridge in triple meter at a slow waltz tempo (as he had on his original version), then doubled the tempo, switching to duple meter in direct emulation of Elvis Presley. It must have been overwhelming for Presley to realize that his first record had influenced one of his idols enough for him to revise his interpretation of one of his signature tunes. The switch in tempo was a device that Presley would use a few months later when he revived "Milkcow Blues."

The brush with Monroe aside, Presley could draw little comfort from his first trip to Nashville; but consolation was just around the corner. Sam Phillips had sent a copy of "That's All Right" to the Opry's rival, the Louisiana Hayride, broadcast on KWKH out of Shreveport, Louisiana. In his covering letter and the phone calls that followed, Phillips stressed that Presley was a "white boy." Horace Logan, who booked talent for the Hayride, understood why when he heard the disc. Under Logan's tutelage the Hayride had developed a flair for experimentation that had already spawned Webb Pierce and Hank Williams. They had even taken Williams back in 1952 after the Opry had dismissed him for habitual drunkenness. Logan, deciding to take a chance on Presley, scheduled him for a guest shot two weeks after his Opry debut.

Hasty acquisition of "attitude"

(G. Geller)

The Hayride emcee, Frank Page, had some insightful words for Elvis Presley on that far-off Saturday night:

"I'd like to know how you came up with that rhythm and blues style," asked Page. "Because that's all it is."

"Well, sir," replied Presley with disarming humility, "to be honest, we just stumbled upon it."

"You're mighty lucky, you know," continued Page. "They've been looking for something new in the folk music field for a long time now. I think you've got it."

Presley sang "That's All Right" and "Blue Moon of Kentucky." Bill Black was barely audible, and the songs were essentially a duet between Presley's voice and Scotty Moore's electric guitar. They were invited back and quickly became regulars, joining Slim Whitman, Red Sovine, Johnny Horton, Jim Reeves, and Jimmy C. Newman. Presley was signed to a year-long contract on November 6, 1954, that called for him to appear every Saturday, although it stipulated that he could miss one Saturday every three months. The starting salary was eighteen dollars per show for Presley, and twelve dollars each for Scotty and Bill. The Hayride added a steel guitar and a drummer behind him on some subsequent shows to help flesh out the sound.

The exposure he gained on the Hayride was crucial to Presley's success. Those Saturday night broadcasts on the clear-channel station established Presley's music in Texas, Louisiana, Alabama, Mississippi, Arkansas, Missouri, and western Tennessee. Presley quit his job and started following up his radio appearances with stage shows, both as a single and as part of the Hayride touring packages. At roughly the same time that Presley was signed to the Hayride, Bob Neal took over from Scotty Moore as Presley's manager. He started Elvis Presley Enterprises from a suite in the Sterick Building at 160 Union Avenue. Both Neal and the Hayride were showing a surprising level of confidence in a kid who might yet turn out to be a flash in the pan.

After they signed the Hayride contract, Scotty Moore and Bill Black quit Doug Poindexter's Starlite Wranglers and started working exclusively with Presley. Years later, Poindexter would assert that Presley "wasn't causing too many riots in them days. Frankly, I thought the boy would starve to death." But Clyde Rush, the rhythm guitar player with the Wranglers, disputes Poindexter's account, attributing it to pique that has barely subsided over the course of thirty years. Rush recalled that Presley's intermission spots quickly became the hit of the Wranglers' show, even in such unlikely venues as the Firestone Workers Union Hall. Possibly coveting Presley's spot on the Hayride, Poindexter found replacements for Moore and Black, but soon quit the music business to sell insurance.

MEMPHIS, TENN.—Elvis Presley, the 19-year-old country songster who clicked with "Blue Moon of Kentucky" and "That's All Right Mama" on the Sun label and was catapulted into a starring spot on the Louisiana Hayride, has signed a personal management contract with Bob Neal, popular WMPS country disk jockey, this city. Although Neal has been in the country music field for eight years, with dj shows, promotions, bookings, etc., this is his first venture into personal management. Pictured above are Elvis Presley (seated), Tom Neal (right) and Sam Phillips prexy of Sun Records.

*H*ayride touring
package '55

(Escott)

Good Rockin' Tonight

It has been recognized by almost every rock writer that the Sun recordings had a sense of fun that Presley rarely managed to recapture. That was especially true of his second single, released on September 22, 1954.

The top side, "Good Rockin' Tonight," was an R&B song heavy with sexual overtones. Both the writer, Roy Brown, and singer Wynonie Harris had scored a hit with the song in 1948. And then, in a display of true musical eclecticism, Presley picked for the flip side a tune from Walt Disney's 1949 animated film *Cinderella*: "I Don't Care If the Sun Don't Shine," a minor pop hit in 1950 for Patti Page, Dean Martin, and others. The strange dichotomy between the innocent and the profane that would exercise such a fascination over teenage girls two years later was played out in microcosm on Presley's second single.

Presley's newfound confidence in front of the microphone is in full force on these sides. It was the first record to bear evidence of the Presley swagger. He is playful, obviously full of energy and enthusiasm. "I Don't Care If the Sun Don't Shine" also sports the first percussion used on a Presley record: in this case, either a set of bongos played by Phillips' neighbor Buddy Cunningham, or Presley himself thumping the back of his guitar.

Inevitably, "Good Rockin' Tonight" cracked the local Memphis country chart—on November 3, 1954—but it failed to show up as strongly as "That's All Right." Precise sales figures are hard to come by, but we do know that "That's All Right" sold 6,300 copies during its first three weeks on the market. By November it had probably sold over 25,000; its impact was sufficiently strong that Marty Robbins covered the song in December and took it into the national country charts early the following year. By comparison, "Good Rockin' Tonight" probably sold less than 20,000 copies during its first few months on the market.

On November 15 and/or December 10, 1954, Presley went back into the studio to record his third single. By this point it was obvious that he was not a songwriter. This meant that Phillips was committed to paying mechanicals (publishing royalties) to companies other than his own unless he could generate some original material. A theater manager from Covington, Tennessee, was the first to come to Phillips' rescue: Jack Sallee ran the Ruffin Theatre, which hosted a hillbilly jamboree on Friday nights. He went to the Memphis Recording Service to record a few promo shots for the show, and listened while Phillips related his dilemma. A few days later, while eating breakfast, Sallee came up with the idea for "You're a Heartbreaker." He made a rough demo for Phillips, who liked it. The song was Sallee's first and last published composition. It was an undistinguished piece of material (one of the few Presley songs that almost no one has attempted to cover or revive), but Phillips owned the rights to it and Presley duly recorded it.

The other piece of original material came from two members of the Snearly Ranch Boys in West Memphis. Trumpeter Bill Taylor and steel guitarist Stan

(Robert J. Dye)

This year's model: 1955

Kesler worked up "I'm Left, You're Right, She's Gone," borrowing the melody from a Campbell's Soup advertisement. Surviving tapes reveal that it was first conceived as a slow blues, and the group recorded it with a guitar figure lifted from the Delmore Brothers' "Blues Stay Away from Me." At some point, however, the group changed their approach and reworked the song into a medium-tempo hillbilly shuffle.

Phillips thought that the arrangement would benefit from the presence of a drummer, so he called Jimmie Lott, who had auditioned at Sun with an East High School jazz band earlier in 1954. "Sam asked me if I would be interested in doing some studio work," recalls Lott, "and I said I would. I was maybe fifteen or sixteen years old, and I was at home one night and took a phone call from Sam Phillips. I had bronchitis at the time, but I loaded up my drums into my mom's car. Elvis was standing in the doorway of the studio. He had long greasy ducktails, which was not too cool with my group. We cut three songs, 'I'm Left, You're Right, She's Gone,' 'You're a Heartbreaker,' and 'How Do You Think I Feel.' I set a Latin tempo to 'How Do You Think I Feel,' which D.J. Fontana used when they rerecorded the song at Victor. Sam asked me if I would be interested in working with the group and I told him I had another year of school and couldn't."

"How Do You Think I Feel" was recorded over except for a rehearsal (issued on *The Sun Country Years* Bear Family boxed set) in which Elvis is off-mike. Scotty Moore is captured rehearsing the guitar part he replicated note-for-note eighteen months later when the song was rerecorded for RCA.

Phillips kept "I'm Left, You're Right, She's Gone" in the can for a while, instead releasing "You're a Heartbreaker," which he coupled with an old blues, "Milkcow Blues (Boogie)." The pairing was issued on Presley's twentieth birthday, January 8, 1955. And the downward sales pattern continued: sales during

"That's a pop song, now!" In the studio with Sam Phillips.

(Escott)

the first six months were a disappointing 20,600. The single became the worst-selling of Presley's Sun singles: After session costs had been deducted, sales of 20,000 would have netted Presley approximately four hundred dollars.

Nevertheless, Phillips and Presley still had much that was positive to reflect upon as they sat down to share a little birthday cake—Sam's birthday fell just three days before Elvis's—in January 1955. For his part, Phillips had just about ceased releasing anything but Presley records. He had canceled the final release he had planned by the Prisonaires, and had shipped one record by a local western swing band, Malcolm Yelvington and the Star Rhythm Boys. He released a final single by Dr. Ross and, on Presley's birthday, issued "When It Rains It Really Pours" by Billy the Kid Emerson. Only six records had been released in six months; three of them were by Presley. Phillips must have known that he was putting too many eggs into one basket. Still, when he expanded the roster in early 1955, it was with local hillbilly musicians. The period between July 1954 and January 1955 was a significant watershed in the history of Sun Records, but neither Presley nor Phillips could have guessed what would happen to the ball they had started rolling.

Enter the Colonel

At some point in early 1955 Presley became associated with another branch of the Nashville establishment, signing a booking arrangement with the team of Hank Snow and "Colonel" Tom Parker. Snow was a Canadian cowboy singer whose steely determination had brought him from grim rural poverty in Nova Scotia to an exalted position in the Nashville oligarchy. Unlike many of his contemporaries, he had neither boozed nor whored away all of his money, splurging only on increasingly luxuriant toupees. "Colonel Tom" was a former carnival barker who many years later was revealed to be an illegal immigrant from Holland. Together, the Dutch carny and the diminutive Canadian cowboy formed a company called Jamboree Attractions, which operated out of Madison, Tennessee. Soon after Bob Neal took over as Presley's manager, he called upon Parker's services as a booking agent.

· Neal was understandably anxious to get his boy exposed outside the school halls and hillbilly nightspots of the mid-South. Parker seemed to hold the key. On February 14, 1955, Elvis Presley appeared as a headliner on a show in Carlsbad, New Mexico. He then swung back through the Southwest on another tour set by Parker that was headlined by Snow's son, Jimmy, together with Mother Maybelle Carter and her daughters and the hillbilly comedian the Duke of Paducah ("Dooka P'dooka"). February 26 found Presley in the frozen north for the first time, playing the Circle Theater Jamboree in Cleveland, Ohio. He was appearing in support of Jimmie Work, who was riding the crest of his only major hit, "Making Believe." Bob Neal accompanied Presley on the trek, and they stopped off to visit key radio stations along the way.

The trips to New Mexico and the frigid shores of Lake Erie represented the first time that Presley and his band had tested the waters outside the Southern states, and marked the inauspicious debut of Presley's alliance with Colonel Parker, a symbiotic relationship that would, of course, endure until the singer's death.

A Pink Cadillac

Success with recordings was still lagging behind Presley's fast-growing popularity as a live performer. When he headlined the Big D Jamboree in Dallas on April 16,1955, he was still billed as "Sun Recording Star—That's All Right Mama."

On April 25 Phillips tried once again to recapture the momentum that Presley had sparked with "That's All Right," issuing one cut from the session held in late 1954, "I'm Left, You're Right, She's Gone." It was coupled with Presley's most aggressive performance on disc to that point, "Baby Let's Play House." The original version of "Baby Let's Play House" had been issued in 1954 by Nashville R&B artist Arthur Gunter. With a strangely countrified charm, enhanced by Gunter's mellow delivery, it had grazed the R&B charts briefly in January 1955. Presley probably recorded it on February 5.*

Once again, Presley made a small but telling change in the lyrics; where Gunter had sung, "You may get religion, baby, but don't you be nobody's fool," Presley sang, "You may have a pink Cadillac, but don't you be nobody's fool." In no other respect, though, had he toned down the original. Scotty Moore enhanced Presley's performance with two bristling solos that were light-years from his fingerpicking roots. The car radio had obviously been tuned to R&B stations along the road.

---

* Gunter is not solely dependent upon the income from *Baby Let's Play House* to fund his retirement. After moving to Port Huron, Michigan, in 1961, he won the Michigan State Lottery in 1973.

At the February 1955 session that produced "Baby Let's Play House," there is evidence that Elvis recorded two other R&B songs: Ray Charles' fast-breaking "I Got a Woman" and the Eagles' "Trying to Get to You," released the previous June. The Sun recording of "I Got a Woman" has never been found, although it was logged as having been received by RCA, and was rerecorded at Elvis's first RCA session. "Trying to Get to You" was attempted at more than one session, and, as drums were not present on "Baby Let's Play House" but *were* present on the issued version of "Trying to Get to You," it may be safe to assume that that version from February 1955 has also been lost. The surviving take is also the only Presley Sun track on which the guitar-bass-drum lineup was augmented by a piano—which, given the evident absence of an acoustic guitar in the mix, may well be Elvis's own.

Hank Snow secured a slot for Presley on the Jimmie Rodgers Memorial show in Meridian, Mississippi, in May 1955. From there Presley embarked on a tour of Texas in the company of the Browns, Ferlin Husky, Onie Wheeler, the Carlisles, and Martha Carson (whose song "Satisfied" was recorded by Presley at Sun but subsequently lost by RCA). When the show got to Lubbock on June 3, Buddy Holly was in the crowd with a friend who had brought along a home movie camera. He shot one minute of soundless color footage of Elvis Presley.

The Holly film offers a glimpse of Presley's burgeoning self-confidence. It also shows just how important Bill Black was to Presley during those early days. Black, who was nine years older than Presley, matched the singer's manic energy level with his own. He thumped his bass, shouted encouragement, and moved his cumbersome instrument all over the stage—in stark contrast to Scotty Moore, who worked away impassively at his licks. In earlier days, Black, pretending to be a rube, would haul his bass to the edge of the stage from within the crowd, asking if he could join the group. Presley would tell him to go away and Black would plead, "Aww, c'mon, man, just gimme a chance . . ." Presley would finally relent, Black would climb up on stage, and the wolf emerged from the sheep's clothing as he and Presley launched into one of their torrid routines.

It was hardly surprising that both Black and Moore were on a royalty deal during the Sun years. Their arrangement with Sam Phillips reflected the fact that they were much more than simply sessionmen—they played an integral role in both Presley's live appearances and the creation of his *sound*.

Despite the momentum Elvis was starting to gather, he was still indisputably a regional phenomenon in 1955. He also embodied a strange paradox. "Baby Let's Play House" was marketed as a country record, though it fit few definitions of country music—and even fewer definitions of pop. To Presley's advantage, though, the climate for R&B–based material in the pop market was improving in the wake of Bill Haley's hits. Since 1951, when he covered "Rocket 88," Haley had been working on a very different fusion of country and R&B, and was finally starting to reap the rewards. He was signed to Decca from the small Essex label in 1954, and by 1955 he had sold 3 million records for Decca.

That statistic was probably discussed by Bob Neal and Colonel Parker as they met in Nashville at the beginning of June 1955. It was agreed at that meeting that Colonel Parker and Hank Snow Enterprises would henceforth represent Presley in "all phases of the entertainment field" and that Neal would continue to be Presley's personal manager. Parker in particular was unhappy about Presley remaining on Sun. He knew that Phillips had no money to promote Presley; after all, Sun was still a two-person operation. Parker also knew that Presley's contract had exactly two years to run, and the likelihood of Phillips selling it was slim, despite the fact that the offers were starting to come in. On June 8, for example, Phillips had received a telegram from Frank B. Walker, president of MGM Records, asking whether "Elvis Presley is available for making records. I have heard that he was and I am interested." Columbia was also interested, and in New York Bob Rolontz at *Billboard* convinced Atlantic Records to mortgage their assets and bid on his contract.

Phillips, however, was determined to hold on to Presley's contract. He knew that Presley could help establish Sun as something other than a regional label. That conviction was reinforced by the success of "Baby Let's Play House," backed with "I'm Left, You're Right, She's Gone," which became his first national chart placing when it entered the country charts in July 1955. Encouraged after the poor showing of the two previous singles, Phillips took out advertisements in the music trade papers for the first time in two years. It was almost exactly one year to the day since Elvis, Scotty, and Bill had stumbled upon "That's All Right" during a coffee break.

During that summer of 1955 Presley also got his first full-page write-up in the doyen of hillbilly fan magazines, *Country Song Roundup*. An article entitled "Folk Music Fireball" revealed that Presley could eat eight deluxe cheeseburgers, two BLT sandwiches, and three milkshakes in one sitting, and that "the big (6 footer) blond guy likes nothing better than to spend an afternoon practicing football with some of the youngsters in his neighborhood." The insidious hand of Colonel Parker was clearly at work in the increasing attention paid to Presley in the media. The old huckster was in his element. It didn't matter whether he was promoting dancing chickens (an early scam) or a wiggling hillbilly. The principle—or lack of it—was the same.

The Mystery Train Departs

Elvis Presley went into the Sun studio again on July 11, 1955, to cut what would become his last Sun single. Once again, Phillips was anxious to ensure that the repertoire was drawn from within his own publishing catalog. The country side was "I Forgot to Remember to Forget," a song composed by Stan Kesler, the co-writer of "I'm Left, You're Right, She's Gone." By Kesler's account, he needed a good demo of the song and enlisted the help of hillbilly singer Charlie Feathers, to whom he gave 50 percent of the royalties in return. By Feathers' account, Kesler started the song and he finished it. Feathers also claims to have worked out the vocal licks, and to have taught Elvis the arrangement.

The R&B side was "Mystery Train," which had been recorded by Junior Parker for Sun two years earlier. In Presley's hands it was transformed from a slow, hypnotic blues to a stunning blend of blues and country in which the elements coalesce to the point where it is impossible to say where one leaves off and the other picks up. Presley's performance is brooding and intense, Phillips' tape delay echo perfectly timed. There are only three instruments on the record, but its sound is as pure, full, and perfect as any record that had ever topped the charts. The single marked Elvis Presley's elevation to greatness.

The drummer on "I Forgot to Remember to Forget" was Johnny Bernero, who worked across the street at the Memphis Light Gas and Water company. Bernero was a capable drummer, with roots in western swing. He had auditioned sometime earlier, and Phillips—still hesitant about using drums—liked Bernero's light touch, which wouldn't drown out the other instruments in the studio.

The success of "Mystery Train" and "I Forgot to Remember to Forget" (the single eventually became Presley's first number 1 country hit) challenged every precept of the record business. Both songs defied categorization, usually a sure predictor of commercial oblivion. They were unpolished—the close of "Mystery Train" sounds as though it has been hurriedly faded over a breakdown. Neither side had a catchy "hook"; in the case of "Mystery Train," the title is never even mentioned in the lyrics. But the record was such compelling listening that it was impossible to ignore.

Presley himself was becoming impossible to ignore, and there was even a plan afoot to break him into the key northern markets.

The sheet music for "Mystery Train"—issued after Elvis's departure for RCA

The Pied Piper of Cleveland

Bill Randle was a top-rated DJ on WERE in Cleveland, Ohio, a market that was always a trendsetter in the North. Randle had a country music counterpart on WERE named Tommy Edwards, and it was Edwards who told Randle about Elvis Presley. Randle saw Presley during his performance with Jimmie Work at the Circle Theater Jamboree back in February 1955, and soon became one of his first boosters in that key market.

In conjunction with Universal Pictures, Randle had set out to produce a film that would serve, among other functions, to document his achievement as an arbiter of teenage taste. The resulting movie has long been rumored to exist, but details about it were sketchy until two local researchers, Bruce Leslie and Chris Hartlaub, started digging. The following account is based largely on their research and subsequent work by Ger Rijff.

Randle gave the project the cumbersome title *The Pied Piper of Cleveland: A Day in the Life of a Famous Disc Jockey*. Elvis Presley, a virtual nonentity in the North, was not the headliner; in fact, he was lucky to have been included at all. The movie's stars were to be Bill Haley, Pat Boone, the Four Lads, and, as one can deduce from the title, Randle himself.

Presley appeared in Cleveland supporting Kitty Wells and Roy Acuff on October 19, and the "Pied Piper" concert with Randle took place the following day at the Brooklyn High School. Arthur Cohen, the director assigned by Universal, thought Presley was pitiful, and would not commit Universal's money to him. Randle, to his credit, paid the cameraman and crew directly to shoot Presley.

Pat Boone remembered the concert well and, in a later conversation with Dave Booth, shared some trenchant insights into the way Presley was perceived on his early forays into the North. "Bill told me, 'I got a guy who's gonna be the next biggest thing—Elvis Presley.' I said, 'Oh yeah?' I had lived in Texas and I had seen his name on some country jukeboxes and I wondered how in the world a hillbilly could be the next big thing, especially with a name like Elvis Presley. Anyway, Elvis came in wearing some odd-looking clothes. I said, 'Hello, Elvis, I'm Pat Boone.' He just said, 'Mrrrbleee mrrrbleee.' Anyway, I was to follow him on stage, so I was watching from the wings. Elvis looked like he had just gotten off a motorcycle. He sang his first song and the kids loved it. I was really surprised. Then he opened his mouth and said something and he sounded so hillbilly that he lost the crowd. Then he sang another song and won 'em over again. As long as he didn't talk he was OK. It took me a long time to win that crowd."

At that point, Boone was making a fat living covering R&B records for the white pop market. As his anecdote shows, however, Northern prejudice extended not only to black R&B artists but to white Southern hillbillies as well. Both were *outside*, though they would soon come in from the cold.

These long-lost photos of Elvis, Scotty, and Bill with Bill Randle were taken during the filming of "The Pied Piper of Cleveland" (Leslie/Hartlaub)

According to Leslie and Hartlaub, Presley performed "That's All Right," "Blue Moon of Kentucky," "Good Rockin' Tonight," "I Forgot to Remember to Forget," and "Mystery Train." Additional footage of Randle was subsequently shot in New York and edited into the movie. It is recorded that Randle previewed the footage at the Euclid Shore Junior High School, and snippets were reportedly aired on WEWS-TV in 1956. From that point, Randle ran into insuperable hurdles with the fourteen unions involved, as well as the record labels and artists' managers, whose clearances were necessary. As late as 1958, Randle was trying to clear an edited fifteen-minute version of the movie without Presley, but he eventually abandoned the project altogether.

Today, when popular musicians of all persuasions and degrees of talent have their activities minutely documented on video, it is ironic to realize that there exists barely an hour's footage of the most influential performer in rock 'n' roll caught at the prime of his career. All but a few minutes of that was shot in the artificial and sterile atmosphere of a network television studio. The *Pied Piper* movie, were it to surface, would represent the missing link between the amateur footage shot in Lubbock and the first Dorsey Brothers television show in January 1956.*

Closer to Being Apart

The success of "Mystery Train"—and Johnny Cash's first single, released within a month of each other in 1955—brought forth more problems for Phillips than they solved. The major problem was cash flow: distributors ordered records, but rarely paid for them until at least three months had passed; even then, they would usually try to work deductions against the total bill, or offer part payment to keep the product flowing. That, of course, would be fine if the pressing plants, label printers, music publishers, trade papers, and other creditors would accept payment on those terms, but few would. In addition, Phillips still owed money not only to Chess Records but also to Jud Phillips, as part of the buyout agreement by which Jud had left Sun in 1954.

Jud reportedly had little faith in Presley and tried to engineer the sale of his contract to Decca via Webb Pierce and Jim Denny. But Decca, like Columbia, MGM, and the others, balked at Sam Phillips' asking price, then hovering around twenty thousand dollars. Jud probably wanted to sell Presley so that he could recoup the money he had invested in Sun when he bought out Jim Bulleit.

The extent of Sam's frustration can be gauged from a letter he wrote to Jud in January 1955:

"I have told you repeatedly that Sun liabilities are three times the assets and I have been making every effort possible to keep out of bankruptcy.

---

* There is reportedly a kinescope in existence of Presley performing with Roy Orbison on the latter's television show, probably on KOSA, Odessa, Texas, c. 1955.

"As you well know, we have had only Presley and with his Union contract of 3% of the 89¢ price plus the fact that songs cost 4¢ a record, it has been virtually impossible to make anything. We have issued merchandise credits to the distributors and as you are aware, artists' royalties, song royalties, excise etc. was already paid on that merchandise, plus the fact that we have to pay song publishers, Presley, the Union, pressing, matrix, label and sampling costs just to give Presley to the distributors against the merchandise credits.

"Surely you see the precarious position of the company and know that we are making every effort to salvage the company and pay off all its obligations and avoid the embarrassment of bankruptcy. Anyone less interested in saving face would have given it up long ago, but I intend to pay every dollar the company owes—including you—even while I know there is no possible way to ever get out with a dollar."

In October 1955 Sam finally paid Jud the remaining fourteen hundred dollars from the buyout agreement, leaving himself as the sole proprietor of Sun Records. The deal drained away the last of his cash, though, and left him with no option but to consider selling Presley's contract. In addition, Colonel Parker was probably breathing down Phillips' neck, possibly threatening legal action if outstanding royalties were not paid.

Parker was angling to become more than Presley's booking agent, a function he shared with Hank Snow; he wanted to become his manager. According to Ger Rijff, there was another contender for the position—Bill Randle. Acting on instructions from Bob Neal, Randle had already tried, without success, to place Presley's contract with Dot, Imperial, and Columbia.

Randle was seriously thinking about leaving his position at WERE to set up a managerial and publishing company bankrolled by Julian and Jean Aberbach, who owned Hill & Range music publishing. The first artist to be covered by the deal would be Elvis Presley. Randle was asked to make up his mind by November 3, 1955, but his lack of success in pitching Presley convinced him that he would probably be better off at WERE. The station ensured his future loyalty by giving him stock and a substantial pay raise.

According to Randle, the Aberbachs then started talking with Colonel Parker, who would secure the deal with RCA by virtue of his relationships with Hank Snow and Eddy Arnold, both of whom recorded for RCA. On November 11, 1955, Steve Sholes, RCA Victor's head of country A&R, journeyed to Nashville with publicist Ann Fulcino for the annual Disc Jockeys Convention. What they expected to find there is hard to say—although Presley had been pre-elected "Most Promising New C&W Artist," there had been no mention that he was scheduled to appear. A later report said that Sholes and Fulcino agreed that they "hadn't seen anything so weird in a long time," suggesting that they had at least seen Presley in an unpublicized showcase.

Sholes, now won over, agreed to the terms that Parker had worked out with Phillips and the Aberbachs. Presley's contract was purchased jointly by Parker, Hill & Range, and RCA. Hill & Range helped to spread the risk by fronting fifteen thousand dollars in exchange for the publishing on at least one side of every Presley record and a co-publishing deal on Phillips' Hi-Lo Music catalog.

"*A* proposition . . .
I didn't think they'd be
fool enough to take."
Elvis with Steve Sholes
of RCA.

On Tuesday, November 15, Phillips sent a telegram to Parker in care of radio station WUX in Madison, Tennessee. It read:

UPON RECEIPT OF CASHIERS OR CERTIFIED CHECK IN THE AMOUNT OF FIVE THOU-SAND DOLLARS NOT LATER THAN MIDNIGHT TOMORROW, WEDNESDAY NOVEMBER 16, WE WILL DECLARE THAT YOU HAVE LEGALLY PICKED UP THE OPTION TO PUR-CHASE THE EXCLUSIVE RECORDING CONTRACT OF ELVIS PRESLEY PURSUANT TO ALL TERMS AND PROVISIONS OF THE AGREEMENT MADE OCTOBER 31, 1955 BY AND BETWEEN SUN RECORDS COMPANY INC. AS FIRST PARTY AND YOU, BOB NEAL AND OTHER INTERESTED PARTIES AS SECOND PARTY.

At 3:40 P.M. the next day Parker sent back a wire to Phillips that read:

AS PER MY TALK ON THE PHONE TODAY, I HAVE MAILED AIRMAIL SPECIAL DELIVERY A CASHIER'S CHECK FOR FIVE THOUSAND DOLLARS AS PER AGREEMENT. LETTER IS ENCLOSED. ALSO WILL APPRECIATE YOUR WIRE AS PER YOUR PROMISE. WILL TRY TO GET EVERYTHING WORKED OUT AS SOON AS POSSIBLE. REGARDS. COL. TOM PARKER.

Altogether, Phillips received thirty-five thousand dollars from RCA, Hill & Range, and Parker. Presley received five thousand dollars in back royalties. At some point in the machinations, Parker took over as Presley's manager. This caused acrimony among several people, including Bob Neal—whose account of the dealings is reportedly detailed in an unpublished autobiography—and Hank Snow, who suddenly found that his and Parker's involvement in Presley's career was now solely Parker's.

It was an unprecedently good deal for Phillips. "I had struggled so long," he recounted to Robert Palmer, "and I made a damn proposition I didn't think they'd take. I didn't think they'd be *fool* enough to take it. And it was the eleventh hour before they *did* actually take it. The price doesn't sound like anything today, but damn! Columbia paid $25,000 for Frankie Laine's contract from Mercury, and they had less time to go on his contract than I had on Elvis's. What I needed was money to just get out of the bullpen so I cou'd maybe get on the mound and throw to a batter. If I've been asked once, I've been asked a thousand times, did I regret it? No. I did not, I do not, and I never will."

Talking to Edwin Howard in 1958, Phillips gave a succinct appraisal of the economic reality underlying Presley's sale: "The record business isn't like any other branch of show business. You can borrow money to produce a movie or a play, but not a record. The record business is so precarious, you can't get financial backing until you don't need it."

It's hard to know what Presley's feelings might have been as he was shuffled around. Although there is no documentary evidence of his having recorded at Sun since July, Johnny Bernero remembers a session shortly before the RCA deal was consummated. "We had cut one side and started on another," recalls Bernero, "when Elvis went up into the control room with Sam. They were up there about thirty minutes. We were just sitting around on the studio floor chewing the fat. Then Elvis came back down and came over to me and said, 'John, we're not going to finish this session, but I really appreciate you coming over.' He gave me fifty dollars. The next thing I knew, Sam had sold his contract."

The songs that were to be used for Presley's sixth Sun single are a matter for some conjecture. Phillips undoubtedly wanted to use his own copyrights, and Presley had started work on Billy Emerson's "When It Rains It Really Pours." For a country flipside, Presley was being pressured to perform another Kesler-Feathers song, "We're Getting Closer to Being Apart." A curiously muffled Sun rehearsal tape of "When It Rains" was discovered by RCA's Gregg Geller on one of his rummages through the vaults, but "We're Getting Closer to Being Apart" has never surfaced.

Bernero never saw Presley again after the aborted rehearsals for the sixth single. "He called me over at the Light Gas & Water Company one day," recalls Bernero, "and asked me to come on the road with him. I was really tempted. I had been with the Light Gas & Water for ten years and wanted to go, but I had five children at that time. The wife and I talked it over and we decided that it wouldn't have been the best thing for me."

As it happened, Presley soon picked up a drummer, D. J. Fontana, from the Louisiana Hayride. On November 12, just as his contract was being peddled, Presley had re-signed with the Hayride for an additional year at two hundred dollars a show. But Colonel Parker soon bought Presley out of the deal so that

Elvis returns to the Hayride, December 1956
(Jack Barham/Escott)

he could take on more lucrative gigs on Saturday nights, although Presley returned for a benefit in December 1956.

Bob Neal remained a DJ on WMPS, started a record store in downtown Memphis, and in April 1956 launched a booking agency in conjunction with Sam Phillips. Scotty Moore and Bill Black remained with Presley, but in the role of backing musicians; they were excluded from future royalties, and were later dismissed or quit in 1958.

Sam Phillips packed up all the little tape boxes with "Elvis Presley" on the spine and shipped them off to RCA. What remained at Sun were tantalizing little snippets of Presley on tapes that had otherwise been recorded over. The full catalog of what Elvis recorded during his days at Sun, of course, will never be known; it's possible that far more was recorded over and lost than was ever recovered. But, as with every aspect of Presley's life, speculation is rife, and the list of songs that *might* have been recorded is long.

One fascinating possibility was brought to light by Johnny Prye, a member of the Jones Brothers, a black gospel quartet that recorded for Sun in 1954. Prye stated that Presley and the Jones Brothers recorded some songs that were transferred from tape to acetate; copies of the acetates, he recalled, were given to Presley and the group members. In view of Presley's fondness for black gospel quartet music, it is entirely possible that they sang together—although Phillips would have known that the results were unreleasable in the mid-1950s. After Prye's death, the loft containing the relics from his recording career collapsed into his son's bedroom. The artifacts were gathered into garbage bags and taken out for collection.

In Their Own Words

Though Elvis Presley never got a chance to tell his tale in the way we might have wanted, fragments like the interview he gave to the Charlotte (N.C.) *Observer* in 1956 showed the remarkable candor that he still possessed before the Colonel started manipulating his utterances. "The colored folks," asserted Presley, "been singing and playing it just like I'm doing now, man, for more years than I know. They played it like that in the shanties and in their juke joints and nobody paid it no mind until I goosed it up. I got it from them. Down in Tupelo, Mississippi, I used to hear Arthur Crudup bang his box the way I do now and I said that if I ever got to the place where I could feel all old Arthur felt, I'd be a music man like nobody ever saw."

And he did. And he was.

Sam Phillips' recollections of Presley have been clouded to some extent by hindsight, although it is beyond dispute that Phillips was the first to see the potential in the singer who would have made most listeners of the time shudder. He then nurtured it until it was hard to separate his contributions from the cross-cultural mishmash emanating from Presley's subconscious.

"The first time I ever saw Presley," Phillips has recalled, "he was without hardly any means at all. He had a style about him, but he was obviously from

With Dewey Phillips
and Joe Cuoghi

(Webbs/Showtime Archive)

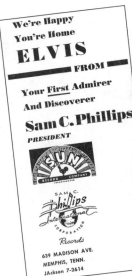

a very humble background. Physically, he had the long sideburns, which was unusual then, and the hair oil—that was unconventional. I later found out that he was disgruntled with his hair—it grew out in all directions—and that was why he combed it *all* the time.

"Apart from that, what impressed me most were his eyes, which were very pure. He seemed to be a genuine sort of person. He was very contrite. Very keen too—but totally lacking in confidence. When I first heard him on microphone I was very impressed with the innate purity of his voice. It seemed to come through even in the audition situation where he was under some stress. I later found out that music was such a great part of his life. He was so desirous of cooperating and being a success. I don't mean he had stars in his eyes. He wanted to succeed like we all did; he was very bright and he comprehended all types of music. He understood and listened to me when I told him that we had to be cautious and take things slowly and come up with something good and new. When I told him something was good, he knew it."

Did Phillips succeed? It's almost an item of faith that Presley never again sounded as good—as fresh, as wild, as loose—as he did at Sun. Whatever he had at Sun Records slowly ebbed away in the years to come, until his style became calcified, teetering between melodrama and an awkward self-parody.

Perhaps the last word, though, goes to the longtime Memphis journalist Edwin Howard, who had the first word on Elvis Presley in 1954. He observed the singer's career from a good vantage point, but with the distance of a member of polite society looking at a proletarian uprising:

"What was sad to me," wrote Howard on the morning after Presley's death, "was that imprisoned within that body was a child who never grew up. He made a huge fortune and could have done great good without depriving himself. . . . Instead he gave nominally to charities and bought expensive cars for strangers—like an ordinary person tossing pennies to ragamuffins.

"He might himself have traveled and studied and grown. Instead he was content to play the games of his youth—renting theaters, rinks and parks for private parties—playing pitch for kewpie dolls.

"Middle age sat unseemly upon him. Old age would have been obscene. His life had become so sad to me that his death seems less so."

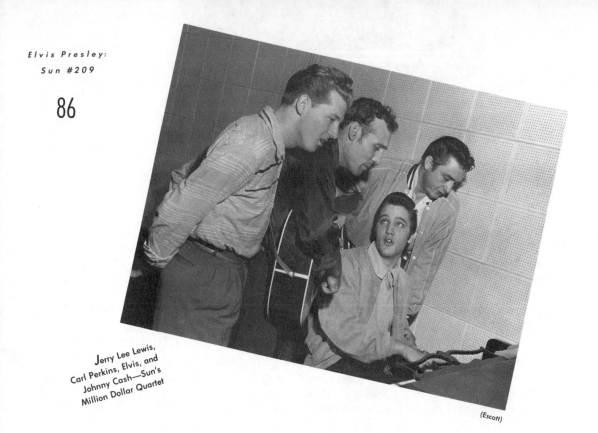

Jerry Lee Lewis,
Carl Perkins, Elvis, and
Johnny Cash—Sun's
Million Dollar Quartet

(Escott)

Postscript #1:
December 4, 1956

Just over a year after he left Sun, Elvis Presley returned one early winter afternoon. A Carl Perkins session was winding down, and Jerry Lee Lewis— just settled in town—was trying to earn some spending money playing backup piano.

Presley listened to the playbacks of the session and pronounced the results to be good. Then, inevitably, they started singing and playing together. Lewis was the only outsider, by virtue of his recent arrival—but, typically, he ensured that he wasn't overlooked. He made a point of auditioning his first single for Presley, who declared to the *Press Scimitar*'s Robert Johnson, "That boy can go. He has a different style and the way he plays piano just gets inside of me."

Very soon the control room and the studio began to fill up. Phillips had called Johnson, sensing that there might be a story and a photo opportunity. With that in mind, he also called Johnny Cash, who dutifully came over to the studio. Another Sun artist, Smokey Joe Baugh, came by, and songwriter Charles Underwood contributed his acoustic guitar and his harmony vocals. Perkins' brothers, Jay and Clayton, hung around for a while. Others came and went.

"If Sam Phillips had been on his toes, he'd have turned the recorder on when that very unrehearsed but talented bunch got to cutting up," wrote

Johnson the following day. As Johnson probably knew, that was precisely what Phillips had done. Using the microphone placements from the Perkins session, Phillips did a rough mix through the board, punched the RECORD button, then joined the melee on the studio floor. He was in his element, holding court and trying to convince Presley to record "When It Rains It Really Pours," on which he held the publishing rights.

Cash left almost immediately after the photo session, but Presley, Lewis, and Perkins sang for an hour or two. They stayed on familiar ground: country, gospel, and the hits of the day were on the menu. Feeling, no doubt, that he had returned home—far from the callousness of the northern media and the tawdry Vegas glitz—Presley let his true musical soul come up for air. That afternoon, he sang an eclectic mix of material, including Chuck Berry's "Brown-Eyed Handsome Man," The Five Keys' "Out of Sight, Out of Mind," Ernest Tubb's "I'm With a Crowd But So Alone," Pat Boone's "Don't Forbid Me," four Bill Monroe songs, and a host of gospel favorites. He did impersonations, tried out new tunes, sang the harmony on "Softly and Tenderly" to Lewis's lead, and left the hillbilly edges intact on his voice.

Reporter Bob Johnson, Sam, Elvis, and Leo Soroka of UPI

(Escott)

With Smokey Joe Baugh and Sam Phillips

(Escott)

With the exception of a few stage-managed moments during the 1968 come-back special, the session represents the only time we catch Elvis talking un-guardedly about music. The studio floor must have been crowded: the drums and piano, the Perkins band, Presley's girlfriend of the season—Marilyn Evans—as well as Joe Baugh, Charles Underwood, and some hangers-on. The terminally withdrawn kid was now the center of attention, talking about Vegas and an R&B act he had caught there:

"I heard this guy in Las Vegas—Billy Ward and his Dominoes. There's a guy out there who's doin' a take-off on me—'Don't Be Cruel.' He tried so hard, till he got much better, boy—much better than that record of mine.

"He was real slender—he was a colored guy—he got up there an' he said . . ." And Elvis leapt into an imitation of this other singer's version of his song, carefully mimicking every changed inflection, every turn of his performance.

"He had it a little slower than me. . . . He got the backin', the whole quartet. They got the feelin' on in. . . . Grabbed that microphone, went down to the last note, went all the way down to the floor, man, lookin' straight up at the ceiling. Man, he cut me—I was under the table when he got through singin'. . . . He had already done 'Hound Dog' an' another one or two, and he didn't do too well, y'know, he was tryin' too hard. But he hit that 'Don't Be Cruel' and he was tryin' so hard till he got better, boy. Wooh! Man, he sang that song. That quartet standin' in the background, y'know—BA-DOMP, BA-DOMP. And he was out there cuttin' it, man, had all'm goin' way up in the air.

"I went back four nights straight and heard that guy do that. Man, he sung hell outta that song, and I was under the table lookin' at him. Git him off! Git him off!"

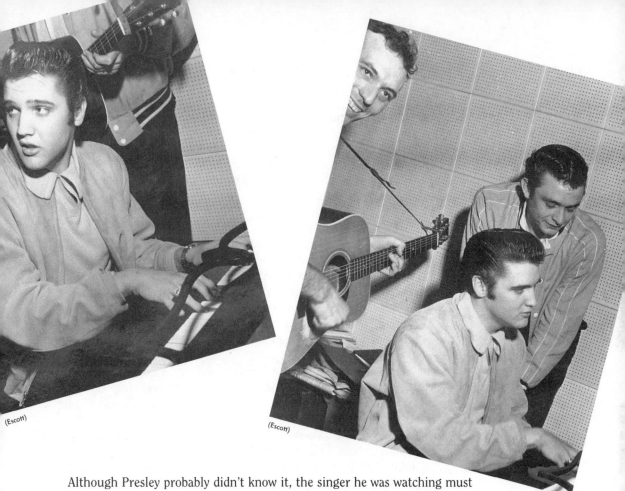

(Escott)

(Escott)

Although Presley probably didn't know it, the singer he was watching must have been Jackie Wilson, then the lead singer with Billy Ward's Dominoes.

After the Christmas break, Presley went out to Hollywood to cut some sessions for RCA. In January 1957 he recorded four of the songs from the December jam session—"Blueberry Hill" (reported by Johnson as having been sung, but as yet undiscovered on tape), "Peace in the Valley," "Is It So Strange," and "That's When Your Heartaches Begin" (one of the first songs he had recorded for Sam Phillips almost three years earlier). In February he recorded "When It Rains It Really Pours."

Toward the end of his life, in an effort to get Presley to record something —*anything*—RCA brought truckloads of recording equipment into Graceland. Twenty years earlier, though, Presley had needed no encouragement to pick and sing all night. "That's why I hate to get started in these jam sessions," he says on the tapes, "I'm always the last one to leave." The surviving tapes from the "Million Dollar Quartet" session (as it was dubbed by Robert Johnson in his feature the following day) hold some of Presley's least-guarded moments on record. The tapes also say more about the origins of rock 'n' roll than a thousand treatises. Presley is loose, effortlessly in command, unself-consciously blending a host of musical disciplines in what amounts to a primer on the creation of rock 'n' roll.

Postscript #2:
August 1958

A touching footnote to Phillips' association with Elvis Presley came immediately after the death of Presley's mother in August 1958. It showed that Phillips the rural Southerner could approach Presley on a level that Colonel Parker and his other handlers never could.

"I called out to Presley's house one day just after his mother died," recalled Phillips. "Vernon Presley told me that there was a problem, that Elvis wanted to go to the funeral home with his mother's body for the embalming. He didn't want to let her go.

"I went out there with Dewey Phillips and I stayed all night. Elvis was with his mother, who was laid out, and he wouldn't leave her. After a time I persuaded him to come to the kitchen and we sat down and I just listened to him. He knew I wasn't going to give him any damn bullshit or try to make him artificially feel good about it. I just explained exactly what the mortician's field of work was, and I got him to accept what was right and proper and what the undertaker had to do now. Elvis kept talking about the body and how he didn't want to give it up to anyone else.

"I eventually got Elvis away from the casket and we sat down by the pool. I'll never forget the dead leaves by the pool. I was able to convince him that he should let his mother go. I knew just enough to know which part of him to touch and in what way."

Phillips' earlier training as a country mortician served him well that night by the pool at Graceland. Like Presley, Phillips had just made the quantum leap from borderline poverty to affluence. Phillips understood why Gladys Presley kept chickens in the gardens at Graceland. He understood the poor white ethos of the South because he, like Presley, had been born of it. To Phillips, there was nothing odd in Presley's behavior; that is why he was able to approach him on a level that few others—certainly not those who saw him simply as a meal ticket—ever could.

The story leaves an imponderable question: What would have happened if Sam Phillips had retained a role in Presley's career? Could he have arrested the sad decline on either a musical or personal level?

Postscript #3:
Scotty and Bill, Jimmie Lott,
and Johnny Bernero

After their parting of the ways from Elvis in 1958, Scotty Moore and Bill Black returned to Memphis where they tried to hustle a little work for themselves backing other singers. Unable to make ends meet, Bill Black took a job servicing air conditioners for Able Appliances. Scotty Moore bought a share in a new recording studio and record label, Fernwood Records.

(Escott)

Bill Black with
Joe Cuoghi of Hi
Records

(Escott)

Black was in dire financial straits when he went to see Ray Harris, with whom he had worked at the Firestone plant. Harris had recorded two singles for Sun before launching Hi Records in 1957. The label was on the point of folding when Black arrived in the summer of 1959. Harris recalled that the habitually amiable bassist became upset when the subject of Presley was raised, perhaps with good reason. Presley had bought one of the most prestigious properties in town and littered it with expensive cars. Black was driving a '49 Studebaker and watching the repo man walk away with some of his household appliances.

Black was in the process of forming a group. After days of rehearsal at Hi, the band members worked up a riff they called "Smokie." Released in September 1959, it became the first hit on Hi and launched a second career for Black. Among those who sent congratulatory telegrams were Elvis Presley and Tom Parker. Black's feelings upon receiving them must have been mixed, although his wife pasted them in the scrapbook.

The Bill Black Combo sold especially well in the R&B market and Hi maintained the illusion that Black might *be* black by never putting his face on an album jacket. In 1962 he started his own studio and record label, virtually bowing out of playing on the road. He obviously sought to emulate Ray Harris and Scotty Moore, seeing his long-term future on the other side of the studio glass. Sadly, Black did not have a long-term future. After experiencing some memory loss and other symptoms, he underwent an operation for a brain tumor in June 1965. After another operation six weeks later, Black was given

Johnny Bernero and
Smokey Joe Baugh

(J. Bernero)

the news that he had only a few months to live. He set his affairs in order and died on October 25, 1965. Presley did not attend the funeral, but sent flowers.

Scotty Moore also struck gold. In 1959 he recorded Thomas Wayne, the brother of Johnny Cash's guitarist, Luther Perkins. The lugubrious ballad "Tragedy" was a hit during the summer of 1959, but Moore quickly bowed out of Fernwood Records and joined Sam Phillips in his new studio as production manager. In that capacity, he produced Jerry Lee Lewis, as well as many of the nonentities who populated the later Sun releases.

In 1963, Moore went to Nashville to manage Phillips' studio there. After it was sold, Moore launched his own studio, Music City Recorders, and subsequently a cassette duplication facility. He played on many of Presley's Nashville sessions and reunited with him for Elvis's 1968 television special, looking as impassive as ever as he joined his old boss for a romp through their hits. He also cut an album of Presley songs for CBS with the hyperbolic title, *The Guitar That Changed the World*.

After turning down Sam Phillips' offer to join Presley, drummer Jimmie Lott had another brief encounter with the group. He had moved to North Carolina with his family when Presley headlined a country package show in Greensboro in February 1956, just as "Heartbreak Hotel" was breaking. "I went to the back door and Scotty and Bill remembered me," recalled Lott. "They let me in. Elvis remembered me. He said, 'Hey, drummer!' and we went and ate breakfast after the show."

Lott joined Warren Smith's band after returning to Memphis. He recorded several sessions with Smith, but eventually left to pursue a career in sales as his family responsibilities mounted.

Johnny Bernero became the staff drummer at Sun between late 1955 and the close of 1956. He was not a rock 'n' roll drummer; his roots were too deeply implanted in western swing. He also turned down an offer from Presley to tour with his band. Bernero subsequently formed a western swing combo that he took to Sun. Phillips recorded them, but wouldn't release the cuts. Bernero recast the band with Ace Cannon and signed with Hi Records. They struck paydirt in 1960 with "Tuff," but Cannon reneged on his deal with Bernero and, after a messy court battle, Bernero received minimal compensation. He retired from the music industry in disgust, sold his drums, and became an insurance salesman.

To some extent, the proximity of greatness brought embitterment to Moore, Black, Bernero, and Lott. Selling insurance—traditionally the musician's nightmare—beckoned warmly by comparison.

For Elvis, the loss of Black and Moore deprived him of two links to the past—in fact, the outside world—and contributed, albeit marginally, to his growing isolation. "Elvis Presley—Scotty and Bill" had a charming, folksy ring to it. When those two names disappeared from the record labels, the change ran much deeper than a renegotiated contract.

Recommended Listening

All of Presley's Sun recordings that were known to exist as of 1987 are gathered on *The Complete Sun Sessions* (RCA [USA] 6414).

The Million Dollar Quartet session tapes were first issued in studio quality on S Records (S 5001), a package subsequently issued by RCA/BMG Records (USA) 2023-2-R.

And, in 1990, RCA finally released one side of Elvis's first personal disc, "My Happiness," on *Great Performances* (RCA [USA] 2227-2-R). The other side, "That's When Your Heartaches Begin," has yet to be issued.

JOHNNY CASH: HILLBILLY HEADS UPTOWN

When the barriers that separated pop and country music began to crumble in the wake of Elvis Presley, Johnny Cash was one of the first young country artists to take a place in the pop charts. Ironically, as hillbilly music slicked itself up in search of the wider market, Johnny Cash broke through with a sound that was so sparse and underproduced that it must have seemed anachronistic even to the more conservative elements of the Nashville establishment.

Cash arrived at Sun Records with a sound that, in the ensuing years of his long, often troubled career, would change remarkably little. It was a sound born of necessity: the minimal backings and the limited range of Cash's vocals defined the full extent of the group's ability. But where other producers might have tried to disguise the shortcomings, Sam Phillips made a virtue of necessity.

Arkansas: The Depression Years

Johnny Cash was born in the remote rural settlement of Kingsland, Arkansas, on February 26, 1932. His birthplace was almost directly across the Mississippi from Lake County, Tennessee, where Carl Perkins was born six weeks later.

In the mid-1940s Cash started work in the fields, habitually listening to Smilin' Eddie Hill on WMPS, Memphis, during the midday break. Hill's "High Noon Roundup" show featured the cream of the local hillbilly talent. Unlike almost all of his Sun colleagues, Cash grew up without the influence of black music: his parents had settled on a government colony in Dyess when he was three years old, from which blacks were specifically excluded. His parents kept the radio tuned to the hillbilly stations, and when Cash went into Dyess with a few nickels to put in the jukebox, it was Roy Acuff and Ernest Tubb that he wanted to hear.

When Cash's voice broke, he realized that he owned something that might get him out of Dyess. He practiced at every opportunity, singing in school and at home. Yet when he left town, it was not to become a hillbilly singer but to work in the auto plants in Pontiac, Michigan. Like many others who took that route, Cash returned home, although he made his return somewhat sooner than most—after three weeks. Still determined to get out of Dyess, he joined the Air Force on July 7, 1950.

By his own account, Cash's "four long, miserable years" in the Air Force were relieved only by playing music with fellow southerners. While stationed in Germany, they formed a group called the Landsberg Barbarians, and Cash started writing material for them—including the quintessential lament of the homesick southerner, "Hey! Porter," which was published as a poem in the servicemen's magazine *Stars & Stripes*.

Before leaving for overseas duty, Cash had gone roller-skating in San Antonio, Texas. On the rink, he crashed into Vivian Liberto, then seventeen years old and in her last year of high school. They dated during his last weeks in the States and wrote to each other constantly while he was overseas. John and Vivian decided to get married after he returned. Cash probably harbored the dream of being able to make money playing music, but up to that point his largest audience had been a gathering of a few dozen Italians who had listened to the Landsberg Barbarians on a drunken furlough in Venice.

(Showtime Archive)

Johnny and
Vivian Cash

Tutwiler Avenue, 1954–1956

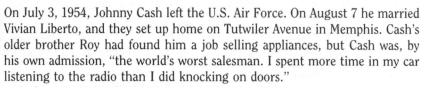

On July 3, 1954, Johnny Cash left the U.S. Air Force. On August 7 he married Vivian Liberto, and they set up home on Tutwiler Avenue in Memphis. Cash's older brother Roy had found him a job selling appliances, but Cash was, by his own admission, "the world's worst salesman. I spent more time in my car listening to the radio than I did knocking on doors."

(Showtime Archive)

Cash's trips into the black neighborhoods of Memphis gave him his first exposure to black music. "I heard a lot of blues," he recalled. "I became friends with some of the musicians. I met Gus Cannon one day on the porch of his home. He had written 'Walk Right In' way back, and he was sitting there playing the banjo. I sat and listened to him, played with him, and it got to be quite a regular affair with me." Once exposed to black music, Cash became a convert, spending money he did not have at the Home of the Blues record store in downtown Memphis. "Southern blues, black gospel, black blues, [that's my] favorite music," he told Bill Flanagan. "People like Pink Anderson, Robert Johnson, Howlin' Wolf, and Sister Rosetta Tharpe . . . *Blues in the Mississippi Night* that [folklorist] Alan Lomax did, is my all-time favorite album."

Trying to break into music any way he could, Cash auditioned for a job as a radio announcer at a station in Corinth, Mississippi, but was turned down because of lack of experience. Taking advantage of the G.I. Bill, Cash enrolled at the Keegan School of Broadcasting in Memphis. Attending on a part-time basis, he had completed half of the course by the time his first record was released.

A few days after getting out of the service, Cash visited his brother in Memphis. Roy Cash had forsaken a musical career and was working at the Hoehn Chevrolet dealership on Union Avenue. He introduced his younger brother to three mechanics who played together at home, at small benefit concerts, and on Sunday morning radio. Marshall Grant was twenty-six years old, sang tenor, and played guitar. Luther Monroe Perkins, also twenty-six, played guitar as well. A. W. "Red" Kernodle, ten years older than Perkins and Grant, played steel guitar. "We mostly played for our own amusement and to aggravate our wives," recalled Kernodle.

Luther's Dream

For all his musical shortcomings, it was Luther Perkins who developed the guitar sound that complemented Cash's stark baritone. Perkins was born in Memphis on January 8, 1928. His father was driving a taxi at the time, but soon returned to farming in Mississippi. The Perkins family—including Thomas Wayne (Perkins), who later scored a hit with "Tragedy"—grew up in Sardis and Como.

Years later, Luther would tell this story: When he was nine years old, he had a dream that he had found the pot of gold at the end of the rainbow. In his dream he knew where the rainbow ended. The following morning he went with his brother to the spot and dug. There they found the remnants of an old house. Luther carried the bricks to a local construction company and sold them at two cents apiece. With the nine dollars he raised in that painstaking fashion, he bought his first guitar.

The Best New Instrumental Group of 1957! Luther Perkins (left) and Marshall Grant.

(Escott)

The family came back to Memphis in 1942. Luther, Sr., worked at Firestone. Luther, Jr. ("L.M." or "Ellum," as he was known), held down a variety of jobs. In 1954 he was installing accessories at Hoehn Chevrolet. He had married in 1947 and already had a young family when he met Cash. "One night we got together at my place," says Cash, "and then we made it a regular thing until we felt that we had it together." At that time Cash was living in a one-bedroom apartment, so most of the rehearsals were conducted at Perkins' house. They rehearsed endlessly, quickly developing a commitment to their music.

"Finally, one day, we decided that we were ready for a shot at the record business," recalls Cash. "I had met Elvis Presley's guitarist, Scotty Moore, and I called him and asked him about the possibility of getting an audition with Sun." Moore probably told Cash that the best approach was simply to go to the studio. It was an approach that had worked for Presley.

In an interview with Peter Guralnick, Cash described how he came to audition. "Sun Records was between my house and the radio-announcing school. I just started going by there and every day I'd ask: could I see Mr. Phillips. And they'd say, 'He's not in yet,' or 'He's at a meeting.' So really it became a challenge to me just to get inside that studio. Finally, one day I was sitting on the stoop just as he came to work, and I stood up and said, 'I'm John Cash and I want you to hear me play.' He said, 'Well, come on in.' I sang two or three hours for him. Everything I knew—Hank Snow, Ernest Tubb, Flatt and Scruggs . . . I even sang 'I'll Take You Home Again Kathleen.'

"I had to fight and call and keep at it and push, push, push to even get into Sun Records. I don't feel like anyone discovered me because I had to fight so hard to get heard."

Phillips liked what he heard and invited Cash to return with his group: "When they came in," recalled Phillips, "Cash apologized to me for not having a professional band, but I said that he should let me hear what they could do and I would be able to tell whether they had a style I would be able to work with. I was immediately impressed with John's unusual voice. I was also interested in Luther's guitar playing. He wasn't a wizard on the guitar. He played one string at a time and he wasn't super good—but he was different, and that was important.

"Their material was all religious at that time. Songs which Cash had composed. I liked them, but I told him that I would not at that time be able to merchandise him as a religious artist and that it would be well if he could secure some other material or write some other songs. I told him that I was real pleased with the sound we were getting from just the three instruments. If I'm not mistaken, I think it was the third occasion in the studio that I actually commenced seriously to get Johnny Cash down on tape. He continued to be very apologetic about his band. However, I told him that I did not want to use any other instrumentation because of the unique style they had. They would practice a lot, but I told them not to be overly prepared because I was interested in spontaneity too."

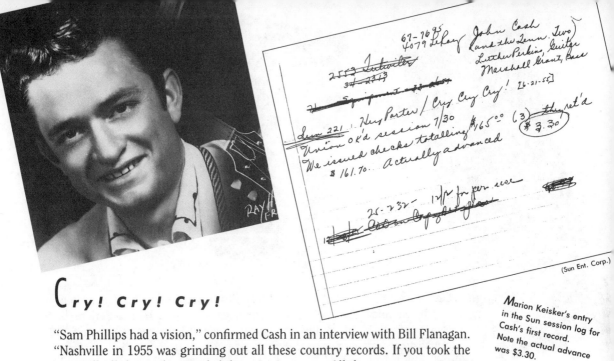

Cry! Cry! Cry!

"Sam Phillips had a vision," confirmed Cash in an interview with Bill Flanagan. "Nashville in 1955 was grinding out all these country records. If you took the voice off, all the tracks sounded the same to me . . . All the arrangements were calculated and predictable. It's kinda that way with my music—but [at least] it's *my* music. It's not done to try and sound like someone else in Nashville."

Red Kernodle played the first session and then quit. "There was no money in it," he contends with little apparent regret, "and there was getting to be too much staying up late at night and running around." His halting attempts at playing the steel guitar can be heard on an early version of "Wide Open Road," proving that his disappearance was no great loss. Luther Perkins' oldest daughter, Linda, recalled that Kernodle's wife had threatened to leave if he concentrated on music. He also held a better-paying job than the other members of the group. His gradual disappearance was taken with some relief by the others.

But Kernodle's shortcomings were certainly no greater than Luther Perkins'. Worse yet, Marshall Grant had only just learned how to play bass. "I'd never held one in my hand and didn't even know how to tune it," he recalled. "I bought one for seventy-five dollars and a friend showed me how to tune it. I figured it out from there. We didn't work to get that boom-chicka-boom sound. That's all we could play."

Needing some secular material in a hurry, Cash resuscitated "Hey! Porter" and previewed "Folsom Prison Blues." The latter was a virtual note-for-note and word-for-word adaptation of a Gordon Jenkins tune, "Crescent City Blues," which formed a segment of a 1954 concept album called *Seven Dreams*, tracing an imaginary journey from New York to New Orleans. Even Jenkins' technique of linking the segments with spoken passages would later be adapted by Cash on his own concept albums. Surprisingly, Cash was not sued by Jenkins until the song was reprised on the bestselling live album recorded at Folsom Prison in 1968.

Cash's early versions of "Folsom Prison Blues" were delivered in a curiously high-pitched voice, although those early takes show that Luther Perkins had already worked out his guitar solo—which would later became a model of minimalist country picking. But Phillips did not want to couple "Folsom Prison Blues" with "Hey! Porter" for the first record.

"I had recorded 'Hey! Porter,' " recalled Cash to Bill Flanagan, "and I'd also recorded 'Folsom Prison Blues,' which [Sam] didn't care all that much for. I saw a note on his desk, a memo to himself, 'Send "Folsom Prison Blues" to Tennessee Ernie Ford?' after I had recorded it. I challenged him on that. I said, 'I know Tennessee Ernie Ford is hot, but I don't want him singing that song. I want to do it myself.' Sam said, 'Well, let's see what else you can come up with. Go home and write me an uptempo weeper love song.' I went home and I heard Eddie Hill say, 'We got some good songs, love songs, sweet songs, happy songs, and sad songs that'll make you cry, cry, cry.' I wrote 'Cry! Cry! Cry!' that night, called Sam the next day, and said, 'I got it.' "

"Cry! Cry! Cry!," backed with "Hey! Porter," was released on June 21, 1955, under the name Johnny Cash. Cash had been christened simply J.R. and had been dubbed John later in life. It was Phillips who coined Johnny. Luther Perkins and Marshall Grant were dubbed the Tennessee Two. They agreed to divide the royalties on a 40-30-30 percent split. The original compositions were credited solely to Cash, although a lawsuit later brought by Luther Perkins' family and Marshall Grant contended that they had contributed substantially to almost every composition during the endless rehearsals.

"Cry! Cry! Cry!" made the local Memphis country charts on August 20, eventually reaching number 1 on September 3, beating out such local favorites as Elvis Presley and the Louvins. It even reached the national country charts for one week in November.

The essential elements of Cash's music were there from the start. The stark, lonesome vocals were front and center, with Luther doing little more than keeping time, even during his solo. Where most guitarists relish the opportunity to solo, Luther seemed to dread it. The fear of failure—of messing up an otherwise good take—seemed to haunt him every time he entered the studio.

For his part, Phillips challenged the conventions of recording balance, placing Cash's vocals more assertively in the mix than had ever been the case in country music. Phillips fattened the sound of the vocals and the rhythm track with slapback echo. Musicians scoffed, but Cash and the Tennessee Two possessed the quality that had been lacking in country music since Hank Williams died: originality.

By this point, Cash was playing a regular fifteen-minute show on KWEM, West Memphis, and he had started playing local gigs arranged by Bob Neal. Though later in his career Cash would deny it, Marshall Grant recalled that the level of the honky-tonks they were playing in those days was pretty low. He remembered "more guns and knives than fans at most of those early gigs." Cash became the hit of Bob Neal's Eighth Anniversary show, just as Presley had been the surprise hit a year earlier. Dick Stuart, who worked as a DJ on KWEM as "Poor Richard," reported to *Billboard* that "this year Johnny Cash broke through as the outstanding new act in Memphis." Stuart promptly signed him to a management deal.

Cash rerecorded "Folsom Prison Blues" on July 30, 1955, together with "So Doggone Lonesome." But "Cry! Cry! Cry!" was still doing good business, and Phillips held off releasing the new single until December. A few weeks earlier, Phillips had acquired a little venture capital from RCA, and he pumped it behind Carl Perkins and Cash. He placed an advertisement in the trade papers touting "handsome and young" Johnny Cash.

Presley, Carl Perkins, and Cash had toured together briefly in 1955. After Presley's departure, Perkins and Cash continued to work show dates together. On December 28, 1955, they played a date in Texarkana supporting George Jones, who was riding his first hit, "Why Baby Why?" "None of us had ever been that far away before," Carl Perkins remembers. "It was the big break. I met John in West Memphis and we had to go 350 miles. I spent most of the time in John's car and we wrote songs together. The next day we were in Tyler, Texas, and the promoter promised us a hundred dollars each. Up to then, our biggest pay had been in Parsons, Arkansas, when Bob Neal stood at the door with a cigar box and charged everyone who came in a dollar unless they were under twelve. We split the take and got eighteen dollars for every guy."

Even in those days, Marshall Grant was convinced that they would see better times. "On a lot of early shows we were openers," he told David Booth, "but I could see the momentum already there. John was becoming popular with that little different sound we had. His big gigantic voice was cutting through something fierce. You could see it grow day by day."

As 1955 ended, Cash and the Tennessee Two were still holding down day jobs. In fact, the only color television set Johnny Cash would ever sell was to Marion Keisker at Sun. Within the next few weeks, though, Cash would sell his last domestic appliance.

Jan 21 '56

50   MUSIC-RADIO   THE BILLBOARD

From The Billboard issue of January 7, 1956

• Review Spotlight on . . .

RECORDS

JOHNNY CASH

Folsom Prison Blues (I) La. #333)

So Doggone Lonesome (I) La. #333)—Sun 232—Cash

"Solid, sincere, genuine"

"Two of the best offerings . . ."

"Both could break out"

HANDSOME AND YOUNG

JOHNNY CASH

CRASHES THROUGH WITH

RED HOT!!

FOLSOM PRISON BLUES

and

SO DOGGONE LONESOME

SUN #232

(STILL HOT–"CRY, CRY, CRY")

(Escott)

January 1956

(Escott)

Cash and the Tennessee Two at the Louisiana Hayride, 1955

Crossing the Line

Good things started to come to Johnny Cash early in the new year. In December 1955 he had played a guest shot on the Louisiana Hayride; in January he was offered a regular spot. Like Elvis Presley and Hank Williams before him, Cash raced down to Shreveport every Saturday night for the precious exposure. The show brought him before more people every Saturday than he could hope to reach all week with a full date book.

The coupling of "Folsom Prison Blues" and "So Doggone Lonesome" raced up the country charts alongside "Blue Suede Shoes." Within a few weeks it was obvious that "Blue Suede Shoes" was also selling well in the pop and R&B markets. Unable to handle the vocal demands of rock 'n' roll, Cash seemed to be doomed to the country charts. He did make his attempts: trying to corner a small role in the new market, he started composing rock 'n' roll songs. One of these, "Rock 'n' Roll Ruby," was pitched to a newcomer at Sun, Warren Smith, in March 1956.* Cash's breathless demo shows how painfully ill-at-ease he was with anything brisker than a medium tempo. He also pitched another rock 'n' roll song called "Little Woolly Booger (You're My Baby)" to Roy Orbison, an effort he would later call "the worst thing I ever conceived." In the demo, again, he continually trips over himself in an inept attempt at stop rhythm. Within a few weeks, though, Cash would no longer feel such an acute need to pander to the nascent rock market. He had written a very adult song that would cross over effortlessly and wholly without contrivance into the pop charts.

* Smith would later contend that George Jones had told him that Cash had bought "Rock 'n' Roll Ruby" off Jones for forty dollars. If that is the case, however, it would appear that Cash amended the lyrics, for they bear the imprint of his writing style.

On April 2, 1956, Cash went into the Sun studio with a beautifully allegorical pledge of love called "I Walk the Line." In an interview with Ed Salamon, Cash recounted the tortuous origins of the song: "While I was in the Air Force I had a Wilcox-Gay tape recorder. I was working the five-to-eleven shift one night, and I came in right after eleven and saw that someone had been fooling with my recorder, so I rewound it and punched the play button. Here was one of the strangest sounds I'd ever heard. At the beginning it sounded like a voice saying 'Father.' It drove me crazy for about a year. I asked everybody I knew if they had fooled around with my tape recorder. I finally found who did it. He put the tape on upside down and backward. All he was doing was strumming chords on the guitar, and at the end he said, 'Turn it off,' which sounds like 'Father' when it's backward. I never got that chord progression out of my mind. It broke all the musical laws but I couldn't forget it. After I started touring, I was playing Gladewater, Texas, one night and Carl Perkins asked me, 'What are you doing?' I was fooling around with those chords. He said, 'That's really different. Sam is always looking for something different. Why don't you write a song and use that progression?' Then a little bit later on we got to talking about our wives and guys running around on the road and so forth. I had a brand new baby and I said, 'Not me, buddy. I walk the line.' Carl said, 'There's your song title.' I wrote it all that night in fifteen or twenty minutes."

(Escott)

The chord progression is not quite as revolutionary as Cash implies, but by reversing the usual country progression—starting on the unstable dominant chord instead of the rock-solid tonic that begins just about every country song—he also begins each verse with the pair of chords that normally *ends* a song. Not only had Cash found the "something different" that Sam Phillips constantly sought, he also had found a way to build a larger framework for the song. After each verse the song moves to a new key, where it hangs tentatively until the next verse, opening with that closing pair of chords, clinches the new key with a feeling of sureness and inevitability. What could more perfectly suit the lyrics' declaration of undying faithfulness?

In the studio Cash set down a version of characteristic simplicity. His aggressive rhythm guitar (with paper woven between the strings to simulate the sound of brushes on a snare drum) backs up Luther Perkins' trademark solo runs on the bass strings. Four bars of sustained humming signal each of the key changes, which gradually move Cash from his upper register, already forced even in his early years, down an octave to the bottom of his range (and then some—he can't quite make the low *D* near the end). It's an uncluttered, remarkably direct performance—compelling, hypnotic, and unlike any other country record that had ever been made. The addition of a chorus or any other instrument would have destroyed its magnetism. As Phillips himself said years later, "Can you hear 'I Walk the Line' with a steel guitar?" Better than most, Phillips knew it was a rhetorical question.

Released on May 1, the song became an immediate success, reaching the number 2 slot in the country charts and number 19 in the pop charts. Cash signed with Bob Neal's new booking agency, Stars, Inc., in May 1956, and on

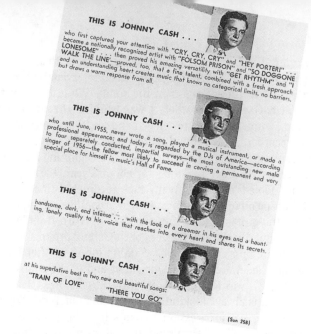

THIS IS JOHNNY CASH . . .
who first captured your attention with "CRY, CRY, CRY" and "HEY PORTER!" . . . became a nationally recognized artist with "FOLSOM PRISON" and "SO DOGGONE LONESOME" . . . then proved his amazing versatility with "GET RHYTHM" and "I WALK THE LINE"—proved, too, that a fine talent, combined with a fresh approach and an understanding heart creates music that knows no categorical limits, no barriers, but draws a warm response from all.

THIS IS JOHNNY CASH . . .
who until June, 1955, never wrote a song, played a musical instrument, or made a professional appearance; and today is regarded by the DJs of America—according to four separately conducted, impartial surveys—the most outstanding new male singer of 1956—the fellow most likely to succeed in carving a permanent and very special place for himself in music's Hall of Fame.

THIS IS JOHNNY CASH . . .
handsome, dark, and intense . . . with the look of a dreamer in his eyes and a haunting, lonely quality to his voice that reaches into every heart and shares its secrets.

THIS IS JOHNNY CASH . . .
at his superlative best in two new and beautiful songs:
"TRAIN OF LOVE"   "THERE YOU GO"

(Sun 258)

July 7 he was offered a place on the Grand Ole Opry. It was barely one year since his first record had been released, and a shade over two years since he had been discharged from the Air Force. It had taken other major country artists years of playing low-life beer halls, county fairs, and five-hundred-watt radio stations to achieve half as much.

"I Walk the Line" still sat at number 3 in the country charts and at number 88 in the pop charts at the end of 1956. Cash's new record, which coupled "Train of Love" with "There You Go," was starting to show up strongly; the year-end results showed that Cash ranked third among best-selling country artists, right behind Marty Robbins and Ray Price.

The Formula Wears Thin

Cash had started to keep a grueling schedule on the road. In later years his concerts would become somber affairs, as Cash, dressed habitually in black, sang selections from his vast repertoire; in the early days, though, he put on a true hillbilly variety show in the manner of his contemporaries. He would do impersonations (including a very realistic parody of Elvis Presley), a calypso or two, and a comedy routine with Marshall and Luther. As always, Luther was the butt of Cash's jokes, playing the role of the hillbilly still life, working away determinedly at his licks. If Luther thought about it, however—and he probably did—he was having the last laugh; the most accomplished pickers in Nashville were now being called upon to emulate his elemental style. It became doubly ironic when Luther, who had exquisite taste in picking, later upgraded his skills, but was called upon only to reprise his original bare-bones solos.

Cash's fifth single, shipped on April 21, 1957, coupled the brooding "Next in Line" with a beautifully vulnerable ballad, "Don't Make Me Go." Despite a brief appearance in the pop charts at number 99, the single did not sell at all well. It only reached number 9 in the country charts, Cash's worst showing since his first record. He had released five singles within two years, and the striking originality of his formula was beginning to wear thin. When Cash went into the studio on July 1 and back in again for an overdub session at the end of the month, his sound was gradually eased uptown by Jack Clement, to whom Phillips had entrusted the supervision of Cash's sessions.

"Home of the Blues" (inspired by the record store Cash had visited in leaner times) is as dolorous as any of Cash's previous efforts, but it sports a piano and a subdued vocal chorus. In contrast, the flip side, "Give My Love to Rose," is more minimalist than ever. A western ballad, it represents the first time that Cash's infatuation with the Old West (which would later consume entire albums) intruded itself onto disc. The slight change in direction brought forth some reward when the single rose quickly to number 5 in the country charts and number 88 in the pop listings before dying away. That showing encouraged Jack Clement to persevere in his attempt at sweetening Cash's sound.

August 31, 1957, found Cash and Carl Perkins playing the Town Hall Party show out on the West Coast. Backstage, they were approached by Columbia's debonair expatriate Englishman, Don Law, who inquired whether either artist would be interested in signing with Columbia at the expiration of their contracts with Sun. Both said they would, but Perkins still had six months remaining on his term with Sun, and Cash still had a year. The discussions proceeded surreptitiously, and Cash eventually signed a Columbia contract on November 1, 1957, to commence August 1, 1958. Blissfully unaware of this, Phillips prepared Cash's—and Sun's—first album, launching it in November at the annual Disc Jockeys Convention in Nashville. At the same function two years earlier, Phillips had been so desperately short of money that he had put his prize asset, Elvis Presley's contract, on the auction block.

The Teenage Dream

After a brief break for throat surgery, Cash reappeared at Sun in November. Jack Clement, convinced that the teenage market did not want to hear any more morbid sagas of the Old West, had written a teen-oriented story song with an ending so sugary it could put a diabetic into a coma. Called "Ballad of a Teenage Queen," it was arguably the worst song Cash cut at Sun, and would have been worse still if some of Clement's original couplets had stood unchallenged ("She was queen of the senior prom / She could cook just like her mom"). Luther sat out the song, and Clement himself played the prominent acoustic guitar. After the session was over, Clement and Sun's new musical director, Bill Justis, brought in a vocal chorus and an ear-rending soprano, Cyd Mosteller, who had sung with Justis's big band. Together, they dominate

BRAND NEW and...
A SOLID *POP* HIT!
JOHNNY CASH

BALLAD OF
A TEENAGE
QUEEN

b/w "Big River"
SUN #283

entire sections of the record, carrying the narrative toward its inevitable and cloying conclusion.

Cash had written one of his more upbeat songs for the session. "Big River" had taken shape after he had read a magazine article bearing the headline "Johnny Cash Has the Big River Blues in his Voice." Once again, Clement's acoustic guitar was prominent, but Luther was also on hand with a typically simple and tasty lick. Cash obviously reveled in some of his own lines, like the one about "cavortin' in Davenport," and, in truth, the song could have been a very credible A side if Clement had not been determined to inflict "Ballad of a Teenage Queen" on the world. "Big River" was banished to the flip, although Shelby Singleton resurrected it as a successful A side after he bought the Sun catalog in 1969.

"Ballad of a Teenage Queen" showed its first signs of life in Canada. Cash, booked on a Canadian tour, asked Sam Phillips how many copies of the record he could expect to sell in Canada. Phillips projected twelve to fifteen thousand. "The fifteen-day tour took us from Prince Edward Island to Vancouver," wrote Cash in 1980. "We filled every hall but, more than that, we sold over 100,000 singles.

"Dan Bass, the promo man for Quality Records [the Sun licensee in Canada] set up a Teenage Queen contest in every city. I flew into a new city each morning and did radio and television interviews. Then in the afternoon I signed records at record shops. My last promo appearance of the day, before the arrival of the Teenage Queen contestants, was to draw a name out of a box at a large department store's record counter and name the Teenage Queen and the runner up. One requirement to enter the contest was to prove the purchase of the record. I autographed hundreds and sometimes thousands of copies of that record in every city. During my concert that evening I crowned the queen and announced the first runner up. In the city of Saskatoon, the Teenage Queen died tragically, leaving the runner up to be enthroned. That runner up was already writing songs and singing. Her name was Joni Mitchell."

"Teenage Queen" was picked by *Billboard* as a "dual market contender" in January 1958, and on February 3 it entered the Hot 100 at number 83, eventually peaking at number 16. It also gave Cash his first number 1 country record. The record sold over 180,000 copies during January alone and another 280,000 before June.

By the time Cash went back into the studio in April 1958 it was apparent that he and Sun would come to a parting of the ways. "I had been out to Cash's house," recalled Phillips, "because I had been hearing rumors. I looked Johnny straight in the eye and I said, 'John, I understand that you've signed an option to go to another label at the expiration of your contract with Sun. I want you to look me straight in the eye and tell me, have you or have you not?' I knew when he opened his mouth he was lying. The only damn lie that Johnny Cash ever told me that I was aware of. That hurt. That *hurt*!" It was doubly galling to Phillips because his old friend Bob Neal had been a party to what Phillips considered double-dealing.

(D. Bass/Showtime)

On the Canadian tour with (top) Dan Bass of Quality Records, and (bottom) Toronto's Teenage Queen

Knowing that Cash was due to depart, Phillips ensured that the market would not lack new Cash product on Sun for some years. "I got an order from Sam Phillips," Cash told Bill Flanagan. "It was a letter [saying] that I *would* go into the studio on such and such a day and record a certain number of songs. That really rankled me and I refused to do it. Then Jack Clement called me and said, 'My job is on the line. I'm supposed to produce you. I think you have to do it. You owe Sam some sessions.' I said, 'I'm not going to sing anything I don't like.' He said, 'Come in. We'll go over songs and find ones you like.' So, I liked the songs but what I hated was that they overdubbed the vocal group on some of them. I *hated* that sound!"

Cash refused to supply new material for the sessions. He was keeping the best for his first sessions at Columbia because he had been promised a better royalty rate as a composer. So it was left to Jack Clement, Bill Justis, and Charlie Rich (who had just been signed as a contracted writer) to fill the breach. It was Clement who contributed the best song, "Guess Things Happen That Way." It had a fine streak of fatalism at its core, and the arrangement was both tasteful and restrained. Released on April 9, it had sold an astonishing 300,000 copies by June, becoming Cash's biggest hit on Sun. It monopolized the number 1 spot in the country charts and reached number 11 in the pop listings.

But there was little rejoicing at Sun. It was now obvious that Cash was departing, as he appeared at the studio on a regular basis during May and July to work off his commitment to the label. In addition, the news of Jerry Lee Lewis' marriage to an underage cousin had broken, and "Guess Things Happen That Way," rising up the charts, met Lewis' "High School Confidential" as it plunged precipitously downward.

On July 17, 1958, Johnny Cash held his last recording session at Sun before moving on to Columbia Records. Phillips placed advertisements in the trade papers assuring DJs and distributors that he had sufficient Cash product to keep the pipeline full for "at least two years." In fact, prodigious recycling by both Phillips and Shelby Singleton ensured that no one would ever want for one of Cash's Sun sides again.

Phillips had apparently asked for a chance to match any offer that another company might make, and he felt betrayed because he had been denied that chance. Bob Neal said in 1973, however, that he had at least informed Phillips of his intentions. "Sam's arrangement with all of his artists involved a royalty rate of 3 percent of 90 percent of retail. When Johnny's contract was set to expire we talked to him. Johnny wanted to get the standard 5 percent royalty, but Sam maintained that he could not afford to pay it. When the deal was announced, he was very upset. He said he would have done the whole deal if he'd thought we'd meant it."

His relationship with Phillips in tatters, Neal folded his management company, Stars, Inc., and managed Cash and Perkins from his house. Two weeks after leaving Sun, Neal announced that Cash was quitting the Opry and that everyone was packing up and moving to the West Coast, feeling that they could storm Hollywood. As it happened, Cash would have to wait almost ten years for a decent dramatic role.

Cash's reasons for wanting to leave were complex. He probably saw a pact with Columbia as a hallmark of legitimacy. Columbia also offered him a chance to do a religious album, something Phillips resisted as strongly in 1958 as he had in 1954. The increased royalty was also undoubtedly a factor. A 5 percent royalty would have meant over ten thousand dollars additional income for Cash in the first six months of 1958 alone. Sam Phillips suggests another potential source of dissatisfaction: "I had given [Carl and Johnny] a lot of time [when they were] getting started. Then I gave Jerry Lee Lewis a lot of time, and they saw it as if we were petting Jerry Lee. They had forgotten that we had brought them along in the same way. They were young people and there was an awful lot of jealousy."

Forging a Legend

Although Columbia recorded Cash with the same instrumentation that Phillips used at Sun, he never sounded quite as good again. Aberrations like "Teenage Queen" aside, Phillips instinctively knew how to record Cash to minimize the group's shortcomings and take advantage of their immense potential. "Luther was the vital player," Phillips contends. "He had real difficulty keeping time; he would lose time or completely mess up during a song, and Johnny would become upset. But I saw something in the plaintiveness of Luther's picking. I said, 'John, it's worth it, you know.' I wanted to make sure that we captured the Luther feel on records and then strengthen it with the slap bass and rhythm. For rhythm we just threaded a little paper through the neck of the guitar and we got a brush-and-snare-drum effect. It was good for Johnny to pick while

Receiving a belated Gold Record for "I Walk the Line" from Cecil Scaife, 1962.

(Escott)

he sang, because he was innately a high-energy person and he worked much better with that guitar in his hand. It was an energy release. I tried to make Johnny's voice outstanding. The three instruments complemented it. I didn't want anything to detract from the command that Johnny had with just the sound of his voice."

Memphis record producer Jim Dickinson has offered another insight into Phillips' work with Cash. "Sam told me that the key to producing Johnny Cash was to 'take it off Luther.' Luther was the brunt of all the jokes: if anyone made a mistake, they'd turn and blame it on Luther, which was not totally fair. Luther only played two strings, but he mostly had those covered. Sam said the pressure made Luther tense, and he said that all you had to do was to take that tension off Luther and you had Johnny Cash produced."

No artist, Johnny Cash included, is truly unique. Cash was obviously influenced by other singers who worked the low vocal range with minimal instrumental support, artists like Ernest Tubb and Jimmie Skinner. His increasingly aggressive rhythm guitar playing came from watching Elvis Presley. "Elvis had a good hard driving rhythm on the bass strings in the key of E," Cash told Bill Flanagan. "A good solid rhythm . . . That's where I was influenced to play that kind of rhythm." The deadened bass string sound had also been used effectively on Hank Williams' recordings, although Williams had used fuller instrumentation. Cash's achievement was to meld these elements together, using songs that were both haunting and, for the greater part, original.

The Sun recordings maximized the effective contrast between the hustling rhythm of the bass and acoustic guitar and the ponderous, sparse vocals and lead guitar. Phillips' achievement was to keep Cash's sound at its bare essentials, and then fatten it up with the use of slapback echo. Subsequent producers and engineers could never quite recapture that formula. Their echo lent distance rather than presence. Worse yet were the early stereo recordings at Columbia, whose primitive separation heightened the unfocused sound.

Johnny Cash's three years of recordings for Sun are a wonderful demonstration of just how far a whole can outclass the sum of its parts. Cash's limited vocals, Luther Perkins' woefully limited picking, and Marshall Grant's strictly functional bass playing jelled magically through Sam Phillips' mixing board to produce perhaps the most original and innovative sound in country music since Hank Williams died.

Recommended Listening

The only complete CD retrospective of Johnny Cash's Sun sessions is contained on *Classic Johnny Cash, 1954–1958* (Bear Family [Germany] BCD 15517), which comprises 3 CDs of Sun material and 2 CDs of Cash's first CBS recordings.

Cash's Sun output has been scattered on countless budget, mid-price, and full-priced albums. The best sampling of his Sun career on CD is *The Sun Years* (Rhino [USA] R2-70950).

CASHING IN

Johnny Cash was neither the first nor the last country artist to appear on Sun Records. In fact, the first artist that Phillips recorded after opening his studio was a local country singer Buck "Snuffy" Turner; more than fifteen years later, the last artist he would record as president of Sun Records was a Johnny Cash sound-alike, Dane Stinit. Though he made his reputation as a producer of blues and rock 'n' roll, Sam Phillips not only began and ended with country music but also kept his hand in it throughout the sixteen years he ran Sun.

As Cash and Presley started to sell in appreciable quantities in the country market, Phillips started to think seriously of Sun Records as a country label. His blues artists had largely disappeared, and rock 'n' roll had yet to explode. In fact, a trade advertisement in January 1956 hyperbolically billed Sun as "America's No. 1 Country & Western Label." But, with the notable exceptions of Presley and Cash, Phillips never achieved anything close to a breakthrough with his country artists during that or any other period.

Rural Electrification

"The very first job I had after opening my recording studio," recalls Phillips, "was in January 1950. I recorded transcriptions for radio with a country singer, Buck Turner. This was for the Arkansas Rural Electrification Corporation. We made fifteen-minute programs that I transcribed onto big ol' sixteen-inch discs. They were distributed to about eighteen or twenty stations."

It is also possible, though unlikely, that the first records Phillips cut were Buck Turner's singles for the Nashville-based Bullet label. Turner had been a featured artist at WREC, where Phillips worked, and when Phillips launched the Memphis Recording Service Turner put up some of the money. He was quickly repaid, however, and the relationship does not seem to have survived beyond 1951.

The mystery surrounding Turner's Bullet recordings notwithstanding, it appears that Phillips' first commercial recordings were made for Bill McCall's

*S*lim Rhodes
and his Mountaineers,
with Sandy Brooks
(top left)

A FOLK SMASH!!

"SWAMP ROOT"

Chess #1475A

backed with

"GOIN' AWAY WALKIN'"

HARMONICA FRANK

CHESS RECORD CORP

750 E 49th Street
Chicago 15 Illinois

Harmonica Frank
after his rediscovery
in the early '70s

4-Star/Gilt Edge company in Los Angeles. Phillips submitted a blues singer, Lost John Hunter, and a local country band, Slim Rhodes' Mountaineers.

Phillips recorded Rhodes on an intermittent basis between 1950 and 1958. Ethmer Cletus "Slim" Rhodes fronted a band that changed with the seasons. When his first sides were sold to Gilt Edge in 1950, Rhodes was working in a strict country format, turning out songs such as "Skunk Hollow Boogie" and "Memphis Bounce." By the time Rhodes appeared in Phillips' studio for the last time in 1958, though, he was sporting a pop-country style redolent of Johnny Cash. In the interim, he had covered all the bases between Hank Williams and Elvis Presley.

Rhodes had a radio show on WMC from 1944, a program that later expanded to television. Without a style of his own, Rhodes stayed abreast of every development within country music until his death from a fall at his home in 1966. He recorded most consistently for Sun between early 1955 and late 1956. His best shot came when he acquired a Presley sound-alike, vocalist Sandy Brooks (born Ronnie Hesselbein), with whom he recorded a creditable rockabilly record, "Take and Give," backed with "Do What I Do." The record sold predictably well in Memphis and got spotty action elsewhere—but not enough action to tempt Hesselbein away from a career with the family tire company.

"I never did see anything particular about Buck Turner or Slim Rhodes' band that stood out as far as style," says Phillips. "They were mainstays on local radio. They were professionals that had well-balanced bands that were easy to record. They were just good, solid local combos."

Harmonica Frank:
Water from an Ancient Well

Harmonica Frank Floyd, on the other hand, was a true eccentric who fascinated Phillips. Their involvement dated back to 1951, when several of Phillips' recording ventures were almost folkloric in nature. "Here was a musician I was very much into," he recalls. "He was a modern-day hobo. It was difficult to find a market for him, because people appreciated what he did without buying his records that much. He was really out of the old school—a one-man band. He played harmonica out of one side of his mouth and sang out of the other side—he didn't use a harmonica bracket. If I had been able to spend the money on Frank Floyd I think he could have become an institution."

Frank Floyd, born to Reuben Brewster Floyd and Estella Miles in Toccopola, Mississippi, on October 11, 1908, was nicknamed "Shank" (he was never christened with a formal name). He spent his earliest years with his grandparents in rural Arkansas, left home in 1922, and rambled throughout much of the Depression. "You say a white boy can't know the blues," Frank said after his rediscovery many years later. "During the Depression I'd sleep in ditches and know if I died that night no one would know who I was or where I come from."

Frank joined a carnival in the early '20s and played for nickels and dimes on street corners. Having already developed his virtuosity on the harmonica, he took up the guitar after hearing the Singing Brakeman, Jimmie Rodgers. The shtick he developed during his spell with the Happy Phillipson Medicine Show was faithfully reproduced on Frank's only Sun record, "The Great Medical Menagerist," in 1954. Occasionally, Frank landed a steady gig at a radio station. It was during a short-term gig with Smilin' Eddie Hill on WMC, Memphis, that he first came to Phillips' attention in 1951.

His credibility high in the wake of "Rocket 88," Phillips persuaded the Chess brothers in Chicago to take two cuts from Harmonica Frank. "Swamp Root" (another song that harked back to Frank's grounding in the medicine shows) was coupled with a primordial blues, "Goin' Away Walkin'." They were released in August 1951. Two weeks after release, "Goin' Away Walkin' " was replaced with a cover version of Big Jeff and the Radio Playboys' hit, "Step It Up and Go." The new pairing apparently sold well, and Frank soon received a royalty check for one hundred dollars, with which he bought a Martin guitar.

By the time Frank's second Chess record was released in January 1952 his steady gig on WMC had ended, Eddie Hill having left for Nashville. When he recorded for Sun in 1954, Frank was working at a station in Dyersburg, Tennessee. The Sun single, which coupled the charmingly anachronistic "Great Medical Menagerist" with "Rockin' Chair Daddy," was released at the same time as Elvis Presley's debut—July 1954. It was Presley's record that sealed Frank's fate. Some reviewers noted that "Rockin' Chair Daddy" was a good blend of black and white musical styles; the problem was that it blended the black and white musical styles of the 1920s.

Still sensing that he could be a part of the rockabilly revolution, Frank auditioned for Meteor Records, and then issued a record on the F & L label, which he co-owned with another would-be rockabilly, Larry Kennon. Disappointed with its failure, Frank moved to Dallas, started hawking ice cream, and got out of the music business.

At some point, Frank returned to Tennessee to work for his cousin. He married a woman he met through a lonely hearts club and settled in Millington, near Memphis. It was there, in the early '70s, that he was rediscovered by

Stephen LaVere, who followed a tortuous path to Frank's door, giving him a second lease on life as an attraction at folk music festivals. First and last, Frank was an entertainer: he had learned his craft on countless street corners, where he had only a few seconds to catch someone's attention. That skill remained intact fifty years later.

After his rediscovery, Frank claimed to have invented rock 'n' roll with much the same cheerful disregard for the facts that Jelly Roll Morton exhibited in claiming to have invented jazz. Yet when Harmonica Frank Floyd died in 1984, a piece of American musical history died with him.

Troublesome Waters

Harmonica Frank's record was not the first country record issued on Sun, it was the sixth; the first two, by the Ripley Cotton Choppers and Howard Seratt, were equally out of date the moment the cutting stylus left the lathe.

Were it not for the presence of an electric guitar, the Ripley Cotton Choppers' single could have been recorded at any point since the mid-1920s. The Choppers had worked on WREC, and Phillips reportedly cut the record as a favor to a member of the group who was dying. Similarly, Howard Seratt was a throwback to an earlier era. Phillips still vividly recalls Seratt, a crippled country gospel singer from Manila, Arkansas. "Oh that man! I never heard a person, no matter what category of music, could sing as beautifully. The honesty, the integrity, the communication. . . . That unpretentious quality. His music just had a depth of beauty about it in its simplicity." Phillips asserted that he would have loved to have recorded Seratt indefinitely, but Seratt remembers that there was a rider attached to that offer: he would have to record secular music, which he was unwilling to do.

On the same day that Seratt's record was issued, Phillips released the first Sun record with an identifiably contemporary country sound. "Boogie Blues" by Earl Peterson was a one-shot release by an artist who dubbed himself "Michigan's Singing Cowboy." A staple of live radio in rural Michigan, Peterson's driving force was his mother, who believed desperately in his talent. In the 1953 family Buick, Mrs. Peterson and her son ventured south to Memphis and knocked on Phillips' door in early 1954. Peterson demoed "Boogie Blues," Phillips liked what he heard, and together with some local backup musicians they cut a session. When Phillips calculated Peterson's royalty statement a year later, "Boogie Blues" had sold 2,868 copies, of which 196 had been returned. Total royalties came to $94.17.

More one-shots followed. In May 1954 Phillips recorded a Memphis group called Doug Poindexter's Starlite Wranglers—a name that would have been enveloped by the mists of time were it not for the rosy future of the group's guitarist and bass player, Scotty Moore and Bill Black. Poindexter's engagingly rural style made even Hank Williams sound uptown by comparison; his solitary

Earl Peterson

(Escott)

Sun recording sold even worse than "Boogie Blues," netting about three hundred copies.

In sharp comparison, Sidney "Hardrock" Gunter had already seen one massive hit, "Birmingham Bounce," when he leased two titles to Phillips in February 1954. Gunter's Sun recording of "Gonna Dance All Night," a song he had already cut for Bama Records in 1950, approximated Bill Haley's fusion of western swing, jazz, and country boogie. It was certainly a mix of black and white musical styles, but it was a fair distance from the magic blend that Phillips would achieve with Elvis Presley a few months later. What Presley would do was evolve a black approach to singing grafted onto a backing that was equal parts country and blues; Gunter merely delivered his cornball vocals over a band that mixed R&B and western swing riffs. As Nick Tosches said of Gunter's single, "Even though it was a bad record, it failed to sell."

In 1956 Gunter leased another single to Sun. He had recorded a rockabilly novelty, "Jukebox Help Me Find My Baby," that was getting a good reaction around his new home base of Wheeling, West Virginia. He rushed a copy to Phillips, who promptly leased it, but again the Midas touch worked in reverse. After it was released on Sun, the record died, and with it, Gunter's affiliation with Sam Phillips.

Through these experiments, Phillips was searching for something different from the Nashville mainstream. The success of Elvis Presley eventually showed him the tack he should take with country music. In February 1955 he launched the Flip label in an attempt to give direction to his country output. Among the first artists on Flip were three of enormous potential: Carl Perkins, Charlie Feathers, and the Miller Sisters.

(J. Huffman/Escott)

Charlie Feathers

Charlie Feathers

In a very real sense, Charlie Feathers has been his own worst enemy. Chewing the fat between sets at countless low-life nightclubs over the last two decades, Feathers recounts the origins of rockabilly music and the "Sun sound" with a strangely skewed perspective, in which one Charles Arthur Feathers plays a starring role. But his larger-than-life boasting merely eclipses the simple fact that the man was a superb stylist who made a handful of brilliant records.

Feathers never really became more than an underground figure in his adopted hometown. Until recently, his convictions for gambling outnumbered mentions of his music in the files of the local newspapers. Yet for a few months in 1956 it seemed as though Feathers might indeed take a place alongside Carl Perkins, Johnny Cash, and possibly even Elvis Presley. But a mixture of impatience, bad luck, and worse judgment brought him back to the bitter reality of endless gigs at local bars, leaving him to eke out an existence on the fringe of the local music scene. To compensate, he has evolved the Feathers Mythology, elaborated with every retelling, in which he is finally a star.

Charlie Feathers was born near Holly Springs, Mississippi, on June 12, 1932. Saturday night in Holly Springs would find Feathers, fifteen years old and already five years out of school, wandering the streets. A black blues singer would be singing with a tin cup in front of him. There might be a bluegrass tent show, high, pure harmonies piercing the night air. Sunday morning would find nothing but preachers on the radio, preachers with a passion that could make a poor unlettered farmer hold a snake or eat rat poison. They all left their mark on Charlie Feathers. Talking about music with his first regular guitarist, Jerry Huffman, Feathers would say he was drawn to music with feeling—or, as he put it, "fillin'."

Feathers left school after the second or third grade and eventually went to work on oil pipelines in Illinois and Texas. He returned to the mid-South and settled in Memphis, where he married in 1950. He had been working in a box factory for a while when he contracted spinal meningitis and had to spend several months in a hospital bed, listening to the radio. When he emerged, he was determined to make a career out of music.

In several interviews, Feathers has claimed to have been hanging around at Phillips' studio since its earliest days, but that seems improbable. What is certain is that in October 1954 Phillips placed him with Bill Cantrell and Quinton Claunch to work up his debut on Flip.

Cantrell and Claunch rehearsed Feathers at a small home studio, and the fruits of their work were released in February 1955. The intensity that Feathers brought to his first record showed that Phillips' hopes for him in the country market were not misplaced. "I've Been Deceived," with its haunting images of recrimination, ranks alongside almost anything that Hank Williams wrote or performed:

> But the Good Book tells us, you'll reap just what you sow
> And your harvest, darlin', will be bitter tears I know
> Oh, I've been deceived.

Charlie Feathers and his Musical Warriors, with Jerry Huffman (top left) and Quinton Claunch (bottom left)

(J. Huffman/Escott)

Feathers and Jerry Huffman

(Huffman/Escott)

Together with the bluegrass-tinged "Peepin' Eyes," the song gave Feathers his first fleeting place on the local country charts.

During 1955 Feathers demoed some songs for Stan Kesler and started spending time at Sun on a regular basis. One of the songs he worked up with Kesler was "I Forgot to Remember to Forget." We will probably never know the truth surrounding Feathers' claim to have worked closely with Elvis on that song and on other occasions between 1954 and 1956. Feathers has made oblique reference to tapes made with Presley at a radio station in 1955, but no such recordings have ever surfaced. Feathers also claims, more plausibly, that another song he co-wrote with Kesler, "We're Getting Closer to Being Apart," was being worked on by Presley at the time his contract was sold.

Feathers' second single, "Wedding Gown of White," was issued on the Sun label because Flip had been shut down after threats from Ed Wells, owner of another Flip label in Los Angeles. Unfortunately, the move to the parent label came at a time when Phillips was placing all of his energy behind Johnny Cash and Carl Perkins, and "Wedding Gown of White" sold fewer than a thousand copies upon release. In January 1956 Feathers returned to Sun with rockabilly looming large in his thoughts, but the session led nowhere. He returned for the last time with a rockabilly version of the R&B standard "Corrine, Corrina." Phillips circulated dubs but didn't release the single. Consumed with impatience, Feathers took his combo across town to the Meteor studio in May 1956, where he recorded the rockabilly classics "Tongue-Tied Jill" and "Get with It," the latter a thinly veiled rewrite of "Corrine, Corrina."

"While we were waiting for Sam to make up his mind on 'Corrine, Corrina,' " recalled Jerry Huffman, "we came up with 'Tongue-Tied Jill,' and Charlie couldn't bear to wait around. Les Bihari at Meteor was after him, saying 'I'll put something out on you right now.' Jody and I were very disturbed at this. We wanted to work something out with Sam."

The Meteor record also led to an offer from King Records in Cincinnati, for whom Feathers recorded several more definitive statements of rockabilly music.

The Feathers trio was booked onto package shows with Warren Smith, Johnny Cash, Jerry Lee Lewis, Johnny Horton, and Roy Orbison. They also held down a regular weekend gig at a skating rink in Cairo, Illinois, for six months and made one guest shot on the Big D Jamboree in Dallas before the good times —such as they had been—came to an end.

Why didn't it happen for Charlie Feathers? According to the man himself, there was a dark conspiracy at work that he will not elaborate upon. Jerry Huffman blames lack of good management. He points to Feathers' lack of a formal education (signing his name was the virtual limit of his literacy). There was also his impatience with Sun, and a measure of sheer bad luck.

Phillips maintains that "Charlie was always a little difficult to work with, and that was why we never got the best out of him. He always felt he knew more than everyone else. He told his stories and got to the point where he believed them. That's too bad, because he was a damn talent . . . and Charlie's talent was in country music—the blues feeling he put into a hillbilly song. Charlie should have been a superb top country artist—the George Jones of his day."

Phillips has a strong case. When Feathers played rockabilly, he used an arsenal of vocal gimmicks—hiccups and stutters—that can soon become tiresome. But when he found a country song that moved him—a song with "fillin' "—he performed it with utterly chilling conviction. If he had stuck with country music and taken a little direction, Feathers might indeed have been a serious contender.

*C*launch and Cantrell:
Daydreams Come True

Sam Phillips worked alone with his blues artists, believing that no one else could do as good a job rehearsing and recording them. But he had fewer reservations about entrusting some of his country music production to the team of Bill Cantrell and Quinton Claunch. "They were old friends I had known for many years," he recalls. "We all lived in the same part of Alabama when we were starting out. I lived in Florence and they worked out of Muscle Shoals."

Claunch and Cantrell had formed a hillbilly band, the Blue Seal Pals, in the mid '40s and had played for a spell on WSM, the home of the Grand Ole Opry. By 1948 the group had disbanded, and both Claunch and Cantrell had moved to Memphis to take up full-time jobs outside music, retaining only a limited involvement.

In 1954 Claunch and Cantrell worked up a song called "Daydreamin'," which they planned to record with a local singer, Bud Deckelman. After they had auditioned it for Phillips, who refused it, they went to see Phillips' local competitor, Meteor Records. With Meteor they were able to make a deal—as part of the arrangement, Cantrell and Deckelman, both engineers, agreed to fix

Bill Cantrell, 1948

Meteor's recording machine—and despite lukewarm reviews in the trade press "Daydreamin' " became a strong-selling record. Jimmy Newman quickly covered the song and scored the hit, but Deckelman's version secured him an MGM contract.

Phillips realized his mistake, which must have been doubly galling given that he had mastered the Meteor disc. By that point Elvis Presley was selling well in the country market, and Phillips' thoughts turned quickly and seriously toward country music. He asked Claunch and Cantrell to work with him rehearsing new country acts, and asked for first refusal on their new material.

Claunch and Cantrell discovered some of the artists they worked with; Phillips found others. Cantrell's protégés included Maggie Sue Wimberly, a fourteen-year-old gospel singer from Muscle Shoals, who sang a "Daydreamin' " sequel called "Daydreams Come True" that betrayed her tender years. After a subsequent session for Sun in a rock 'n' roll vein, Maggie Sue retired from secular music for a while, re-emerging as Sue Richards in the early '70s. She scored a few minor hits under her own name and then joined up with Tammy Wynette's group.

The Miller Sisters were an act in whom Phillips had infinitely more faith. They were actually sisters-in-law: Elsie Jo Wages was married to Mildred Miller's brother, Roy. The two "sisters" and Roy worked as the Miller Trio around their hometown of Tupelo, Mississippi, and eventually auditioned for Sun in 1954 at the suggestion of a DJ on WTUP. Phillips was immediately struck by the unerring vocal harmony and the heart-stopping innocence that Millie and Jo projected in their singing.

Phillips was never able to understand why his faith in the Miller Sisters couldn't be translated into record sales. Sister acts were selling, and the Millers' clean harmony was surely as good as anything on the market. He gave them three shots; the first, on Flip, and the second on Sun were achingly pure country music. Their final shot, "Ten Cats Down," was a rock 'n' roll novelty concocted by Claunch and Cantrell. The sisters returned again in 1957 and strayed even further from their roots, recording a version of the R&B classic "Got You on My Mind," but Phillips would not release it. Shortly afterward the sisters-in-law went their separate ways: Millie to the North, Jo and Roy to the countryside near Tupelo, where their involvement in the Pentecostal faith hardened to the point where Jo found it difficult to talk about her days on the fringes of secular music.

By this point, Claunch and Cantrell were becoming disillusioned with their deal at Sun. They had worked with Carl Perkins on a song called "Sure to Fall" that was to be placed on the flip side of "Blue Suede Shoes." At the last moment, Phillips decided to replace "Sure to Fall" with another rocker, "Honey, Don't." "Sure to Fall" was re-scheduled with "Tennessee" on an all-country single that was never released. Cantrell estimates that he lost $140,000 from that decision. At roughly the same time that "Blue Suede Shoes" was sitting near the top of all three trade charts, Claunch and Cantrell received a statement of earnings from Phillips that reported that Sun had overpaid them on the first Charlie Feathers single, and consequently owed them only $21.75 for sales on Maggie Sue Wimberly and the second Feathers single.

"From that moment on," recalled Cantrell, "Quinton and I decided that we should put our songs on the back of every record we could. The only way to control this was to have our own record company." In partnership with a failed rockabilly singer, Ray Harris, and a local record store owner, Joe Cuoghi, Claunch and Cantrell formed Hi Records in 1957. Their first big seller, Bill Black's "Smokie, Part 2," came in 1959.

Cantrell stuck with Hi through good times and bad, eventually quitting his job with the city of Memphis and becoming a full-time vice president. By the time Hi was sold in 1976, he and Cuoghi's lawyer were the only partners remaining from 1957. Claunch left Hi with considerable ill will on all sides in 1960 after he recorded a Bill Black sound-alike for another label. He eventually formed Goldwax Records, which for a brief period came close to rivaling both Stax and Hi.

The records by the Miller Sisters and Charlie Feathers, along with Carl Perkins' early recordings, exemplified all that was best in the last flowering of hillbilly music. The painfully intense vocals were matched by beautifully executed steel guitar solos from Stan Kesler and percussive electric guitar parts from Quinton Claunch. Drums were still taboo in country music productions, so Claunch accented the rhythm by thumping on the muted bass strings of his electric guitar. "We had a pretty good country house band," asserted Phillips, "but I knew that cutting Nashville-style country music was not what I wanted. I knew I *could* cut it, but I knew it wasn't what I hoped to get."

After the rock 'n' roll explosion, Phillips continued to record country music sporadically. He rarely stuck with an artist for more than one release, though, and virtually none of his latter-day country acts had the stilling quality of Charlie Feathers or the Miller Sisters. The best of the new crop was Ernie Chaffin.

Feelin' Low

After 1956 the character of country music changed. The success of country boys such as Elvis Presley, Carl Perkins, Sonny James, and Marty Robbins in the pop charts held out the alluring promise of crossover. The country music that Phillips and virtually everyone else released after 1956 was recorded with at least one eye on potential crossover sales. When Phillips signed Ernie Chaffin in 1956 he found a singer whose voice had few alienating hillbilly edges and thus seemed ripe with pop potential.

Born in Water Valley, Mississippi, on January 1, 1928, Chaffin relocated to Gulfport in 1944, hoping to break into country music. He met a local songwriter, Pee Wee Maddux, in the early 1950s while playing at a pavilion on the waterfront in Biloxi. By the time he received the news from Memphis that Sam

*E*rnie Chaffin

(Escott)

Phillips liked his work and wanted to sign him, Chaffin had already been recording for over two years.

In its way, Chaffin's Sun debut, "Feelin' Low," is as good as any other country record issued on Sun. Breezy and hypnotic, its unusual chord changes underpin a warm, understated vocal. Chaffin could have been a major figure in country music: he had an intimate vocal presence that appealed to the same market that would later make Jim Reeves a star. He also had the benefit of some top-class material from Maddux.

"Feelin' Low" did well in some markets, encouraging Chaffin to record another three singles. Yet, as Chaffin himself put it, "I always felt like the Lord came first, my family came second, and my career came third." From a commercial point of view, Chaffin had a dangerously skewed perspective, but his priorities have brought him peace of mind—something to which few of his contemporaries at Sun can lay claim.

Cashing In

After Carl Perkins and Elvis Presley showed the path to commercial salvation for Sun Records, Phillips recorded remarkably little pure country music. Despite the fact that Johnny Cash became a staple of his album catalog (seven of the twelve original Sun albums were by Cash), Phillips was rarely tempted to try and repeat his success with Cash in the country market. Between Ernie Chaffin's last single in April 1959 and Dane Stinit's first single seven years later there were only a few isolated experiments with country music.

"I think," Phillips concluded in 1985, "I could have had a darn good country label. Had I stayed in country music alone and dedicated myself to it, then I had the nucleus of several fine artists who could have made it—in particular Ernie Chaffin and Charlie Feathers. I just loved stylists. People you *knew* the minute you heard them on record. That's what it's all about. I had a different sound in country music, and I knew I would have had difficulty in orienting the taste of people and getting the radio play."

The fact that RCA signed Elvis Presley with the firm intention of marketing him as something other than a country music act started to turn Phillips' head away from country music. Then, in the early months of 1956, he gained first-hand experience of the difference that pop sales made to a country product when "Blue Suede Shoes" started to sell outside the country market. Sun Records' brief fling as a country music label had effectively ended.

Recommended Listening

The Sun Country Years (Bear Family [Germany] BFX 15211) contains 11 LPs and a book detailing Phillips' involvement in country music.

Memphis Ramble (Rhino [USA] R2 70963) is a single CD drawn from *The Sun Country Years*, containing recordings by Harmonica Frank, Howard Seratt, Hardrock Gunter, Doug Poindexter, the Miller Sisters, and others.

Charlie Feathers' early recordings not included on *The Sun Country Years* can be heard on *Rock-a-Billy* (Zu-Zazz [UK] ZCD 2011).

(Escott)

CARL PERKINS: PROPHET IN BLUE SUEDE SHOES

T
h e r e i s an enduring belief among Carl Perkins' diehard constituency that if fate had just taken a few different turns—if he had not suffered an automobile accident at a critical juncture in his career, if he had only had a manager as wily as Colonel Parker, if Sun had not deserted him to concentrate on Jerry Lee Lewis—then Carl would have been as big as Elvis.

Elvis Presley and Carl Perkins leaped into the public consciousness at approximately the same time, each with a brand of music that broke down well-established barriers. Indeed, both were nourished by the same musical wellsprings; but the similarity ends there. It's not that Perkins was an inferior musician to Presley, for in many ways he was superior; it's not even that Perkins' potential was sapped by his fifteen minutes of fame back in 1956. Rather, the fact is that Presley had the personal and musical malleability to sustain a career in an orbit beyond the one that had spawned him. Carl Perkins did not. His music was born and bred in the barrooms of the mid-South. The rhythms that underpinned his music and the images in his songs were pure honky-tonk. He got lucky with one song near the dawn of his long career, and he certainly deserved that luck, but you could never take the country out of Carl Perkins.

Lake County Cotton Country

Although Perkins is closely associated with his current hometown of Jackson, Tennessee, he was born in the far northwest corner of the state, close to the banks of the Mississippi. His birth certificate gives his parents' address as Route 1, Ridgely, and their names as Fonie "Buck" Perkings (*sic*) and Louise Brantley. Their second child, born on April 9, 1932, was christened Carl Lee Perkings. The misspelling of the family name suggests that the literacy of government employees was barely a notch higher than that of the people they were cataloging.

Carl's birth certificate

A 1956 publicity photo

Perkins in the early '50s

It was the height of the Depression, and Buck Perkins was a sharecropper without a market. The family lived first in a three-room shack and then in a one-room storehouse. "Mama hung a sheet for partition," recalls Perkins in his autobiography, "and our stove was an old tin barrel Dad set upon some bricks in the middle of the floor." The kids in the neighborhood brought cast-off clothes for the Perkins brothers, and Carl has often told the story of how one kid asked for his pants back after Carl had tackled him in a football game.

Music entered Carl Perkins' life from two directions: the Grand Ole Opry from Nashville, and a black sharecropper from across the field. The Opry was inevitable: "My daddy only liked country music," Perkins remembers. "He was the one that turned the radio on and off because we didn't have electricity, just a battery that we'd buy once a year when the crops came in."

The black sharecropper was named John Westbrook (or Westbrooks), and Perkins called him Uncle John. "He used to sit out on the front porch at night," Perkins told Lenny Kaye, "with a gallon bucket full of coal oil rags that he'd burn to keep the mosquitoes off him, and I'd ask my daddy if I could go to Uncle John's and hear him pick some."

In the same way that Perkins rarely sings a song the same way twice, he never seems to tell a story exactly the same way. In some versions, Uncle John gives Carl his guitar on a Saturday and dies the following Wednesday. In another, Buck Perkins buys the guitar for three dollars. Whatever the case, the older musician's influence on Perkins was incalculable: "It was his inspiration that made me know what it was I wanted to do for the rest of my life."

Shortly after the end of World War II, Buck Perkins moved his family to Bemis, Tennessee, where his brothers worked in the cotton mills. Buck was refused a job in the mills because of his deteriorating lungs, and the Perkins family went back to sharecropping, although by this time they had a house with electricity and a refrigerator. Perkins soon found a use for the electricity when he bought a cheap Harmony electric guitar and plugged it in.

Although he will generally claim to have no direct influences, Perkins' style was obviously formed by listening to the guitarists who worked on the Opry. In particular, he remembers "Butterball" Page, who played single-string leads with Ernest Tubb for a few years in the late '40s. Another important influence was probably Arthur Smith, whose 1946 hit "Guitar Boogie" influenced a generation of pickers and set a new standard for sheer technique.

And then there was the blues. It's unlikely that Perkins was allowed to listen to the R&B stations, but he never forgot the lessons that Uncle John had taught him. "I liked the slur he put on the blues things," he recalled to Lenny Kaye. "I could never get away from what was buried in my mind of the sound he made on that simple little guitar. I just sat and constantly worked on that."

The Perkins Brothers Band

There can be little doubt that Carl's older brother Jay and his younger brother Clayton would never have thought of a career in music had it not been for constant badgering from Carl. He wanted a backup group, and his two brothers were the prime candidates.

The choice of venues available to the brothers was limited, virtually confined to church socials and honky-tonks; the Perkins Brothers Band gravitated naturally toward the latter. Jay Perkins handled some of the vocals, singing in a rough-hewn voice modeled on Ernest Tubb's. But it was Carl who was both principal vocalist and lead guitarist. By 1954 their repertoire included a fair sampling of hillbilly standards—"Always Late (With Your Kisses)," "Jealous Heart," "Honky-Tonk Blues," and the inevitable "Lovesick Blues"; there was also a little pop music, in the shape of "I'll Walk Alone," and a pointer toward the future, "Carl's Boogie." Thousands of bands in similar dives across the mid-South were playing an identical repertoire. From among their number, the Perkins Brothers Band found themselves at the top of the pop charts two years later.

The reason revolves around Perkins himself and the nature of his music. By 1954 he had evolved a unique style, not pure honky-tonk music but a hybrid that borrowed much in terms of feeling, phrasing, and rhythm from black music. "I just speeded up some of the slow blues licks," said Carl. "I put a

little speed and rhythm to what Uncle John had slowed down. That's all. That's what rockabilly music or rock 'n' roll was to begin with: a country man's song with a black man's rhythm. Someone once said that everything's been done before—and it has. It's just a question of figuring out a good mixture of it to sound original."

The honky-tonks were also a good place to experiment. Mistakes would go unnoticed, and by listening to the audience Perkins could determine the type of music that went over best. One of his first moves was to bring in a drummer. Drums, of course, were forbidden on the Grand Ole Opry, but Perkins decided that he needed them to reinforce the rhythm and keep it danceable. His first drummer, Tony Austin, lasted no more than a few gigs in 1953. He was replaced by W. S. "Fluke" Holland, originally from Saltillo, Mississippi, who had gone to school in Jackson with Clayton Perkins. Not only did he show real promise, he was able to buy a set of Brecht drums and—just as important—a reliable automobile for the group. Holland frequented many of the black nightclubs in town because, as a drummer working in country music, he had few role models.

With a steady backbeat maintained by the bass and drums, Perkins would accentuate the rhythm by hitting the bass strings of his electric guitar while he sang. He also developed the technique of singing and playing fills around his vocal, in the manner of a blues singer. Like most singers, Perkins was looking for a compatible lead guitarist who would complement his work with tasty fills, and he found the most compatible lead guitarist of all in himself. He would use the little runs on the guitar as extensions of his vocal lines, working a dialogue with himself, scatting a line and then completing it with a lick on the guitar. His finesse was probably wasted upon most of his clientele, but Perkins evidently did not care. He worked hard on his music, for he saw in it a deliverance from an otherwise bleak future as a barely educated country boy trying to scratch out a living in Jackson.

Between 1953 and 1955 most of Perkins' income came from working at the Colonial Bakery in Jackson. The honky-tonks paid only two or three dollars a night, but they enabled the Perkins brothers to practice their music and cultivate their drinking habits at minimal cost.

"I would mix beer with whiskey," wrote Perkins in his autobiography (published by an evangelical publishing house), "and, with soul on fire, I'd stand on the table tops striving for the attention I thought my music deserved. The booze was free at most of the places I played at and it eased the pressure. My intentions seemed good. I wanted to try and help the drunks, give them some happiness, maybe a little hope. But I was in the Devil's playground and it wasn't long before some old boy would shout, 'Give that Carl another drink and he'll really pick and sing.' "

On January 24, 1953, Carl Perkins married Valda Crider from Corinth, Mississippi. They moved to a government housing project in Jackson as the children started appearing. But Valda encouraged Carl to work on his music and try for a career in entertainment. Her support has nourished Perkins through a long career as a musician, and through many bouts with the bottle and his own self-doubt. In fact, it was Val who heard a record on the radio that would alter the course of Perkins' career.

"One of the Greatest Plowhands in the World..."

As Perkins observed, there were many country boys who were playing with a blues feel and working on the hybrid that later became known as rockabilly music. One of those who had independently worked up a similar style of music, of course, was Elvis Presley. "The first time I heard Elvis was when my wife was in the kitchen," recalled Perkins to Dave Booth, "and she said, 'Carl, that sounds just like y'all.' Hearing him do 'Blue Moon of Kentucky' set a flame afire in me. And oddly enough, I'd been doing that song, too."

It did not take long before Perkins found out that the singer of "Blue Moon of Kentucky" recorded for the Sun label. A few weeks later, the Perkins Brothers Band headed for Memphis. Marion Keisker apparently shooed them away, but they met Sam Phillips outside on the street. Perkins was impressed by Phillips' car and his matching suit and shirt. For his part, Phillips encountered someone whom he later described as "one of the greatest plowhands in the world," adding, "There was no way Carl could hide that pure country in him—although pure country can mean an awful lot of soul."

"Sam later said he felt sorry for me," recalls Perkins. "He said I looked like I would have died if he hadn't listened to me. And I might have. He said he liked 'Turn Around' although he later said that he wasn't knocked out by anything else I did." Phillips remembers seeing more promise than fulfillment:

"He was a tremendous honky-tonk picker. He had this feel for *pushing* a song along that very few people had. I knew that Carl could rock and in fact

On stage 1955 or '56

he told me right from the start that he had been playing that music before Elvis came out on record. I was so impressed with the pain and feeling in his country singing, though, that I wanted to see whether this was someone who could revolutionize the country end of the business. That didn't mean we weren't going to rock with Carl. That was inevitable because he had such rhythm in his natural style."

It seems fairly certain that Perkins first appeared at Sun in October 1954. Phillips placed him in the hands of Bill Cantrell and Quinton Claunch, who worked to perfect a hillbilly single that was issued in February 1955 on Phillips' new Flip subsidiary. The sincerity that Phillips responded to was in full flower on "Turn Around." Both song and performance owed a measure of debt to Hank Williams, but it was immediately apparent that Phillips' hopes for Perkins in the country market were well founded.

Shortly after the Flip release hit the market, Perkins began to work with Claunch and Cantrell on a second single, this one to be brought out on the Sun label. The formula of coupling a slow country ballad with an uptempo rhythm novelty remained unchanged: "Let the Jukebox Keep On Playing" saw the ghost of Hank Williams looming large again. But the flip side, "Gone, Gone, Gone," owed an obvious debt to no one, and was an entire dimension beyond the uptempo hillbilly flipside of his first record. The steel guitar sat out the song, the fiddle ghosted far back in the mix, leaving Perkins front and center. It gave the first indication of Perkins' amazing rapport with himself, as he scatted phrases vocally, completing them on guitar. In delivery and feel, it was pure R&B.

Surprisingly, W. S. Holland was barely audible on either of the two uptempo numbers Perkins had released to that point. He was playing with brushes, and Phillips mixed him as far back as he could manage in the cramped studio. It seems Phillips shared the prevailing aversion to using drums on country records. "Sam said, 'What do you need 'em for?' " recalled Perkins to Dave Booth. "I said, 'W.S. just plays, he don't play loud.' Sam came to agree. He said, 'He don't sound like drums, he sounds like clickin'. Sounds good.' "

"Gone, Gone, Gone" was released on August 1, 1955, the day that Elvis Presley's last Sun single was released. By the time Perkins went back into the studio, Presley had departed and Phillips had a little money to throw behind a new song that Perkins had written.

BLUE SUEDE SHOES:
CHRONOLOGY OF A HIT

"Blue Suede Shoes" has been called the first true rock 'n' roll hit, in the sense that it was an "all market" hit. Some R&B hits had sold well in the pop market (most notably Chuck Berry's "Maybellene," which had even outsold the white cover versions); likewise, some country records had crossed over into the pop market, and Bill Haley had defined his own pop/R&B hybrid. But there had never been a record that had sold well in all three markets.

While it seems almost pointless to try to pinpoint where rock 'n' roll began, it's fairly clear that the music incorporated elements of blues, country, and pop. "Blue Suede Shoes" was the first record to borrow from all three categories *and* become a hit on all three charts. *That* is Carl Perkins' achievement, and it is worth a detailed look at exactly how it happened.

Fall 1955. Johnny Cash joins Carl Perkins for a show in Amory, Mississippi. He suggests that Carl write a song based on a saying he had heard in the chow line while he was in the service, "Don't step on my blue suede shoes."

A few nights later Perkins is playing in Jackson, Tennessee, when he sees a dancer in the crowd trying to keep his girlfriend away from his new blue suede shoes. It connects with the idea that Cash had given him. At three o'clock the following morning, Perkins awakes with the genesis of the song in his head. He goes downstairs and writes out the lyrics in pencil on an empty potato bag. *Suede* is spelled *swaed*.

Early December 1955. Perkins and his brothers have worked up the new song to the point where they feel comfortable auditioning it for Sam Phillips. For his part, Phillips is unsure about the future of "hillbilly bop" music, but now that Presley has departed, he is willing to let Perkins experiment in the new style.

Perkins runs through the song for Phillips in the studio. Phillips commits three cuts to tape. On the first take, Perkins sings " . . . three to get ready, now *go boy go*!" Phillips suggests that Perkins change it to "*go cat go*!" They also change "drink my corn" to "drink my liquor" as the song is gradually eased uptown.

Three other songs are recorded at the same time: "Sure to Fall" (with Jay taking the lead), "Tennessee" (with Jay joining Carl on the chorus), and "Honey, Don't."

December 19, 1955. Phillips listens to the tapes and decides to master two singles from the sessions. He assigns master numbers as follows:

U-176	"Blue Suede Shoes"
U-177	"Honey, Don't"
U-178	"Sure to Fall"
U-179	"Tennessee"

There is some talk immediately after the session of keeping the old formula of coupling a rockabilly tune with a country weeper, but Phillips decides to go with one rockabilly single to be released under Carl's name and one country single, coupling "Sure to Fall" and "Tennessee," under the name of the Perkins Brothers Band or, possibly, Carl and Jay Perkins.

Phillips cuts masters on both singles and ships acetates via Air Express to Jack Rosen at Superior Records in Los Angeles. He instructs Rosen to process the acetate masters and ship sets of 45-rpm and 78-rpm stampers (the metal parts used to press records) to Plastic Products in Memphis. "Make all shipments by air," adds Phillips, "and we surely will appreciate your doing a RUSH job on these—especially 176 and 177."

Late December 1955. Phillips circulates dubs (acetates run from the tapes) to local radio stations and confirms that his hunch is correct; "Blue Suede Shoes" is the side to watch. Plastic Products has the first commercial copies ready by the last week in December.

January 1, 1956. "Blue Suede Shoes," backed with "Honey, Don't," is released. "Sure to Fall"/"Tennessee" is held back, probably because Phillips does not want to risk splitting airplay.

January 20–21, 1956. Based on its local reception, Phillips suspects that there will be a heavy demand for "Blue Suede Shoes" and instructs Superior to ship stampers to Paramount in Philadelphia and Monarch Manufacturing in Los Angeles. "We anticipate that this number will be very big," adds Phillips.

Billboard reviews "Blue Suede Shoes" in their country music review section: "Perkins contributes a lively reading on a gay rhythm ditty with a strong R&B styled backing. Fine for the jukes." The rating is 76/100.

February 1956. "Blue Suede Shoes" enters the local Memphis country charts on February 11 at number 2.

The following week it is number 1, where it remains for three months. *Billboard* picks it as a "Country Best Buy." "Interestingly enough," adds *Billboard*, "the disk has a large measure of appeal for pop and R&B customers." It starts to sell in huge quantities throughout the South.

Early March 1956. *Billboard* picks "Blue Suede Shoes" as one to watch for the pop market. It features in their "Coming Up Strong" picks. The cover versions start appearing. The first is probably by western swing bandleader Pee Wee King, to whom Carl had given a prerelease acetate when both artists played for the Milk Fund in Memphis. King's version, recorded on February 7, hits the street in early March. It is followed in short order by versions from Boyd Bennett, Bob Roubian with Cliffie Stone's Orchestra, Sid King, Lawrence Welk, Roy Hall, Sam "The Man" Taylor, and Jim Lowe. It is also covered by Elvis Presley, but Presley's version is initially available only on his first album and an EP drawn from it. Presley performs the song during his appearance on the Dorsey Brothers television show on March 17.

"Blue Suede Shoes" appears on *Billboard*'s Hot 100 on March 3. Presley's debut RCA single, "Heartbreak Hotel," makes its appearance on the charts the same week. *Billboard* dubs both songs "mongrel music" and notes that Perkins is showing up on seven territorial R&B charts.

Perkins returns to the studio to cut a follow-up. Four songs are recorded, but the intense action surrounding "Blue Suede Shoes" convinces Phillips to delay mastering a new single. "Blue Suede Shoes" is selling over twenty thousand copies a day.

March 10, 1956. Carl Perkins becomes the first country artist to reach the national rhythm and blues charts ("Blue Suede Shoes" eventually peaks at number 2). He is followed three weeks later by Elvis Presley with "Heartbreak Hotel" (which peaks at number 3).

March 21, 1956. The Perkins band together with manager Dick Stuart are driving to New York for a taping of the Perry Como television show. They leave Norfolk, Virginia, and get lost in Delaware. With Dick Stuart asleep at the wheel, their huge eight-seater Chrysler slams into a poultry truck near Dover, Delaware. The driver, Thomas Phillips, a forty-four-year-old farmer from nearby Paradise Valley, is killed. Jay Perkins suffers a fractured neck and several internal injuries. Carl and Clayton suffer injuries when they are thrown from the vehicle. Carl has a broken shoulder, cracked skull, and lacerations.

April 1956. "Blue Suede Shoes" finally tops most charts. Although it spends almost five months on *Billboard*'s country and pop charts, it is excluded from the number 1 position by "Heartbreak Hotel." By early May both Perkins and Sun Records have logged their first million-seller.

Memphis Singer Hurt in Crash

Carl Perkins and Troupe in Delaware Hospital—Cancel Date on Como Show

By ROBERT JOHNSON, *Press-Scimitar Staff Writer*

Carl Perkins, the rags-to-riches singer from Jackson, Tenn., and Memphis, whose smash hit recording of "Blue Suede Shoes" carried him from obscurity to stardom within six weeks, was hospitalized with his entire troupe in Dover, Del., after a pre-dawn crash this morning, in which one person was killed.

Perkins, his manager and musicians were on their way to New York City to rehearse for a appearance on the Perry Como Show on NBC-TV Saturday night.

W. S. Holland, drummer, was the only occupant of the Perkins car who was able to leave the hospital.

Call to Sam Phillips

He phoned Sam Phillips, owner of Sun Record Co. of Memphis, in New York. Perkins and his party were to have met Phillips at 6 a.m.

Dick Stewart, until recently a disk jockey on KWEM, who had become Perkins' personal manager, was driving, Holland said.

All the others were asleep, and Holland didn't know how the crash occurred. An occupant of the other car was killed, and Holland said both cars were smashed and strewn along the highway.

Perkins received head injuries and a fractured shoulder.

His brother, Jay, guitarist, was thrown from the car and received chest injuries.

Extent of injuries to another brother, Clayton (Buck) Perkins, bass player, and to Stewart had not been determined.

Up to two months ago, Perkins had earned a precarious living as an obscure musician.

To the Top

"Blue Suede Shoes" spun him to the top with jet speed.

This week it had climbed to 12th place among best selling records of all types in Billboard's statistical chart. Last week Billboard said it was the first record in memory which had appeared simultaneously in the best seller lists of country and western music, rhythm and blues, and pop music.

Perkins will not be able to keep his engagement on the Como show, the most important appearance so far in his career. He was on the Red Foley show on ABC-TV last Saturday night. As a reward for his sensa-

tional success, Sam Phillips had presented him with a new Cadillac. The car ordered was not ready yet, however, and Southern Motors had loaned him a limousine. It was described as "completely demolished."

News of the crash was phoned to Memphis by Phillips to Marion Keisker, who is associated with him in Sun Records.

CARL PERKINS
Spinning records, spinning wheels, in a spin . . .

Into the Major League

In November 1955 Sam Phillips had been on the point of going bankrupt. The banks wouldn't lend him money against the dubious assets he had accumulated. The pressing plants were screaming for money; he owed publishing royalties, artist royalties, an unrecouped advance to Chess, unrepaid funds from the buyout deal with Jud . . . and probably more. Exactly six months later Phillips was flush with money. The slim profit he made on every single hadn't made him a millionaire, but it enabled him to buy a new house and lay the foundation of a sizable fortune.

The experience of hard times, together with Phillips' innate frugality, meant that his overhead was very low. His rent on the property at 706 Union was still less than two hundred dollars a month. He paid Marion Keisker and his new assistant Sally Wilbourn less than twenty-five dollars a week, and the rest of his overhead was minimal. Most of his warehousing and shipping was done by the pressing plants. His only challenge was to collect from his distributors, and that was hardly a problem with "Blue Suede Shoes" and "I Walk the Line" in the charts. Phillips was approaching the volume of a major label, with the overhead of the smallest independent.

Phillips also owned the publishing rights to "Blue Suede Shoes," although the song was represented by Hill & Range as part of the Presley deal. That meant that every record company who pushed a version onto the market owed Phillips two cents for every copy sold. The success of "Blue Suede Shoes" also enabled Phillips to assemble the nucleus of his foreign deals, which saw Sun product go to British Decca's London subsidiary for most of the world.

The reel of tape, the bottles of bourbon, and the night's work that Phillips invested in "Blue Suede Shoes" on that December evening paid a dividend more handsome than anything he could have dared dream as he locked up the studio and walked to his car that night. The record business is a lottery, and Phillips had hit the jackpot. More than that, he was a success on his own terms. He had recorded music that no one else believed in. He recorded it his way. He released it on his own label. And he reaped the colossal rewards.

Carl Perkins, too, had been vindicated. But, for Perkins the struggle was just beginning. Although he would write songs that were, in some respects, better than "Blue Suede Shoes," he could never recapture the commerciality of the muse that came to him at three o'clock that morning when he went downstairs and scratched out his anthem on a potato bag.

Dixie Fried

The ensuing months on Sun were marked by disappointment for Carl Perkins, as he struggled to recapture the seemingly effortless success of "Blue Suede Shoes." They were also tinged with envy, as he saw labelmates Johnny Cash

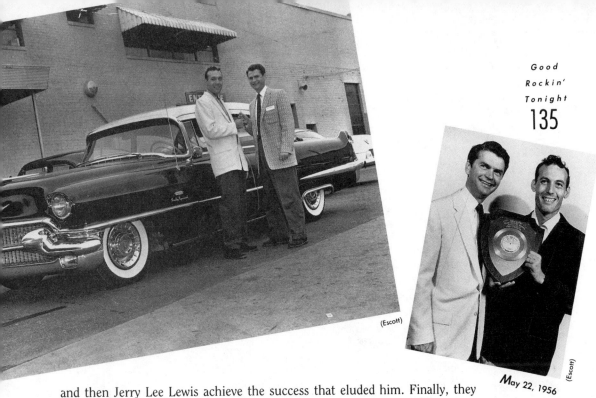

(Escott)

(Escott)

May 22, 1956

and then Jerry Lee Lewis achieve the success that eluded him. Finally, they were darkened by grief as he watched his brother Jay slowly fall victim to cancer.

After a short hospital stay, Perkins was back in Memphis at the beginning of April 1956. The huge Chrysler that was ruined in his wreck had been a loaner from Southern Motors while Carl awaited the delivery of his obligatory Cadillac. Rarely one to miss a photo opportunity, Sam Phillips handed him the keys to the shiny new blue '56 Fleetwood as he and Perkins stood at the dealership on April 11. Perkins told the press that the car was a gift from Phillips, who had sworn that the first artist to sell a million copies of a record on Sun would receive a Cadillac. "Carl says he'll drive it mighty careful," said the report in the Memphis *Press Scimitar*—although the car would be wrecked on August 29 near Brownsville, Tennessee, when Perkins was speeding.

Perkins resolved that he would not go back on the road before his wife had given birth to their third child, but the pressure from promoters grew too intense. With Jay still in the hospital, Carl hit the road as part of a Big D Jamboree package working out of Dallas. His booking fee was as high as fifteen hundred dollars a night. Perry Como held the invitation open for Perkins to appear on the show, but Perkins would not fulfill the engagement until Jay was ready to perform. They eventually worked the Como show with Jay sporting a neck brace.

"Boppin' the Blues," the follow-up to "Blue Suede Shoes," was released in May. Intended to capture the essence of the new music, instead it showed how closely Perkins was tied to the country tradition. By contrast, Elvis Presley's second RCA record, "I Want You, I Need You, I Love You," fit no known

definition of country music. "Boppin' the Blues" reached number 9 in the country charts, but did no more than dart in and out of the lowest reaches of the pop charts while Presley's song jumped straight to the top.

The next record, "Dixie Fried," was arguably the high point of Perkins' career on record, and probably the best song he had a hand in writing. But it was an almost willful act of commercial hara-kiri, so determinedly rural in content and execution that Phillips couldn't conceivably have entertained serious hopes for it in the pop market. Gogi Grant was sitting atop the pop charts with "Wayward Wind" on the day that "Dixie Fried" was released; the two songs could have come from different planets.

"Dixie Fried" was a slice of life from the Jackson honky-tonks:

On the outskirts of town there's a little night spot
Dan dropped in about five o'clock
He pulled off his coat, said "The night is short"
Reached in his pocket and he flashed a quart, hollerin'
"Rave on, children, I'm with you, rave on, cats" he cried
"It's almost dawn and the cops are gone
Let's all get Dixie Fried"

Dan got happy and he started ravin'
He jerked out a razor but he wasn't shavin'
All the cats knew to jump and hop
'cause he was borned and raised in a butcher shop . . .

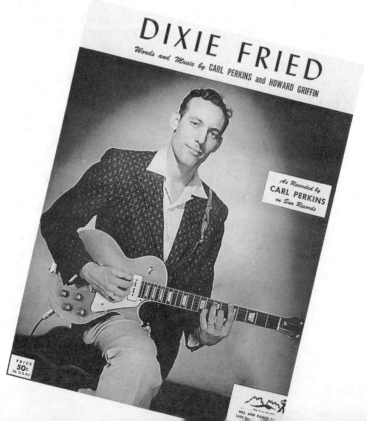

Perkins co-wrote the song with Howard "Curly" Griffin, a DJ from Jackson. Whatever Perkins' role in the composition might have been, it is "Dixie Fried" rather than "Blue Suede Shoes" that is the proof of his skill as a songwriter. The song is born and bred of illicit liquor, delivered with throwaway humor worthy of Chuck Berry. You could make a movie out of it. And every record producer in New York, Nashville or Los Angeles would have said, "I'm sorry, Carl . . ." after hearing the first run-through. Phillips released it in August 1956; "Dixie Fried" did some business in the country charts on the lingering strength of "Blue Suede Shoes," but—inevitably—failed to show up in the pop charts.

December 4, 1956, found Perkins back in the Sun studio seriously trying to recapture his place in the pop market. Jerry Lee Lewis was sitting in on piano, trying to make enough money to buy his folks some Christmas presents. Elvis Presley dropped by to see what was shaking at his old stomping ground. Before the so-called Million Dollar Quartet session started, Presley listened to the tapes of Carl's newest songs and declared that they had real potential.

It is hard to know exactly what songs Presley might have heard that day. Perkins had originally planned to couple an old blues standard, "Matchbox," with "Her Love Rubbed Off," a recording on which he is audibly drunk and mumbles the lyrics in a manner that would have done credit to Jimmy Reed. But shortly before release, and with the dismal failure of "Dixie Fried" looming large in his thoughts, Phillips decided to take his chances with a very self-conscious shot at the pop charts. Called "Your True Love," it was as innocuous as it sounded. Phillips even decided to knock a few years and some hillbilly edges off Carl's voice by speeding up the tape. He almost overdid it; the vocal chorus sounds like the Chipmunks, and Perkins sounds pre-pubescent. The high point of the record for many was the wonderfully aggressive guitar intro.

The ploy almost worked. "Your True Love" climbed to number 67 on the pop charts before running out of steam. Ironically, it was the flip side that would reap the big pay-off, albeit ten years later: with Perkins in the studio, the Beatles would record their version of "Matchbox." Of course, the song was no more from Perkins' pen than it was from Lennon and McCartney's; one of the first recorded versions was Blind Lemon Jefferson's, which dated back to

October 1927. Still, the Beatles attributed the song to Perkins, having learned it from his *Dance Album*. Thus, Perkins began receiving astronomically high airplay and publishing royalties from a song that had been a throwaway flip side to perhaps his least creditable Sun single. To add to the story's irony, his earnings from the Beatles were compounded when they released their versions of two more Perkins songs that weren't strictly original: "Honey, Don't" and "Everybody's Trying to Be My Baby," which had both been adapted from 1930s records.

Of course, no artist is completely original, and Perkins' versions of "Matchbox," "Honey, Don't," and "Everybody's Trying to Be My Baby" showed how successfully he had assimilated all the music he had heard while growing up. He had a rich and varied heritage to draw upon and, during his early days at least, unself-consciously mixed and matched all the disparate elements, coming up with a fresh, exciting new sound. After being hailed as one of the fathers of rock 'n' roll, Perkins made some stilted attempts at rendering his own versions of its creation, among them the song "Birth of Rock 'n' Roll," which opened 1986's artistically arid *Class of '55* album. Perhaps he never came closer to summing up the essence of the music than in couplets like the one eventually omitted from the final version of "Everybody's Trying to Be My Baby": "They're squallin', ballin', runnin' down the hall / I guess ol' daddy's got a lot on the ball . . ."

Perkins, like Hank Williams, was essentially a rural poet. His best music was always rooted in the western Tennessee barrooms that spawned him; only when he was forced to appeal to the teenage market did he run into problems. Unlike Chuck Berry, who could sit in his hotel room, guitar in hand, and trade the voice of a middle-aged black R&B singer for that of a pimply white teenager, Perkins never achieved a real understanding of the audience that made rock 'n' roll.

With Johnny Cash

(Escott)

Indeed, Perkins and Berry were not entirely dissimilar as writers; their songs shared an anecdotal style and a sense of abandon that represents the best of early rock 'n' roll. But even though Perkins was in some ways closer to the teenyboppers—he was white, and younger than Berry—Chuck Berry had grown up in urban St. Louis, while the grim rural poverty of the Depression years meant that Perkins had never enjoyed the spare time nor the spare change that had come to define the teenage market. Carl Perkins had never really been a teenager, and ultimately he found it difficult to identify with them.

Sweethearts or Strangers

By the beginning of 1957, bitter disillusion was setting in for Perkins. He had started off on an equal footing with Elvis Presley: they had both played for pennies off the back of a truck on Bob Neal's forays into Mississippi, and they had both shot up the charts with their "mongrel music." By 1957, however, Perkins was competing with Bill Haley for the honor of becoming rock 'n' roll's first casualty. He had sold 1 million copies of "Blue Suede Shoes," only to slip into almost total obscurity. Elvis Presley went on to sell 12.5 million singles and 2.75 million albums in 1956.

Perkins made two more singles before his divorce from Sun. The first paired another gritty honky-tonk number, "That's Right," with a country ballad, "Forever Yours." This coupling failed even to make the country charts. "That's Right" was a grim song delivered in the vernacular of the barroom:

> *If what they say is true and there is another joker*
> *Well you'se a number five in this game of poker*
> *When I find the cat that's been gettin' my sugar*
> *It's gonna be rough when I catch that booger*
> *And THAT'S RIGHT!*

The entire verse was excised before the song was issued in England. With even less regard for the creative process, Quality Records in Canada only took out the line containing "booger."

As 1957 wore on, Perkins saw Johnny Cash become the best-selling country artist of the year, and then saw Jerry Lee Lewis, who had begun his career at Sun playing backup on one of his sessions, become the hottest new property in rock 'n' roll. Every time Perkins went to the Sun studio the talk was always of Jerry Lee: they were charting his airplay and logging his sales on a blackboard. Jud Phillips was cutting deals to get him on the Dick Clark show or an Alan Freed tour. It was galling, and no words from Sam Phillips' silver tongue could assuage the frustration that Perkins felt. In later years, Perkins would say that they were all pulling for each other, but Jimmie Lott, who played drums for Warren Smith on Bob Neal's package shows remembers differently: "Warren and Carl Perkins constantly fought Jerry Lee Lewis. They'd sit around in the dressing room before the show on steel chairs with a fifth of Old Crow.

Jerry would say, 'I got a big record out now, I'm going on last.' Clayton Perkins would stick his jaw out and say, 'If you're going on last, we're gonna fight.' "

The final blow came with the movie *Jamboree*. Originally titled "The Big Record," the project had been initiated while Carl was still a hot property. He had been signed to the production as a star, and Jerry Lee Lewis as an afterthought. Otis Blackwell (who had written "Don't Be Cruel" and "All Shook Up" for Elvis Presley) was music director, and he sent down a set of dubs for Perkins and Lewis to consider for the movie. Perkins reportedly passed on "Great Balls of Fire" and chose instead to perform "Glad All Over."

By the time the single hit the market, Perkins had quit the label. He and Cash had been approached in August 1957 by Don Law from Columbia Records, who proposed that both artists move to Columbia. Like Cash, Perkins signed an agreement on November 1, 1957, and the Columbia deal became effective when his three-year Sun contract expired on January 25, 1958.

With the heady days of 1956 long gone, Perkins faced an insuperable uphill battle to resurrect his career. He tried again to become a teen poet, writing or recording such songs as "Pop Let Me Have the Car" and "Pink Pedal Pushers," but they didn't sound nearly as convincing as the dark backwoods humor of "That's Right."

It may be that Carl Perkins recorded more memorable music during his three years at Sun than he has recorded during the balance of his career to date. No one but Sam Phillips could seem to draw the rough edges out of Perkins and capture the bite in his guitar playing. A comparison of Perkins' Sun recordings with the remakes he cut for a variety of labels makes an eloquent case for the chemistry at 706 Union. Even "Dixie Fried" sounded like a report of a church social when Perkins rerecorded it for Mercury. The edge had gone.

Twenty years later, his frustration and bitterness dimmed and his place in the history books assured, Perkins characterized Sam Phillips as a man who was "as near a genius as any man I ever met. He didn't have a light in the studio saying READY, or a clock on the studio wall to scare you. There was no such thing as a standard three-hour session. He said, 'Get in there and pick, boys. We'll find the record when we get through.' There was a feeling there that I've never found since. We were trying 100 percent, and Sam Phillips captured it."

Hero in a Foreign Land

His short-lived career as a teen poet fading fast, Perkins turned back to the honky-tonks. He also turned to the bottle. His alcoholism was precipitated by the death of his older brother Jay, who succumbed to a malignant brain tumor in October 1958. The respect in which Jay was held was evidenced by the roster of artists who performed at a memorial concert held in Memphis on November 14 of that year. Johnny Cash organized the event and enlisted the help of Jerry Lee Lewis, Webb Pierce, Dickey Lee, Ernest Tubb, Hawkshaw Hawkins, Sonny

Carl Perkins,
1958

(Escott)

Burgess, Slim Rhodes, Thomas Wayne, Curtis Gordon, Merle Travis, Lefty Frizzell, the Collins Kids, and Joe Maphis.

Early in 1959 W. S. Holland quit the line-up and tried artist management before joining Johnny Cash. Clayton Perkins quit a little later to return to Jackson, where he too became an alcoholic, eventually committing suicide.

Disillusioned and resigned to his status as a has-been, Perkins decided to give up the music business in the early '60s. He returned to Jackson, tired of playing "Blue Suede Shoes" twice a night for an ever-diminishing crowd. He had been dropped by Columbia in 1963 and signed by Decca, but that affiliation also failed to yield that elusive second major hit. Even the country audience would not embrace him. Perkins decided to return to farming, or possibly open a small store.

Then, early in 1964, Carl received a call from Nashville booking agent "Lucky" Moeller, who told him that there was a tour awaiting him in England working with Chuck Berry. Nervous and apprehensive, but trying to stay clear of the bottle, Perkins walked onstage for the first date of the tour to find a sea of banners saying "Welcome Carl 'Beatle Crusher' Perkins" and "Welcome King of Rock 'n' Roll."

"Tears filled my eyes as I felt the love and appreciation from them," wrote Perkins in his autobiography. "I performed with a vitality I had never known before. The standing ovation at the end of the show was too much to handle. The tour lasted four weeks and during that time I never once got drunk. For the first time since Jay's death I felt that there was still a place for me in music."

Britain was consumed with a musical war between the hard-core traditionalists ("rockers") and followers of the new British beat groups ("mods"). Perkins was a conquering hero to the rockers (explaining the title "Beatle Crusher"). More than most, however, Perkins had a vested interest in remaining distant from the squabble.

On the last night of the tour, Perkins was invited to a party. There he met the four young men who had meant nothing to him when he arrived but loomed large in his thoughts by the end of the tour. "Someone brought a guitar," recalled Perkins, "and I sat on the couch with the Beatles sitting around me on the floor. At their request I sang every song I had ever recorded. They knew each one. I was deeply flattered when George asked, 'Hey Carl, how did you kick off "Movie Magg"?' I showed him and he jumped up and said, 'See, I told you we didn't do it right!' "

Very little rockabilly music had been made available in England between 1956 and 1964. The centerpiece of every record collection was Carl Perkins' *Dance Album*. George Harrison, together with virtually every other would-be guitarist from that era, had cut his teeth on the licks that Perkins had hit on his Sun sessions.

Perkins was invited to a recording session the following night. He cancelled his return flight and attended. "During that session," he recalled to Don Bird, "Ringo turned to me and said, 'I certainly would like to record some of your songs.' I'll be truthful with you. Right between his eyes on that famous nose I saw the prettiest dollar sign I had ever seen in my life. I said, 'Help yourself, son. The whole catalog's yours.' " The Beatles recorded more songs by Perkins than they recorded by any composer other than themselves. For the Beatles and countless others who have come to meet him, Perkins was that rare specimen, a hero who turned out *not* to be an ass.

The first British tour rejuvenated Perkins' career and helped establish his reputation as one of the godfathers of rock 'n' roll. He could never quite understand how or why it happened, and in particular he could never understand why it happened where it did—in Europe. The best explanation that Perkins could suggest was that his good-time music helped the Europeans to forget their blighted lives. "England's a beautiful country," he told Dave Sholin, "but, let's face it, those people eat what's on their plates. We throw a lot away. Maybe the music helps them feel good, loosens them up and helps them forget about some of the things they don't have."

The adulation in Europe continues to the present. On October 21, 1985, Perkins decided that he would try to get all of his disciples together in one place. That place turned out to be the Limehouse studio in London's born-again dockland. George Harrison and Eric Clapton were among those who attended. Dave Edmunds stage-managed the event. Perkins fought back tears as he thanked them after the inevitable encore of "Blue Suede Shoes."

"Sometimes in your twilight years," said Perkins to Don Bird with his characteristic humility, "you see these boys come along with the flying fingers and knowledge of the guitar, and you get the feeling that you're way over the hill. Then, for example, a guy like Eric Clapton will visit and say how proud he is to meet me. Now we all like to drive new cars and wear pretty clothes, but you can't explain how it feels for an older guy like me to have these boys say these things about me. I feel like I've left something in the world that people can enjoy. If you do that then it ain't so bad to leave the world, because part of you will always be here."

And the part of Carl Perkins that he will leave behind consists of a handful of recordings, only a few of which were released during his tenure with Sun, but recordings that still form the bulk of his stage repertoire today. They also remain, all told, one of the landmarks of pure, carefree rock 'n' roll.

Recommended Listening

The most complete retrospective of Perkins' career is contained in *Classic Carl Perkins, 1954–1965* (Bear Family [Germany] BCD 15494), 5 CDs comprising his Sun and early Columbia and Decca recordings.

The best single CD anthology of Perkins' Sun recordings is *Original Sun Greatest Hits* (Rhino [USA] RNCD 75890).

Honky Tonk Gal (Rounder [USA] CD/SS 27) contains a selection of lesser-known Sun cuts and alternate takes.

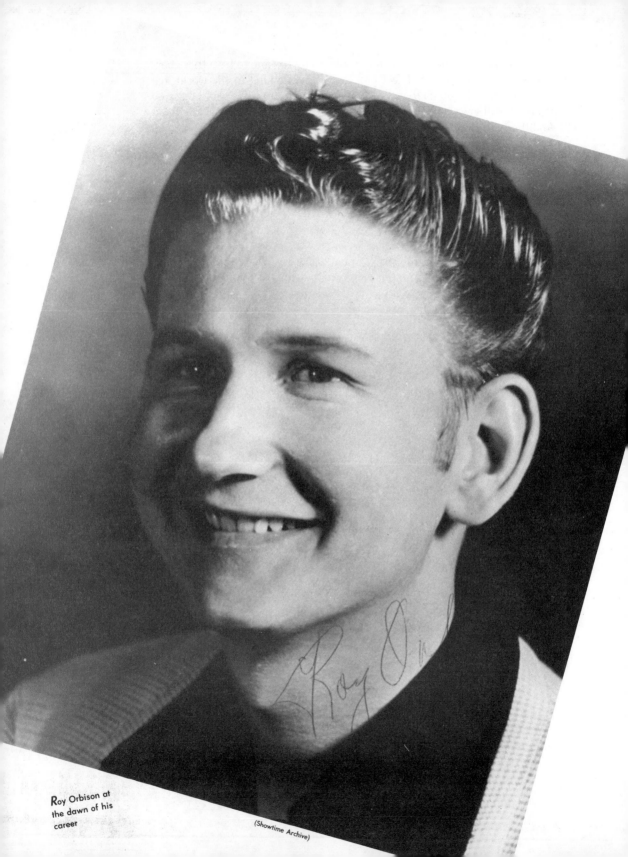

Roy Orbison at
the dawn of his
career

ROY ORBISON: A CADILLAC AND A DIAMOND RING

The **sight** of Roy Orbison playing with George Harrison, Tom Petty, and Bob Dylan as a member of the Traveling Wilburys shortly before his death was unexpected testimony that Orbison survived better than most of his contemporaries. His lately acquired ponytail was his only concession to the changing times; the character of his music remained remarkably consistent. In fact, the most uncharacteristic music Roy Orbison ever made was for Sun Records.

One of the many who came to Sun in the wake of Elvis Presley and Carl Perkins, Roy Orbison tried for a few years to become a rock 'n' roll singer. By his own admission, his heart remained elsewhere. Despite the fact that Orbison made periodic forays back into the country and rock music of his youth, the heart of his style was rooted in pop ballads. Hillbilly and rockabilly were essentially southern musics; the hits Orbison scored in the 1960s were timeless and placeless. Like Elvis Presley, but unlike Jerry Lee Lewis and Carl Perkins, Roy Orbison transcended his roots.

The Wink Westerners

Orbison was born in Vernon, Texas, on April 23, 1936. His parents, Orbie Lee and Nadine, gave him a guitar for his sixth birthday and taught him the chords to "You Are My Sunshine." Orbie was an auto mechanic in Vernon, but during the war he moved the family to Fort Worth so he could find work in the defense plants. "My first music was country," Orbison recalled to David Booth. "I grew up with country music in Texas. The first singer I heard on the radio who really slayed me was Lefty Frizzell. He had this technique which involved sliding syllables together that really blew me away."

An outbreak of polio in Fort Worth during the war caused his parents to send Roy back to Vernon. After V-J Day they moved back to Vernon as well, soon moving on to the West Texas town of Wink, an oil-boom town close to the Mexican border where Roy grew up in a shotgun shack. His father worked for Olson Drilling, across the state line in Jal, New Mexico. When he was thirteen Orbison formed his first band, the Wink Westerners. His talent had never been in doubt: he had had his own radio shows from the age of eight, and when he was ten years old he had played his first paying gig—a medicine show, where he sang the Cajun novelty "Jole Blon." After the Wink Westerners won a talent contest organized by the Pioneer Furniture company in Midland, Pioneer sponsored a weekly television show for them on KMID-TV.

The character of the Westerners' music can be judged by their name and the Roy Rogers bandanas they tied jauntily around their necks. "We played whatever was hot," recalls mandolin player James Morrow. "Lefty Frizzell, Slim Whitman, Webb Pierce—we did all of their numbers. We also played a lot of Glenn Miller–style songs like 'Stardust' and 'Moonlight Serenade,' which we adapted for string instruments." Morrow amplified his mandolin through an Echoplex amp, giving it an eerie, haunting tone that can be heard on "Trying to Get to You" and some of the other ballads they recorded later.

For his part, Orbison had discovered what he wanted to do in life: "I remember we played a free gig for the principal of our school, and someone came up to us and asked if we'd play a dance. I was going to say that we only knew about four or five songs when they said, 'We'll give you four hundred dollars.' I said, 'Yes sir, we'll make the date. We'll be on time and you'll love us.' That was the first time I realized that I wanted to be an entertainer. I enjoyed it—and you could make money at it."

In his 1954 high school yearbook Orbison spelled out his ambitions:

To lead a western band
Is his after school wish
And of course to marry
A beautiful dish.

Immediately after graduation, Orbison worked in the oil fields, playing music at night; then he went to college at North Texas State, transferring to Odessa Junior College for his second year. Ever conscious of security, Orbison studied geology, preparing to follow his father into the oil fields if all else failed.

While at North Texas State, Orbison visited the Big D Jamboree in Dallas. It was there that he saw Elvis Presley for the first time. "First thing," he recalled to Nick Kent, "he came out and spat out a piece of gum onto the stage. He was a punk kid. A weird-looking dude. I can't over-emphasize how shocking he looked and sounded to me that night. He did 'Maybellene,' and the kids started shouting. There was pandemonium 'cause the girls took a shine to him and the guys were getting jealous. Plus he told some real bad crude jokes. Dumb off-color humor. His diction was real coarse—like a truck driver's. But his energy was incredible and his instinct was just amazing."

One of Orbison's contemporaries at North Texas State was Pat Boone, who had been raised in Nashville but had eloped to Texas with Red Foley's daughter, the one wild-ass move of his life. After a false start on Republic, Boone resumed his recording career for Dot shortly after he arrived in Denton, and achieved immediate success with his insipid versions of the R&B hits of the day.

"All these people were doing what I wanted to do," recalled Orbison, "but it seemed as though I was in the wrong place at the right time. I wanted to get a diploma in case I didn't make it in the music business. In the end, though, I decided I didn't want to do anything half-way so I jumped into the music business."

The Teen Kings

In Odessa, Orbison roomed with James Morrow, Jack Kennelly, and Billy Pat Ellis, who recast themselves as the Teen Kings. The original bassist from the Wink Westerners, Charles Evans, had quit to get married and had been replaced by Kennelly. The Teen Kings were joined by the diminutive Johnny "Peanuts" Wilson on rhythm guitar, and with that line-up they secured themselves another television show on KOSA, sponsored by the local Pontiac dealer. In 1955 Johnny Cash appeared on the show and implanted the idea of recording for Sun.

Orbison had also returned from Denton with an original song, "Ooby Dooby," that he had acquired from Wade Moore and Dick Penner, who had written it in fifteen minutes on the flat roof of a frat house at North Texas State. It was copyrighted in May 1955, and Orbison apparently first recorded it at some point in late 1955 during a demo session for Columbia Records at Jim Beck's studio in Dallas. That session also yielded a version of the Clovers hit "Hey Miss Fanny."

Columbia saw no merit in the singer, but gave the acetate to one of their contracted artists, Sid King, who recorded "Ooby Dooby" on March 5, 1956. A day earlier, Roy Orbison had rerecorded the song at Norman Petty's studio in Clovis, New Mexico. That session (and possibly others for Petty) also yielded "Domino" and "A True Love Goodbye," which were later reworked at Sun. Another song, "An Empty Cup (And a Broken Date)," was pitched by Petty to Buddy Holly two years later. In the Petty sessions the Teen Kings sang backup vocals similar to those popularized by R&B groups.

Orbison's version of "Ooby Dooby" from the Petty sessions was quickly released on Je-Wel Records, the name a rough acronym from *Je*an Oliver and *Wel*don Rogers. The label was underwritten by Oliver's father, Chester, an executive at Gulf Oil. The Teen Kings had met Jean, who played accordion and sang, and her boyfriend, Weldon Rogers, at some of the Friday night jamborees they played in West Texas.

For a flip side to their first single, the Teen Kings chose "Trying to Get to You." Never a real lover of rhythm and blues, Orbison had latched on to an obscure song by the Eagles (ironically, the first production by Fred Foster, who later signed him to Monument). Orbison recorded it at roughly the same time that Elvis Presley recorded a version for Sun that remained unissued until 1956. It is conceivable that Presley sang the tune on one of his forays

Orbison with the
Teen Kings

(Showtime Archive)

through Texas (possibly even on Orbison's television show), and that Orbison learned it from him: Orbison used the same shuffle rhythm and made the same minor lyrical change that Elvis did. An additional wrinkle was added to the story when Orbison's Je-Wel cut was later sent to Imperial Records (together with Weldon Rogers' version) and inadvertently used as a B side for Rogers' single "So Long, Good Luck and Goodbye" in 1957.

At Johnny Cash's suggestion, Orbison had already approached Sam Phillips at Sun Records, but Phillips had rebuffed him, declaring, "Johnny Cash doesn't run my record company." But Orbison had a stronger ally in Cecil "Pop" Holifield, who operated the Record Shops in Midland and Odessa and had booked Elvis Presley into the area. Holifield played a copy of the Je-Wel record over the phone to Phillips, who heard something unique in the strangely fragile voice, and asked him to send along a copy. "My first reaction," recalled Phillips many years later, "was that 'Ooby Dooby' was a novelty-type thing that resembled some of the novelty hits from the '30s and '40s. I thought if we got a good cut on it we could get some attention. Even more, I was very impressed with the inflection Roy brought to it. In fact, I think I was more impressed than Roy."

Go! Go! Go!

Sensing that "Ooby Dooby" might break like "Blue Suede Shoes," Phillips moved fast and brought the Teen Kings to Sun in late March or early April 1956 to rerecord the song. Phillips wanted one of his own copyrights on the flip side, so they cut "Go! Go! Go!," a composition by Roy and his drummer, Billy Pat Ellis. The coupling was released in April 1956. *Billboard* praised its "spectacular untamed quality" and surmised that it would "cash in for plenty of loot in the rural sectors."

The Teen Kings returned to West Texas immediately after the session and heard nothing until Sam Phillips called them one day in early May and told them that the record was breaking in Memphis and other markets. Phillips placed the Teen Kings with Bob Neal's booking agency, Stars, Inc.

Orbison and the Teen Kings hit the road as part of a package show headlined by Johnny Cash and Carl Perkins. "We played all these unbelievable little towns," Orbison remembered. "We were trying to make stage show out of one hit record, which is very difficult, so we jumped around on stage like a bunch of idiots. We even had this song called 'The Bug,' where we had an imaginary bug we would throw on each other. When it hit you, you had to shake." Orbison would begin his segment by playing everyone else's hits and close, naturally, with "Ooby Dooby."

"Ooby Dooby" did good business nationwide, eventually reaching number 59 on *Billboard's* Hot 100 and selling roughly 200,000 copies. It would be the biggest hit that Orbison would have for four years. He bought his first Cadillac. "That's what we all wanted," he asserted, "a Cadillac and a diamond ring before our twenty-first birthday."

Orbison quickly developed a fascination for studio work—and it was the studio, rather than the stage, that became his true medium. He worked sessions at Sun for other artists and performed on the commercials and radio spots that Sam Phillips continued to engineer, just in case the rock 'n' roll craze blew over. "I don't think people know how good a guitar player Roy was," asserted Sam Phillips. "He used the bass strings and played combination string stuff. He also had the best ear for a beat of anybody I recorded, outside of Jerry Lee Lewis. If we had a session going, Roy would come in early and pick an awful lot just warming up and getting his fingers working. His timing would amaze me. He'd play lead and fill in with rhythm licks. I'd kid him. I'd say, 'Roy, you're trying to get rid of the band and do it all yourself.' He just hated to lay his guitar down. He was either writing or developing a beat. He was totally preoccupied with making records."

Orbison had also started to write prolifically: "I'd write in the car when we were on tour," he told Penny Reel. "Even when we'd take a break alongside the road I'd jump on the fender of the car and play the guitar and sing. Then we'd go back [to the studio] and get somebody to turn on the machine and we'd play this thing in some form or another to see if it would make a record."

Like Carl Perkins, Orbison was unable to find a follow-up to his first hit. He recorded "Rockhouse," a song that another aspiring Sun act, Harold Jenkins (a.k.a. Conway Twitty), had worked up as a theme song for his group, the Rockhousers. It was coupled with Johnny Cash's execrable song, "You're My Baby," originally "Little Woolly Booger." *Billboard* once again was effusive in its praise of Orbison's "sock showmanship," but its recommendation failed to take account of the fact that "Rockhouse," released in September 1956, was already behind the times.

Orbison sought to rectify that problem when he returned to the studio to cut his third Sun single, "Sweet and Easy to Love," backed with "Devil Doll," in December. Taking his cue from Elvis and the Jordanaires, Orbison had brought a vocal group, the Roses, in from Texas for the session. The mid-paced ballad "Devil Doll" allowed Orbison's true musical soul to come up for air for the first time.

During the rehearsals for "Devil Doll" and "Sweet and Easy," Orbison split with the Teen Kings. "It happened right in the studio," recalled Sam Phillips. "They had some difficulty among themselves, and the band broke up then and there. Really it was nothing more than their being extremely young."

"We had a commonwealth drawn up," asserts James Morrow, "in which the royalties would be split equally five ways. At first the group was to be called 'The Teen Kings,' but Sam Phillips and Bob Neal wanted it as 'Roy Orbison and the Teen Kings.' Bob also did not want an equal five-way split of royalties, and evidently Roy didn't want it either. We hadn't actually signed anything, and that was where the disagreement arose. Jack, Billy Pat, Peanuts, and I went back to West Texas and formed another group for a few months."

Orbison completed the sessions with the Sun house musicians. When he went out on the road, he used other artists' groups to support him. "The first time I met him," recalls Warren Smith's drummer, Jimmie Lott, "was at the Club Zanzibar in Hayti, Missouri. I never realized that Roy had a sight problem until he got ready to go on stage. He took his glasses off, and Warren had to lead him to the microphone like he was blind. He worked hard at being a rock 'n' roller, but even then you could see his heart wasn't in it."

Claudette

The change in direction and the fuller sound did nothing to revive Orbison's sales, so Sun's new musical director, Bill Justis, gave Orbison one of his first efforts at rock 'n' roll composition, "Chicken Hearted." It was a novelty song, the quintessential nerd's lament. Roland Janes, who played guitar on the session, recalled that Orbison was bitterly unhappy with the material—and with good reason—but didn't complain. The flip side, "I Like Love," was as trite as its title suggests. Released in December 1957, the single was Orbison's last shot on Sun as a contracted artist.

Wrapped in shadow, 1957

Orbison was disillusioned with the way Phillips was handling his career as a recording artist. He was locked into recording rock 'n' roll novelties and, with hindsight, would even come to look askance at Sun's primitive recording conditions. "We had to make do," he recalled. "I had to write the songs, sing the songs, arrange the songs, and play the guitar." Yet to Orbison it was that independence that, he would reflect later, enabled his musical ideas to start taking shape in his own mind —even if they never crystallized in the Sun studio. Many years later, he would say, "I'm glad now there was no one to call on." Perhaps he had a point; one of his

(Showtime Archive)

favorite stories involved a warning from Jack Clement that he should stay away from ballads—that he would never make it as a ballad singer.

Shortly after "Chicken Hearted" flopped, Orbison returned to Texas with his new bride, Claudette Frady, from Odessa. She had joined him in Memphis; for a while before their marriage in 1957, they chastely slept in separate rooms at Sam Phillips' house.

At Sun, Orbison was only one of a stable of young rockabillies, one who became easily lost in the shuffle after his first hit. It was a legacy that Orbison would be eager to disown after his huge success on Monument, but one from which he drew in subtle ways throughout his career. "Neither Elvis nor I thought our work for Sun was any good," he was fond of saying. "Then, around 1970, the era of instant history came along. Everybody saw it as a beginning."

In one of the least commercially astute moves of his career, Sam Phillips had kept Roy Orbison on a steady diet of rock 'n' roll. Phillips' golden ear told him once again that he had heard something unique; yet in Orbison's case, he didn't know what to do with it. "Roy had a definite feel for rock," claims Phillips. "I think that if we had been able to keep his band together I would not have let Roy go. I really have to take the blame for not bringing Roy to fruition. It's still my regret that I didn't do more promotion [for him]."

Orbison knew that his talent was being misdirected at Sun, and events to come would prove it. As he returned to Texas though, he was beginning to question whether he wanted to continue as a performer at all. He admitted to a measure of jealousy over the fact that Buddy Holly, a fellow Texan who had joined Norman Petty's musical frontier in Clovis a year after Orbison had left, had started to score heavily, while his own career seemed hopelessly roadblocked.

At Sun Orbison had started writing quite prolifically, and he scored a fleeting Hot 100 hit for Warren Smith with "So Long I'm Gone." He had done even better when Jerry Lee Lewis revamped what he could remember of "Go! Go! Go!" as "Down the Line," giving Roy a free ride to the top of the charts on the back of "Breathless." He also submitted a few songs to the departing Johnny Cash, who recorded Orbison's "You Tell Me" during the final crush of sessions that marked his exit from Sun.

But it was the success of a song called "Claudette" that made Orbison's thoughts turn seriously toward writing. "I was back in West Texas," he recalled, "and I stopped by Memphis to put it on tape. Bill Justis was there and he's been a lifelong friend, so I expected to get the tape but never did.

"I'd just about stopped performing, but I'd gone to Indiana to do a show with the Everlys, and everyone was pitching songs to them. I wouldn't do that. I just said hello and was headed for the door when they asked if I had any material. I said I had one song and played them 'Claudette' and they said, 'Write the words down, Roy.' So I tore off this cardboard box top and wrote down the words to 'Claudette.' "

After "Claudette" rode to the top on the flip side of "All I Have to Do Is Dream," Orbison bought himself out of his Sun contract by signing over all

of his copyrights (except "Claudette") and affiliated himself with the Everlys' music publisher, Acuff-Rose. It was Wesley Rose who secured Orbison his one-year term with RCA, an affiliation that spawned two mediocre singles that hit the market to even less acclaim than the last Sun singles.

Only the Lonely

During the last RCA session, Orbison had a conversation with the session bassist, Bob Moore, who was buying himself a stake in Monument Records, a small Washington, D.C.–based label. "Roy said RCA wasn't going to renew his contract," recalled Moore, "so I called Fred Foster, the owner of Monument, and said, 'You know what I heard today? RCA's letting Roy Orbison go.' Fred took the bull by the horns, and the next thing I knew we had Orbison signed."

There is an apocryphal story that Foster confused Orbison's "Ooby Dooby" with Warren Smith's "Rock 'n' Roll Ruby" and believed that he was signing Smith. It is a rumor that Foster is eager to scotch, but each artist had scored a big hit with his first Sun record in 1956 and had then sunk into oblivion; to confuse the two would have been understandable.

Back in Texas, Roy had started writing with Joe Melson, who led a local group called the Cavaliers in Midland. "A mutual friend, Ray Rush, was dealing around in management," recalls Melson, "and he loved my songwriting. I played him a song one night and he said, 'I want you to meet Roy Orbison.' I think Ray wanted to show Roy that someone in that area could write songs besides him. I went to Odessa, where Roy and Claudette lived with Claudette's mother. They had just released his first record on Monument, 'Paper Boy.' He loved my song and got a dub of it. When I was leaving I said, 'Roy, I really love your singing' and his whole face just brightened up. We became friends right then.

"One night I was at the drive-in and Roy drove up in his Cadillac. I got in his car and we had the normal musicians' conversation. Finally, he said what I wanted him to say. He said, 'You write a pretty good song and I write a pretty good song. I believe if we put it together we could write some great ones.' I said, 'Let's do it.'

"I was studying rhythm and blues at that time and I was studying themes that were selling in the market. We'd ride around in the car and play the pop stations and try to write. We tried for a year."

After some false starts, Orbison and Melson came up with the song that would set the stage for his unprecedented success. "We were in adjoining motel rooms in Odessa, trying to write," recalls Melson. "I hit a melody line on the guitar and Roy really liked it. He said, 'That's a real uptown melody. Uptown. Uptown.' We wrote 'Uptown' that night. We moved from rock 'n' roll to class rock right then."

"Uptown" sold better than any Orbison record since "Ooby Dooby," peaking halfway up the Hot 100. Looking for a follow-up, Melson showed Orbison a fragment of a song he had been working on called "Only the Lonely." They

(Escott)

honed the song to perfection over a period of weeks and crafted an epic, the first song that truly probed the frightening potential of Orbison's voice.

Reviewing the charts in 1960, Sam Phillips found four of his departed protégés doing well: Elvis Presley, Johnny Cash, Warren Smith, and Roy Orbison. Phillips was already assiduously recycling his Cash repertoire, and Orbison's success convinced him that it was time to look through the tape vault and get a little mileage from another departed star.

To his chagrin, Phillips found tape boxes filled almost exclusively with rockers that had been cut at his behest. He gave the stash of tapes to Vinnie Trauth and Scotty Moore, who added some extraneous instruments and a chorus to the masters. They reissued "Devil Doll" together with a complete album of doctored masters titled *At the Rockhouse*.

The album justifiably infuriated Orbison, who went to see Phillips in 1961 and reportedly demanded, unsuccessfully, that he hand over all of Roy's unissued tapes. The tapes that remained at Sun have been prolifically recycled since the Sun catalog was sold in 1969. With hindsight, one can hear the roots of Orbison's future success in his phrasing and delivery on the slower Sun cuts, like "Trying to Get to You," "This Kind of Love," and "It's Too Late." But over the best of these recordings hangs a feeling of missed opportunity, of perhaps the most singular chance Phillips failed to take.

Recalling his 1961 meeting with Phillips in a conversation with Nick Kent, Orbison said, "Sam looked at me and smiled and said, 'You'll be back.' His brother Jud was in the room—he just looked at me, rolled his eyes, and said, 'The hell he will!'"

Recommended Listening

The most complete anthology of Roy Orbison's Sun recordings can be found on *Roy Orbison: The Sun Years* (Bear Family [Germany] BCD 15460); a selection of the best is on *Roy Orbison: The Sun Recordings* (Rhino [USA] R2 70916).

Some additional Sun cuts are on *Problem Child* (Zu-Zazz [UK] Z 2006).

The best overview of Orbison's career, including a selection of the Sun masters, is on *The Legendary* (CBS [USA] A4K 46809).

Orbison: late '50s

(Escott)

Chapter Nine

THE STUDIO AT WORK

"Sam Phillips knowed somethin' *different*," concluded Ray Harris, reflecting on the vicissitudes of the record business by the light of the Donut King in Tupelo, Mississippi. "You've got to know talent in this business, and Sam knowed talent. He was in the right place at the right time, but just look at the bushel barrel of top talent that came out of there."

Phillips' achievement rests in three things he did that—due to luck or judgment—were intrinsically right. First of all, he settled in Memphis, a unique and largely untapped musical community. Once there, he found talent all around him, talent in performers whose styles were unswayed by the accepted norms of commercial American music. And once he had found these artists, he developed ways of working with them to capture their talent and discovered ways of introducing it to a broad, national audience.

The fact that Phillips was not a musician was a distinct advantage. Schooled musicians continue to wince at the sour notes, botched chord changes, and off-key vocals that populate some of his recordings. But Phillips responded to the *feel* he heard in an artist, not to technical expertise. A trained musician behind the board would have shooed both Elvis Presley and Johnny Cash back out onto the street; Sam Phillips saw two diamonds in the rough. Where others shied away from the unpolished, Phillips gravitated toward it.

He wasn't without his limitations, though. Ray Harris, in another trenchant observation, said, "Sam was a genius with three- or four-piece bands. When it got beyond that—boom!" Once the intimacy of the small group was gone, Phillips was less effective. The one-on-one rapport that he cherished—and with which he was most effective—was impossible with a large group. The only Top 20 hit on Sun Records that had more than four instruments was Charlie Rich's "Lonely Weekends" (and that only had five).

In a one-on-one situation, though, Phillips could work his spell. "You could look into his eyes," said Jim Dickinson, "and see whirling pools of insanity. You knew that he was looking down into your guts and you think at that moment, 'That's how he looked at Howlin' Wolf. That's the way he looked at Elvis Presley. Something happened. Maybe it can happen to me.' That's what he does that's magic."

The producer in his element: Sam Phillips at the Sun console, 1958

"It was spontaneous," said Dickey Lee, who cut his second and third records for Sun. "You didn't have to watch the studio clock. In fact, the clock never worked. It was stopped at four-thirty. You shouldn't be tied down to a time schedule when you're creating. Everything was loose, but we were always on edge too—we were always going for it. Today no one worries about getting their part right, because they can overdub. The feel has gone. Back then, the adrenaline was going."

Phillips himself seems to understand the effect he had in the studio: "I saw my role as being the facilitator, the man who listened to an artist for his native abilities, then tried to encourage and channel the artist into what would be a proper outlet for his abilities. I wasn't interested in just a good singer. There had to be something distinctive there for me to want to spend time with an artist."

As recording technology evolved from single-track to multitrack, the "producer" (a coinage adopted from the movie business) worked as the liaison between the technology and the talent, controlling the increasing number of options open for postproduction, such as overdubbing. The producer's function was an outgrowth of the established role of the recording supervisor. At major labels, this was the person with creative responsibility: selecting repertoire with—or for—the artist, booking the studio time and musicians, and representing the company at the session. By the mid '60s, the advent of multitrack recording allowed producers more latitude to add to, subtract from, or otherwise alter performances. From that point, the finished product increasingly bore the imprint of the producer.

Sam Phillips was both an engineer and a producer; his level of involvement in the creative process marks him as possibly the first producer in the later sense of the word. His options for postproduction were few: he could do limited overdubs and edits; he could add a little echo or change the tape speed; but to do any more was against his philosophy. "Too many people go into a studio depending on overdubbing and covering up," asserted Phillips in 1982. "There's too many musicians doing too damn much. I don't go for it. I understand all the techniques and the bullshit, but I just don't see the spontaneity. I'm not saying you shouldn't overdub the occasional instrument, but you can have too many crutches. People think, 'Well, that track wasn't bad, but we can always bring him back in again, drop the voice in here or take that instrument out of there.' The result may be a little prettier, the tonal quality may be good, but an awful lot of the essence is gone.

"Today I see and hear too much of the lack of the real soul that comes from knowing, 'This is it. I can do it. It might need one, two, four, or five takes, but I can do it myself *right here and now.*'

"Atmosphere is so important. There is so much psychology in dealing with artists. If you don't know what you are doing with people and don't care about them individually—their strong and weak points—both psychologically and musically, you are bound not to get the best from them."

Phillips also approached sessions with one overriding concern: to keep things simple. He can be heard on tape again and again in the hundreds of sessions he produced, telling the musicians not to overplay. On a Presley outtake of "When It Rains It Really Pours," Phillips warns Scotty Moore—hardly prone to overplaying anyway—"Scotty, don't get too damn complicated in the middle there." He also wanted the vocals to be direct and honest. "I wanted to feature the person who was supposed to be featured and set up the atmosphere that got the best results [for the singer]," he said later.

Evolving a philosophy of record production and applying it on a day-to-day basis made Phillips one of the most important innovators in the business. But there's a paradox in all this. Phillips was one of the first engineers to bring an artistic vision to the process of recording (that is, to *produce*), yet the genius of his recording philosophy dictated that the technology should never become an end in itself—should never sacrifice the virtue of simplicity that he cherished.

Forty 'Leven Dollars

Virtually everyone who worked at Sun Records—the artists, the backing musicians, those who worked behind the scenes—have a general recollection of the studio, with only a blurry grasp of what the actual recording process was like. Of course, we can hardly blame them; after all, by Sam Phillips' own reasoning, if they had been more concerned with making history than music, they likely would never have created the fresh, unguarded music that they did. Fortunately, though, journalist Edwin Howard, the entertainment editor of the Memphis *Press Scimitar*, persuaded Phillips to let him cut a record and document the odyssey in print. The following is extracted from his account, and is probably the most objective and detailed portrait we have of the Sun studio at work during the late '50s.

"Behind the dusty, bent Venetian blinds in a three-desk office at 706 Union stands the man who, in six years, has brought a brand new industry to Memphis. The office is identified only by a small neon sign in the window, which says Memphis Recording Service. The man is Sam C. Phillips. [He] stands because, although he has made roughly $2 million for himself in those six years, he has no desk at which to sit. 'If I have a real long telephone call,' he admits, 'I will ask someone to get up and let me sit down.'

Edwin Howard, writer . . .

(Mississippi Valley Collection)

. . . and singer

(E. Howard)

Our newest artist is Edwin Howard, and he's a newspaper reporter, but that doesn't mean he can't sing. His record has been out only one day, at this writing, and our Memphis distributor called very excitedly this morning to report that his juke box operators are going nuts over the side called, "Forty-'Leven Times." This is a modern-day "Barbry Allen"—pleasingly different.

The other side is an updated, and somewhat popularized version of "More Pretty Girls Than One."

Since he's a free lance magazine writer and entertainments editor of the local daily, Edwin has capitalized on the possibilities for publicity. NEA Features and a popular fan magazine have had big spreads.

We think his record quite as good as his stories. Since we're looking for reaction, would surely appreciate hearing from you re. your opinion of the record.

"Even without a desk, Phillips somehow manages to run eleven corporations from the building at 706 Union, which consists of a tiny reception room (two desks), a studio which doubles as a mailing room, a control room with attached half bathroom, a promotions office (one desk), and a storage room.

"Some have wondered why Phillips never dressed up the studio at 706 Union or hung out a sign identifying it as the Sun Record Company. Phillips has several reasons: 'I just felt like if I put up a big sign on this little building or tried to fancy it up, it would look all out of proportion. There's something about that little Memphis Recording Service sign that just goes with it. As for a desk, well, I'm not the kind that runs things by bangin' on a desk, so I didn't figure I needed one. Anyhow, I've got four girls and a man at the three desks and they know how to handle the desk work. Everyone around here has a smattering of knowledge of the whole business, and I've got no secrets. Our informality is what gives us our hit records. Our artists just get the feeling we're goofing off. As I tell 'em, there's no sense being nervous, because there's nobody else here can do any better.' "

Howard went on to describe how he came to make his record.

"Phillips turned me over to his director of A&R, Bill Justis. A big part of his job is auditioning talent. 'They come in from all over the sticks, man,' Justis told me. 'We end up recording maybe one out of a hundred.' He auditions songs too. 'Everybody wants to do the songwriting scene. We get like fifty or sixty a day through the mail on tapes. Most of them are real nothing. We use one out of every four hundred we listen to.'

"One of Sun's regular composers is Jack Clement, who handled the control board for my sessions. Office space is at such a premium that business is often transacted and lead sheets written in Taylor's restaurant next door (plate lunch sixty cents). In fact, Taylor's has been to rock 'n' roll what Pee Wee's saloon on Beale Street was to the blues. It was in a booth at Taylor's that Justis first heard my idea for the record. He was unimpressed. 'But that's probably a good sign, man. If I hate something it usually turns out to be a hit.'

"I wrote the 'B' side of my record, 'Forty 'leven Times,' on a piece of copy paper, using the studio piano as a desk. Justis liked it even less than the other side, and I was encouraged. He made an arrangement (all in his head: he writes music but nobody there reads it), using three guitars and a vocal trio. Now he thinks it stands a good chance of becoming a hit.

"I spent fifteen hours working on the record. Phillips himself listened to the various cuts and offered suggestions as to how they could be improved. Once Justis got the echoey sound he wanted from my record, Phillips had to give his final OK and set a release date. He listened to the final tape of 'Forty 'leven Times' over and over again, waxing more enthusiastic every time."

Howard's record was finally released in April 1959. A few months later he wrote a follow-up report containing reflections, then surprising but now familiar, on the tyranny of Top 40 radio programming and the difficulties inherent in breaking new artists. They are worth repeating, for they proved to be factors that contributed heavily to the decline of Sun Records as the new decade dawned.

"Bill Fitzgerald, former manager of the South's oldest independent distributor, Music Sales, and now general manager of Sun Records [told me]: 'The fallacy in the system is this: since it is the Top 40 records that the retailers stock, they are obviously the records that they are going to sell. And as long as those records are selling, they are going to stay on the list. So, it's as hard to get a record off the Top 40, and make way for a new one, as it was to get it there in the first place. And ironically, the more a record is played after a certain point, the less likely people are to buy it. It reaches saturation point. In other words,' he concluded, 'we can't live without Top 40—and we have a hard time living with it.' "

Howard's record charted locally on the strength of his stories in the press but, as Howard was quick to point out, Memphis represented only 1.3 percent of the national market. Six months after release, he got a royalty statement. "So far," he wrote, "it has sold 975 copies. With a contract rate of 3% of the 98¢ list price, minus 10% for promotions, my royalty on paper is $25.81. However, since recording costs must be paid first, and they amounted to $181.50, I am $155.69 shy of earning my first penny as a recording artist. However, since I took the precaution of recording my own songs and songwriters get three-fourths of a cent on every copy sold, I have made something after all—$14.62."

There was a little postscript. Howard put some new words to the old gospel tune "Down by the Riverside" in the first flush of enthusiasm following the release of his record, and showed them to Sam Phillips. Rockabilly singer Billy Riley later planned to record the song, and he gave 50 percent of the writer's share to Howard as a token of goodwill because Howard had originally conceived the idea. Riley's record sold 10,633 copies during its first six months on the market, giving Howard $39.86 in writer's royalties, which, "added to my $14.62 for 'Forty 'leven Times,' " concluded Howard, "gives me a little over forty 'leven dollars for my excursion into the record business."

As Howard's account shows, even by 1959 Phillips was delegating an increasing part of the recording function to others. Howard mentioned a few of them in passing, but it is worth looking a little closer at some of the sessionmen who made part of their living at the studio during the years in which Sun Records rose to prominence. Every one of them contributed to the unfettered atmosphere that Phillips cherished, and were as resilient and adaptable as he needed.

Roland Janes

"I don't know why Sam hired me—probably took pity on me, I guess," is Janes' typically self-deprecating way of explaining his arrival at Sun. But Phillips knew that he had found in Roland that most precious commodity: a guitarist who could submerge his own ego and virtuosity for the good of a session. He also knew that Janes was supremely adaptable, able to fire sparks off Jerry Lee Lewis one moment and play the gentlest fills the next.

Janes was born in Brookings, Arkansas, on August 20, 1933, and grew up in St. Louis, Missouri. He met Jack Clement in 1956, when Clement was planning to launch Fernwood Records with aspiring rockabilly singer Billy Riley. Janes was recommended as a picker who might fit in, and he soon became a part of Riley's group.

After Riley's contract was bought by Sun, Clement came on board as an engineer, and Janes and his partners in Riley's band became the de facto house band. Janes was without obvious influences, sporting an eloquent and fluid style. He cherished innovation, and his curiosity would lead him to experiment with new sounds at Sun and later in his own Sonic studio. He was a pioneer in the technique of playing two strings at once, best exemplified on Billy Riley's recording of "I Want You Baby." In an interview with Rob Bowman and Ross Johnson, he characterized it as a "funky sound—at that time. Most blues guitarists were playing single string back then, and we wanted something that wasn't country but wasn't blues. [We said] 'What can we do that's different to set this apart?' "

After quitting Riley's band, Janes worked on the road with Bill Justis and Jerry Lee Lewis until 1959. At first Janes, Riley, and Sun's recently dismissed musical director, Bill Justis, had an involvement with Top Rank/Jaro Records. They recorded pseudonymously as the Spitfires. Then Janes and Riley decided that they wanted to move to the other side of the studio glass. They talked to Phillips about leasing the old Sun studio, which was about to be made redundant. The resulting product would have gone to Sun, but the idea never came to fruition. Janes and Riley eventually formed Rita Records, and scored an immediate hit with Harold Dorman's "Mountain of Love" in 1960, eclipsing virtually everything released on Sun that year. Rita soon fell apart, however, and Janes moved back to St. Louis for a while. When he returned to Memphis in 1962 he opened Sonic Sound, on Madison Avenue.

Sonic operated primarily as a custom studio and a preproduction studio, although Roland cut some hits there: Travis Wammack's "Scratchy," Jerry Jaye's "My Girl Josephine," and Matt Lucas' "I'm Movin' On." After Sonic folded in 1974, Janes eventually got back into the business as an engineer at Sounds

Roland Janes (left) picking with his brother, Delmar, c. 1947-48

(R. Janes/Showtime)

The morning after: Billy Riley with Roland, Corning, Arkansas, December 1959

(R. Janes/Showtime)

of Memphis, and then at the Phillips studio. In between, he worked as an instructor in recording technology at a primarily black community college in Memphis.

In recent years, as visitors have come to the Phillips studio and lectured Janes and the other resident engineer, Stan Kesler, about how it *really* was back in the heyday of Sun Records, Janes has kept enigmatically quiet. Perhaps better than most, he knows *exactly* the way it was at Sun. He worked there virtually every day, saw it all, and, unlike most of the others who walked through the door, he didn't strive to lead the parade. In watching the procession of inflated egos, Janes conspicuously avoided developing one.

J. M., bassist Pat O'Neill, and Billy Riley at Niagara Falls, 1957

(R. Janes/Showtime)

J. M. Van Eaton

J.M. Van Eaton

Looking back on his career at Sun Records, J. M. Van Eaton recalls that he was "proud of my work. I was doing something no one else could do." Smacking of immodesty, that assertion is nevertheless demonstrably true. Van Eaton was a true rock 'n' roll drummer, which his predecessor, Johnny Bernero, was not.

Van Eaton, born in Memphis in December 1937, took up drums in the ninth grade at school. His first influences were the propulsive drummers with the big bands. He also sought out black gospel rhythms, attending a church on Trigg Street. "It had a feel like Ray Charles and Aretha Franklin," recalled Van Eaton to Johnson and Bowman. "I was in awe of all this. We wouldn't miss it for the world. It was an every-Sunday-night thing."

Van Eaton started playing with Billy Riley's group at the tender age of sixteen or seventeen, and at eighteen he started working regularly in the studio. No one at Sun made a living from studio work, however, and Van Eaton also played on the road with Riley, Roy Orbison, and Conway Twitty.

It was as a studio drummer, though, that Van Eaton left his mark. His perfectly timed rim shots and fills and his subtle control of tempo imparted spontaneity to a session; his lack of rigidity helped to keep the other musicians loose. Van Eaton's style combined the swing-era shuffle with a backbeat. "A lot of people try to copy [the sound we got with] Jerry Lee Lewis," said Van Eaton, "but they'll never copy it, because they're trying to play a straight [4/4 beat] and in fact it's a shuffle with the backbeat. I never could play that straight country shuffle—maybe for eight or sixteen bars, but after that I start falling off the stool. I've got to concentrate, and when you concentrate, you lose the feeling."

Van Eaton grew dissatisfied after Jack Clement and Bill Justis were dismissed in 1959, and he effectively quit Sun at the same time as Roland Janes. He recorded for Janes' and Riley's Rita label and, in 1961, decided to quit the business. He was twenty-three years old. The looseness and unpredictability of his drumming may sound out of place in the modern era when most drum tracks are derived from a computer sample repeated with mathematical precision. But the sound of surprise that he captured in his playing was the pulse of Sun Records.

Jimmy Wilson

The profoundly strange Jimmy Wilson remains something of a mystery man. Another of Riley's Little Green Men, Wilson was co-opted for session piano work in late 1956, and played regularly at the studio until he left for California in 1958.

Wilson had an obsession with guns, and preferred working on his gun collection to playing session piano. He lived in a room above Taylor's Café, next door to the studio, but not even his proximity to the studio could lure him away from refurbishing or otherwise caring for a new firearm. Gene Simmons (who began his career with Sun and later broke through on Hi Records with "Haunted House") remembered him firing indiscriminately at passers-by from a tour bus that was taking them through southern Ontario, and he was eventually evicted from the rooms above Taylor's after he launched a home-made rocket from his apartment.

Wilson's strangeness appears to have stemmed from more than a bad attitude; most agree that he was mentally disturbed. He had a pet raccoon that he later stabbed and let die in the studio with the knife embedded in it. His bizarre conduct continued on stage, as Billy Riley recalls: "Wilson was not like anyone I knew. He had nothing in common with anyone in the world. He was in one minute and out the next. I've seen him on stage playing a rock number just great, then, all of a sudden, he'd have a change come over him and he'd just quit playing and be staring straight ahead. Then he'd start playing Chopin or something right in the middle of the song. We'd holler at him and he'd start playing rock 'n' roll again. He played with us for five years and nobody knows where he came from or what happened to him."

Never an outstanding pianist, Wilson nevertheless fitted in well on sessions, playing with Johnny Cash, Billy Riley, Warren Smith, and many others. He also worked professionally in Memphis under the pseudonym of Jan Dillard. At some point in 1958, Wilson bummed twenty dollars from everyone he knew

*Jimmy Wilson—
disturbed*

(R. Janes/Showtime)

and headed out to California, where he later married the daughter of Nudie the Rodeo Tailor—the man responsible for Elvis Presley's gold lamé suit. Nudie promised to bankroll his career if he went straight, but the news soon reached Memphis that Wilson had been committed. Besides the recordings that bear his stamp, Wilson left one enduring contribution to the Sun sound: he was the man who showed Phillips how to place tacks on the hammers inside his piano to achieve a harsher, more metallic sound.

Bill Justis
and Sid Manker

The onslaught of rock 'n' roll and its impact on the music scene in Memphis brought forth some strange new converts. Few were stranger than Bill Justis and Sid Manker, and few less converted.

William E. Justis, Jr., was born in Memphis on October 14, 1926. His father was an affluent roofing contractor, and Justis grew up riding show horses and playing tennis—in sharp contrast with most of those with whom he would one day work. After graduation from college, Justis returned to Memphis to work in his father's office. In 1951 he started a dance band, which became very popular locally. Beginning as a trumpeter, Justis took up the sax just before the advent of rock 'n' roll. After his father closed the office where Justis worked, he decided to try to make a career out of his music.

The first session he arranged was for O-J Records. Dewey Phillips, who engineered the session, suggested that Justis take the tapes to Sam Phillips as a calling card. By that point Justis had "learned" rock 'n' roll. "One night I was reading a newspaper article about a guy in New York named Buck Ram," he recalled in 1973. "Ram had a lot to do with the success of the vocal group scene. I read about how much money he had made out of rock 'n' roll so I said, 'That's for me!' So I immediately set out for a record store and bought eighty dollars' worth of the all-time rock 'n' roll hits. I studied the stuff and found it was so simple, yet basic and savage, that it was difficult to perform." Sam Phillips, hearing something he liked in the O-J sessions, hired Justis and gave him the official title of Musical Director. In May 1957 Justis decided that he would try to record a rock 'n' roll tune. He invited Sid Manker over to his house to play riffs while Justis worked out a melody. The results sounded commercial, and Justis decided to record it. Before the session he had read a glossary of teenage jargon in a magazine. He found *raunchy* in there. After the session, saxophonist Vernon Drane said, "That's the raunchiest damn thing you've ever done. You'll miss a hit if you

Bill Justis

(Escott)

don't release it." The two ideas connected and Justis had his tune named.

Part of the charm of Justis' version of "Raunchy" missing in all the cover versions was the off-tone of his saxophone. It was not wholly intentional: Justis had called in another sax player who had begged off, forcing Justis to play the lead part himself. He hadn't touched the sax for a while, and his rusty chops accounted for the strange tone.

After "Raunchy" became a hit in the late months of 1957, Justis began touring. He had started balding at age 17 and was self-conscious about both his age and his appearance; he felt woefully out of place on package shows. Roland Janes recalls one occasion in Los Angeles. Justis used the opportunity to hire some of his favorite big-band musicians. They sat around all afternoon poking fun at rock 'n' roll, but when it came time to play, Justis found they couldn't hit the licks.

Justis recorded some very creditable follow-ups, none of which recaptured the excitement of "Raunchy." On the session reels, he can be heard between takes chiding the musicians in the hipster's patois he had adopted: "OK, girls, let's get real bad now so we can sell some records. Instant crapsville, girls. Here we go . . ."

In March 1959 Justis and Phillips came to a parting of the ways. In circumstances that are still not entirely clear, Justis and Jack Clement were fired for insubordination. Each started his own label, looking to emulate Phillips' success. Justis started Play-Me Records, but found the road Phillips had traveled to be a hard one. Economic necessity forced him to take on a job as a PR rep for a trucking line until Bill Lowery at NRC Records offered him a job working in A&R. Justis commuted to Nashville and Atlanta for sessions, eventually moving to Nashville in 1961 to become a freelancer. Between 1962 and 1966 he usually had at least one of his arrangements on the pop or country charts. His clients included Bobby Goldsboro, Brook Benton, Roy Orbison, Bobby Vinton, and countless others.

In early 1966 Justis moved to Los Angeles to take on more legitimate work and possibly get into film scoring, but he returned to Nashville in 1972, his ambition to work on movies still unfulfilled (although he later wrote the

(Escott)

*J*ustis plays for
the young society crowd,
mid-'50s

Smokey and the Bandit scores). Justis remained in Nashville until his death from cancer in July 1982, doing what he did best: arranging. His wife, Yvonne, whom he married in 1954, remembered that in church everyone would sing the melody and Justis would hum an arrangement around it. The huge crowd that attended his funeral attested to the respect in which he was held.

In contrast, Sid Manker remains a shadowy figure. Born in Memphis in 1932, he lived there until he was drafted at age 20. After his return to Memphis, he went to the Academy of Art to study design until the guitar (or "starvation box," as he called it) entered his life. Abandoning art for music, he quit the academy and went to work with Bill Justis.

The sales of "Raunchy" enabled Manker to concentrate upon his Memphis Jazz Quartet, although he continued to work sessions at Sun and tour with Justis. During one of the follow-up sessions to "Raunchy," Manker received a phone call telling him that his mother had died. "I was so close to her that her death left me in a state of mental collapse," recalled Manker to the Memphis *Press Scimitar* in 1959. "The day after her burial I went to a friend's house and he told me he would give me some sedation. I didn't know it was heroin. Well, that was it. I was hooked. The friend gave me about five shots over the next three days, and I was a full-fledged addict. From then on, it was three shots a day, seven days a week. I spent over $200 a day on dope."

Sid Manker   (Escott)

Manker's account sidesteps the fact that heroin was the final stage in a long career of substance abuse. On a tour of Canada in 1957, Manker was so stoned after consuming all of his drugs before going through customs that even a head-on collision between the tour bus and a car only elicited the comment, "Far out, man." Along with the argot of the jazz musician, Manker had acquired the penchant for narcotics that neatly took care of all his royalties from the 3 million sales of "Raunchy."

In April 1960 Manker was sent to the penal farm for six months. After his release, he married and dropped out of sight. He and his wife, Linda, moved to Biloxi, Mississippi, in 1969. Manker continued to compose and worked at the Axent studio in Biloxi until his death, of a heart attack, on December 15, 1974.

Jack Clement
and Stan Kesler

Jack Henderson Clement, known as "Cowboy Jack," has enjoyed a career so long and multifaceted that it almost defies condensation. Peter Guralnick, in his essay "Let's All Help the Cowboy Sing the Blues," captured the spirit of the man; but whenever he tried to pin down the facts, Clement threw up a verbal smokescreen: "Asked another question, he winces slightly, suggests, 'Well, that's kind of a long story. It's not a particularly interesting one either. Why don't you make up another?' then relates the tale in its entirety." When we first talked with him about his Sun career, then almost fifteen years past,

Jack Clement

he sat in a darkened studio, which he owned. To pointed questions he offered elliptical replies, delivered to the trilling notes of a mandolin.

Born in Memphis on April 5, 1931, Clement started his musical career in Washington, D.C., while he was in the Marine Corps. Having acquired a taste for bluegrass music, he started playing the local bars in the company of Roy Clark, later a star of "Hee Haw" and then a struggling picker. After his discharge from the Marines in 1952, Clement returned briefly to Memphis before heading back east. He formed a duet with mandolin player Buzz Busby, which they called Buzz and Jack, the Bayou Boys. Working the eastern seaboard, the duo made their first record for the Sheraton label in Boston using two of Clement's compositions. After the record flopped, Clement went to Washington and played briefly in a Hawaiian band before returning to Memphis to work at the Arthur Murray School of Dancing and study English at Memphis State University.

On weekends, Clement played country music with Slim Wallace. Together, they planned to launch a company called Fernwood Records. Billy Riley was to be the first artist, but Clement took the tape to Sam Phillips for mastering and parlayed it into a contract for Riley and a full-time job as an engineer for himself.

Clement was the first person to whom Sam Phillips entrusted the technical side of his operation, although Phillips soon discovered that he had hired someone with views radically different from his own. "I was into making things musical," recalled Clement, "and Sam was not. But Sam understood one thing that I didn't at that time: he understood *feel* in music. I was interested in machines and the way recordings could be made better. The first time Sam gave me an artist to work with, it was Roy Orbison, and we recorded 'Rockhouse.' Sam also gave me Johnny Cash from 'Home of the Blues' onward."

In the studio, Clement would work with the pickers, changing keys, chord progressions, and arrangements—something that Phillips, with his lack of musical knowledge, was unable to do. Clement favored a light, acoustic, and folky feel, and cherished musical technique and virtuosity, virtues reflected in records he made himself as well as those he produced. Hoping to take advantage of the vogue for pseudo-folk music that followed in the wake of the Kingston Trio, Clement recorded a pair of singles under his own name that combined elements of folk, country, and pop; he also recorded an instrumental single under the pseudonym of the Clement Travelers. Despite a big push from Sun's in-house promotional department, Clement's records died on the vine. They stand among the least interesting records issued during Sun's golden era. Technically perfect but emotionally vapid, they share none of the rawness that characterized the best music issued on the label.

Dismissed from Sun with Bill Justis in March 1959, Clement formed his own record label, Summer Records, which folded after a few releases. He remained in the city working at the Echo studio (which he co-owned) and as a freelance engineer. After the money ran out, Clement took a job with Chet Atkins at RCA for a few months.

In 1961 Clement and Bill Hall formed a little musical outpost in Beaumont, Texas, operating both the Hallway label and Hall-Clement Publishing. Their successes included Dickey Lee's "Patches" and a song that Lee co-wrote, "She Thinks I Still Care." In 1965 Clement finally moved to Nashville and became a linchpin in the studio scene, discovering and recording Charley Pride, Don Williams, and a flock of others. His diverse activities include production, publishing, video, songwriting, and perpetuating his own legend.

At Sun he was, as he put it, "a malcontent. I was trying to make more sophisticated music than Sam. Less gutsy. Looking back, he was right and I was wrong."

Among the many others who worked regularly at Sun was Stan Kesler, who played with the Snearly Ranch Boys and contributed some luminous steel guitar solos to early recordings by Charlie Feathers, the Miller Sisters, and others. Kesler also wrote some early material for Elvis Presley, including "I'm Left, You're Right, She's Gone" and "Playing for Keeps." After the onslaught of rock 'n' roll, Kesler learned the electric bass and worked countless sessions between 1956 and 1959, when he left to launch the Echo studio with Jack Clement and start up Crystal Records. Although Crystal didn't last long, Kesler eventually prospered during the Memphis recording boom of the mid-to-late '60s, scoring big with Sam the Sham and the Pharoahs, whom he cut at Sam Phillips' new studio on Madison Avenue.

After a few years out of the music business, Kesler came back to roost at the Phillips studio, where he signed on as an engineer. His renewed involvement with the music business took a new turn when he dusted off his electric bass in 1986 to join Roland Janes and J. M. Van Eaton in the Sun Rhythm Section band. Janes and Van Eaton soon bowed out, but Kesler seemed to delight in being before an audience again after thirty years. Part of the reason why the Sun Rhythm Section has been so successful at clubs and festivals in the past few years is that they capture the irrepressible joy of playing that the real Sun rhythm section caught in their day.

Never a musician, Phillips was fortunate to find a staff band who knew instinctively what he was after when he had neither the vocabulary to explain nor the expertise to demonstrate. Phillips' little group of pickers knew what he wanted, and gave it to him at $2.50 an hour, night after night. Although their identities were little known outside the small circle of Memphis musicians, their contribution to Phillips' success was integral.

Recommended Listening

Roland Janes' solo recordings for Sun, Judd, and his own labels are on *Guitarville* (Bear Family [Germany] BFX 15340), which also includes J. M. Van Eaton's solo recordings.
Bill Justis' Phillips International album was reissued in 1969 as *Raunchy* (Sun [US] LP 109).
Jack Clement's Sun recordings are included on *The Sun Country Years* (Bear Family [Germany] BFX 15211).

(J. Bernero/Showtime)

*W*arren Smith on
stage with Marcus Van Story
(bass) and Al Hopson
(guitar)

Chapter Ten

THOSE WHO WOULD BE KING

For a few months rockabilly was a contender for Next Big Thingdom. Some of those who followed in Presley's wake, like Roy Orbison, eventually developed an individual approach and survived in the music business. Some returned to country music and view their flirtation with rockabilly as an aberration. Most, however, simply returned to the mundane reality of making a living outside the music business, coming to see with thirty years' hindsight that they never stood a chance of making it.

"Rockabilly," asserts producer Jim Dickinson, holding up two fingers held close together, "is about *that* wide. Revivalists treat it as if it were all kinds of other things too. Once you get past Sonny Burgess, Billy Riley, and Johnny Burnette, there ain't much more." It's still unclear who coined the term but it was in fairly common use by early 1956—usually, as Dickinson indicates, as misapplied then as today.

Once Sam Phillips' achievement with Presley and Perkins became common knowledge, his little studio became a mecca for a generation of young singers who stood at the door where Elvis had stood, hoping against hope that the magic would rub off on them. And it was Elvis—not really Carl Perkins, despite his role in shaping the rockabilly sound—that the new generation sought to emulate. For some, Presley was an enigma they hoped to unravel; but it's easy to forget that for many of the teenage boys who auditioned at Sun, he was a frustratingly real person. He might have shared a Coke with them backstage at the local high school gym after a gig. Yet he had passed from their midst, had suddenly become a vision of the success that was tantalizingly close and desperately unreachable. Many could never find the answer to the question: "Why Elvis and not me?"

Like those who straggle up and down Music Row in Nashville today, they came to the Sun studio from a variety of backgrounds. The cross-section that follows reflects the different musical strands that went to make up the great catchall, rockabilly.

(Showtime)

Yelvington with
the Star Rhythm Boys,
1954

(Showtime)

Malcolm
Yelvington

Malcolm Yelvington

The first record issued on Sun after Presley's debut was by Malcolm Yelvington. Presley's first two records were Sun 209 and 210; Yelvington's first record was 211. A more unlikely candidate to follow in Presley's footsteps would be hard to find.

Yelvington and his group were firmly rooted in the western swing tradition; any black music they absorbed came second- or third-hand. Yelvington, born in Covington, Tennessee, started singing in the late '30s. After the war he joined Reece Fleming's Tennesseans (Fleming had recorded before the war as part of the duo Fleming and Townsend), playing schoolhouse dates around Covington. In 1952 they merged with another local group, the Star Rhythm Boys, and secured a daily gig on a local radio station.

At some point in the winter of 1953–54, the Star Rhythm Boys' guitarist, Gordon Mashburn, learned that there was a record company in Memphis that had just issued a disc by another local group, the Ripley Cotton Choppers. "We went down to see Sam," recalls Yelvington. "He asked us what type of music we played and we said, 'Country.' He said he wasn't interested, so I asked him what he wanted. He said, 'I don't know, but I'll know when I hear it.' Gordon said, 'Mr. Phillips, that means you'll have to listen to every single person who comes in off the street.' Sam said, 'I intend to.' "

Yelvington and his group eventually persuaded Phillips to take a listen. "We couldn't come up with anything that Sam wanted," recalled Yelvington. "I wanted something like Hank Williams or Moon Mullican, but Sam kept saying no. Then I decided to try 'Drinkin' Wine Spo-Dee-O-Dee.' Sam poked his head around the door and said, 'Where did you get that from?' I said, 'Man, we've been playing that every week for a long time.' "

Yelvington and his group worked up "Drinkin' Wine," which had been an R&B smash for "Stick" McGhee in 1949; their version was released on November 10, 1954. Essentially a country record, it nevertheless had the loose-jointed swing that Phillips cherished and that he was nurturing in Elvis Presley. Still, it failed to create even a shadow of the impact that Presley was already making.

In 1955 Yelvington sidestepped his Sun contract and recorded pseudonymously as Mac Sales for Phillips' competitor, Meteor Records, with equally poor response. The following year, Yelvington returned to Sun with a rockabilly novelty, "Rockin' with My Baby." Sounding a little uncomfortable with the brisk tempo—and slurring the lyrics because he had removed his dentures—Yelvington nevertheless turned out a very creditable piece of the new music. Yet his fortieth birthday wasn't too far away, and with his youth went his faint chance of stardom. His music was a curious hybrid that never strayed too far from his group's hillbilly roots. Yelvington's bullfrog baritone was a fair distance from the primal yawp of Gene Vincent, but his music had an engagingly lazy quality that has weathered well.

In 1961 Yelvington finally gave up his club dates to concentrate on his day job, his bowling, and family life. But his Sun career had one belated postscript. In 1988, six months before his seventieth birthday, Malcolm Yelvington journeyed to England and Holland, where several thousand fans (many young enough to be his grandchildren) gathered to hear him play the old songs. The gentle roll of his music was still with him, and the applause was a sweet consolation prize for the acclaim Yelvington felt he had been denied in 1956.

Harris in 1984

Ray Harris:
"Rack 'em up, boy"

(Escott)

Ray Harris

Tall and imposing, with sharp, angular features, Ray Harris carries about him a frightening intensity, and speaks with an impenetrable accent that almost demands subtitles for a listener not from Mississippi. He sat in his wife's Chrysler one humid summer night a few years ago, holding a cassette of a band he had just recorded. As it played, his eyes burned as it reached the parts he liked. He stabbed at the cassette deck. "There! There! I tell you, them boys have got it!" As abruptly as it had arisen, though, the energy subsided. Ray Harris was sixty years old, recovering from a heart bypass operation, with an operation pending to remove a cancerous growth in his throat. He also hadn't cut a hit in almost twenty years. "I ask myself," he said finally, "do I wanna go beatin' my head against the goddamn wall at my age?" Better than most, Harris knew it was a rhetorical question. But, as he well knew, there was no good answer.

Homer Ray Harris was one of the unlikeliest pretenders to Elvis Presley's throne. His brand of music was so raw and Southern that airplay outside the South would have been unthinkable. Acknowledging that fact with grim, self-knowing humor, Harris quit the performing end of the business and launched a record label that would let him experience success vicariously. But not even the proximity of success in those years gave him the impetus to resume his recording career, which began and ended with two luminous singles on the Sun label.

The son of sharecroppers, Ray Harris was born in Mantachie, Mississippi, on September 7, 1927. "I come from the rural areas," he says. "We listened to the Grand Ole Opry. We didn't listen to colored music. We just kept the radio tuned to Nashville. We was country folks, and we listened to country music."

By 1953 Harris had married and moved to Memphis. He took a job on the graveyard shift at the Firestone plant working next to Bill Black. "One day we was taking a break," he recalls, "and I asked Bill what he was doin' in music. He said that on Saturday nights he was playin' down at the State Line, some li'l ol' club down on the Tennessee-Mississippi state line. He also said he was tryin' to cut a record up at Sun with a boy named Presley. He asked me to come by during the next session.

"I went up there one afternoon. I was shy, sat in the car and waited for Bill. We went inside and Bill introduced me to Sam, Elvis, and Scotty. They was cutting 'Good Rockin' Tonight.' I sat with Sam up in the control room. He would listen to the playbacks and say, 'This is it! This is it!' I didn't see it at first, 'cause you gotta remember I was raised on Hank Williams, but even before the end of the session it was startin' to hit me. I'd played a little back around Tupelo—wienie roasts and the like—and I listened to Presley and thought, 'Hell, that boy ain't doin' anything I cain't do!' "

Armed with that certainty, Harris recruited a band led by guitarist Wayne Cogswell, who had moved to Memphis from Connecticut with his wife and children in search of the shaking music. "We disturbed the neighborhood every night," Harris remembers. "Told everyone they would get a copy of the record when it come out. We was huntin' somethin' different like everyone else. We just decided to go as wild as we could."

Bill Cantrell met Harris while he was working up his debut single. "Ray wanted to be another Elvis. He couldn't sing and he wasn't good to look at, but he didn't care. You'd go visit him and you could hear him practicing from two blocks away. He would open the door wearing nothing but his overalls, dripping with sweat. He had an old portable recorder, and he'd go back to singing and sweating. In the studio, he'd throw himself around, arms going like windmills."

Harris took his songs to Sun. Phillips, surely knowing that he couldn't sell Harris to the mass market, nevertheless responded to his maniacal energy. "I'll never forget it, he was so intense," says Phillips. "He looked like he was going to have a heart attack every time he played. 'Rack 'em up, boy, let's go!' That was Ray's saying."

"Come On Little Mama" was recorded in June 1956. It was a definitive statement of supercharged rockabilly: a world apart from country, but not identifiably R&B or pop. The lyrics were virtually unintelligible, the musicianship limited, and the production sparse, but the performance was irresistible.

"Come On Little Mama" apparently sold well locally, and Harris was invited back to cut a follow-up. Casting around for material, the group lighted upon the old hill country ballad "Greenback Dollar," and they worked up a surprisingly commercial version of the song. There was a contagious party atmosphere on the record, highlighted by whistles and hollers during the instrumental breaks. "A lot of people thought I was gonna have a big one," recalled Harris, "so I got carried away and went and bought a new Mercury. Ended up diggin' ditches for six months to pay for it."

Harris provides his own epitaph on his Sun career: "I never did get a hit. Probably had too much country in my style. I tell ever'one I sure had a good time tryin', though."

Later in 1957, Harris happened to meet one of Jerry Lee Lewis's cousins, Carl McVoy, on a construction site. McVoy, a pianist and singer, played a goosed-up version of "You Are My Sunshine," and Harris, no stranger to the recording studio, saw a chance for a career on the other side of the glass. Together with Bill Cantrell and Quinton Claunch, he invested $3.50 in recording a demo of "Sunshine" that they pitched to Joe Cuoghi, the owner of a local record store. Cuoghi was intrigued, found some other investors, and launched Hi Records in 1957. On the strength of artists like Bill Black, Ace Cannon, and especially Al Green, Hi would eventually eclipse Sun.

After ten years as the éminence grise behind the hits of Black and Cannon, Harris quit the business in 1970. He was sick of the control room, having engineered and mixed sessions twelve hours a day for most of the previous decade. In particular, Harris could see no future in Al Green, in whom the other partners seemed to have an inordinate amount of faith. Burned out, Harris retreated to a house on the Tennessee River before starting a construction company in Tupelo.

In the mid-'70s Harris and Sam Phillips built the Trace studio in Tupelo with a commitment from Playboy Records, but the deal went sour and Harris lost a considerable amount of money. By this point, Harris's daughter had married Phillips' younger son, Jerry, but the failure of Trace Recording gave

Harris little enthusiasm for another partnership with his new in-law.

Harris still owns a stake in a small studio near Saltillo, Mississippi, and every so often he gets excited about a new band or a new song, and wants to re-enter the business. Unfailingly, though, the pendulum will swing the other way. On one such occasion, Ray Harris took all he tapes he had accumulated over the course of a thirty-year involvement in the music business, loaded them in the back of his pickup truck, and drove them to the Iuka, Mississippi, dump—where they remain.

B*illy Riley*

It was rare for an artist who didn't have a hit to see more than one or two singles on the Sun label. One notable exception was Billy Riley. Riley recorded sporadically for Phillips between early 1956 and late 1959—four years that produced seven memorable singles, but also gave rise to a bitterness that has barely subsided in three decades. Riley is still convinced he could have made it had Phillips not been concentrating all of his energies on the career of Jerry Lee Lewis.

Riley was born on October 5, 1933, in Pocahontas, Arkansas. Like many from that area, Riley had some Indian blood in him, evident in his high cheekbones. His father, a painter, decorator, and sharecropper, moved the family around Arkansas and Mississippi during the Depression in search of work. Like so many others, Riley learned country music from the radio and black music from the sharecroppers across the cotton patch.

Billy Riley,
1957

(Escott)

"FLYING SAUCER ROCK & ROLL"

IN PERSON

Billy Riley & "His Little Green Men"

Plus

LOCAL TALENT CONTEST FINALS

Sunday Afternoon March 24th 2 - 5 PM

AT THE BLUE MOON   3600 N. Cincinnati

ADVANCE TICKETS $1.00

at

Bill's "T" Record Shop, 17 W. 7th

Harvard Record Shop, 2620 S. Harvard

Roof Terrace Music Center, Sheridan Village

Everybody Welcome

For More Details Listen to

"THE DON WALLACE SHOW"*

over KTUL   2:30 - 6:45 P.M. Daily

* Tulsa's Top Disc Jockey Show

Sun Makes His Star Shine

(R. Janes/Showtime)

Billy Riley Signed For 1957 County Fair

Riley entered the Army in 1949 and stayed in until 1953. After his discharge, he married and brought his wife to Memphis, where he joined a country band that included Jack Clement and Ronald "Slim" Wallace. When Clement and Wallace decided to start Fernwood Records in early 1956, they signed Riley as the first artist. They recorded two songs, "Trouble Bound" and "Think Before You Go," in a primitive studio Clement had built in Wallace's garage. Clement took the masters to Sam Phillips, who responded to the eerie, bluesy intensity of "Trouble Bound" and offered a job to Clement and a contract to Riley. Phillips counseled against releasing the countrified "Think Before You Go," so Riley concocted a rockabilly novelty, "Rock with Me Baby," that he recorded at the WMPS studio. Purchasing the masters from Fernwood, Phillips issued Riley's debut single in May 1956.

Casting around for a follow-up, Riley's guitarist, Roland Janes, remembered a song called "Flyin' Saucer Rock 'n' Roll" he had heard on a demo tape from Ray Scott. With Jerry Lee Lewis on piano and Janes thrashing his tremolo bar, Riley delivered the song in a newfound rasping voice that owed more than a passing nod to Little Richard. Released in January 1957, it had sold only a disappointing fifteen thousand copies by June—though it gave Riley's band their unforgettable name, the Little Green Men. Undeterred, Riley returned to the studio to start work on a rockabilly version of an old Sun copyright, Billy "The Kid" Emerson's "Red Hot." As always, the rhythm section, featuring Janes and drummer J. M. Van Eaton, played with telepathic cohesion. Win, lose, or draw, Riley always had one of the hottest working bands in the mid-South.

By the end of 1957, "Red Hot" had sold only thirty-seven thousand copies, and Riley was furious. To compound the insult, he had stood in the office one day only to hear Phillips cancel orders for the record, telling distributors to work "Great Balls of Fire" instead. The upstart pianist who had played on "Flying Saucer" was now usurping Riley's fleeting place as Phillips' Great White Hope. Riley drove over to West Memphis, bought a half-gallon of cheap wine, and returned to the studio drunk and vengeful. He started taking the studio apart, beginning by kicking a hole in the string bass and pouring some of his wine over the tape machines. Sam Phillips was called in and his silver tongue said the words that Riley, through the haze, confusion, and vitriol, wanted to hear. "We went back into his little cubbyhole," recalled Riley, "and talked 'til sunup. Sam said, ' "Red Hot" ain't got it. We're saving you for something *good*.' When I left I felt I was the biggest star on Sun Records."

Riley's next record was released at the same time as Jerry Lee Lewis's "Breathless." It sold thirty-two hundred copies. Its title: "Wouldn't You Know."

Riley quit Sun in disgust soon thereafter and went to Nashville to cut a painfully contrived single for Brunswick. It fared no better than his Sun releases, and Riley considered an approach from Steve Sholes to record for RCA and another from Dick Clark to record for one of the labels in which Clark had an interest. "We drove up 'specially to see Clark," Riley told Bill Millar. "He asked if I wanted to record, and he set up a session at a studio in Philadelphia for the same afternoon. On the way over to the studio we said, 'Aw,

Riley on stage with Roland Janes, 1957

(R. Janes/Showtime)

(R. Janes/Showtime)

let's go back to Sam, he's the only one that understands us,' and we just drove back to Memphis, didn't tell nobody. We were just suspicious of anyone from the North. I was a dumb country boy and I didn't have enough self-confidence, I guess."

Hittin' the highway: Roland, J. M. Van Eaton, Marvin Pepper, and Riley, 1957

Riley stayed a year at Sun during his second go-round, recording two singles and working countless sessions for a recently humbled Jerry Lee Lewis and every other artist on the roster. "Every session we got drunk," asserted Riley to Millar. "It was fun getting in there and getting drunk. Sam usually got tight with us. We had respect for each other, but we never did get along too well. I didn't appreciate the lack of promotion, but I appreciated his talent. He knew I had the band that could work with anybody, and he needed us."

The final single was as good as anything Riley had ever—or would ever— cut. The top side was a raspy cover version of the Regals' "Got the Water Boilin'," but the reverse was a haunting, melancholy blues, "One More Time." Riley had learned the song from an obscure blues record by Country Paul, and he sang it, as he said, "like a tenor sax." Van Eaton set a ponderous beat, and Martin Willis contributed some dark, bluesy fills on the saxophone. It was a magnificent record.

"Riley was just a damn good rocker," Phillips concludes, "but, man, he was so damn weird in many ways. He interested the hell out of me, but he was not the easiest person to deal with. When he took a drink he'd become almost a different person. He just never achieved his potential in my studio. I'm sorry I didn't do more with him. I was disappointed we never broke him into the big time. His band was just a rockin' *mother*!"

After Riley and his longtime guitarist Roland Janes quit Sun in September 1959, their new label, Rita Records, scored an immediate hit with Harold Dorman's "Mountain of Love." But Riley quit the label just as it was getting off the ground. After starting and folding two more labels in Memphis, he eventually left for the West Coast. He slept on Charles Underwood's floor (Underwood had been a writer and later an A&R man for Sun). He played

(Escott)

Billy Riley: businessman

guitar on a few sessions, including Herb Alpert's "Lonely Bull" session, which Underwood engineered, and he recorded for a plethora of labels.

The story repeated itself for years. Riley was never able to find a winning groove. Part of the problem was that he lacked an identifiable style—like Little Milton, he was a musical chameleon with an undeniable talent but little sense of direction. When he came to Memphis he was a hillbilly singer; then he tried becoming the white man's answer to Little Richard; then he went on to record trite rock 'n' roll novelties, pseudonymous instrumentals, pseudonymous blues tunes, Whiskey-a-Go-Go albums, country soul, and so on, and so on.

Despite his frustration, though, Riley could never quite let go of his grounding at Sun. After returning to the South, he became the first artist on the reborn Sun International label in 1969, cutting a luminous single, "Kay," in a country soul style. He also worked for Sam Phillips' son Knox, recording a rockabilly session for Knox's Southern Rooster label. After feeling once again that his hour had finally come when Robert Gordon and the rockabilly revivalists started doing good business with what was essentially *his* music, Riley saw his star eclipsed for the last time and retired from the music business to work in construction.

Blues singers without enough money to put gas in their cars often hear that they are idolized by white guitar heroes who fill fifty-thousand-seat venues. Riley suffered the same fate, with understandably little good humor. The maniacal, raucous overstatement of his records became part of the vocabulary of rock 'n' roll, and his influence wasn't restricted to revivalists such as Robert Gordon. Yet he was unable to translate his undeniable talent into even one bona fide hit. All he could do was look at the charts and conclude—in Ray Charles's immortal plaint—"It should have been me."

Hayden Thompson

In a two-bedroom apartment in a Chicago suburb lives another man who has never fully resigned himself to his fate. Hayden Thompson drives an airport limo by day, and the promise of what should have been still gnaws at him.

Thompson was born a few miles north of Tupelo, Mississippi, in the town of Booneville, on March 5, 1938. He formed his first band when he was in his early teens, and played the predictable round of local radio stations and Saturday night dances. In 1955 Thompson and the Southern Melody Boys recorded for the small Von label in Booneville (on which Johnny Burnette also made his debut). After Thompson graduated in 1956, the group hit the road. "We bought a trailer," he recalled, "and we carried the movie *Rock Around the Clock* in that trailer together with our instruments. We'd go into a town, do a show, they'd play the movie, and then we'd do another show. It cost the punters fifty cents or a dollar. We did that until late 1956."

After only a few months on the road, however, Thompson's band decided to call it quits. "I wanted to play rock 'n' roll, but most of the guys in the group

(R. Janes/Showtime)

Hayden Thompson

(R. Janes/Showtime)

*Hayden Thompson,
on stage, 1957*

said rock 'n' roll would never last, and they wanted to stick with country music. The final straw came when two of them got married. They wanted to stay home and had no dreams of doing anything more in music than they had already done." Yet Thompson had no intention of abandoning his dreams, and he found temporary salvation with the Billy Riley band. "I'd met them before my group broke up—I had been in and out of Sun quite a lot—and I found that Riley and I worked good together. We'd do a finale in which he'd do a Little Richard impersonation and I'd do Elvis Presley. We were making seventy or eighty dollars a week—which was good money for guys without hits."

Thompson hoped to improve that situation when he went to Sun in October 1956 with the nucleus of the Riley band behind him. They cut the old Junior Parker song "Love My Baby," with the newly arrived Jerry Lee Lewis strengthening the rhythm track. Once recorded, the single was held back for nine months; finally, in September 1957 it was issued in the first batch of Phillips International releases. Wide-eyed in Babylon, Thompson was ready for the acclaim that would surely follow. The portents seemed excellent: "I went by the studio and Jack Clement was there. We left and went to pick up Jack's wife and went to a drive-in movie. I listened to Dewey Phillips on WHBQ rather than the movie—Dewey played my record. After the movie, we went back to the studio. Sam was still there. He invited us back to his place to spend the night. We got there about two in the morning. Sam called his wife on the intercom and she came down and fixed breakfast for us. He put 'Love My Baby' on the turntable and spun it over and over. I was thinking to myself, 'This is really something.' "

Thompson had fallen prey to the premier illusion of the record business. The industry gives everyone the equivalent of Andy Warhol's fifteen minutes of fame; virtually anyone who puts a record out gets at least one good review, a slot on a playlist, or a word of encouragement from one on whom Fortune has smiled. The problem lies in the capriciousness of the market; the following week there is a new crop of records, a new set of reviews, a new set of playlists.

Last week's Best Bet is next week's unreturned phone call. It was Bill Justis's "Raunchy" that was the surprise hit from the first batch of singles on Phillips International. As Phillips probably knew, "Love My Baby" was too primitive for the ever more sophisticated teenage market. Thompson went back to the studio, but never got another shot on Sun. Disillusioned, he headed north to Chicago in 1958.

Thompson's best chance came with a series of uptown country singles he recorded for Kapp Records in the mid '60s. The Kapp singles secured him a guest appearance on the Opry that seemed for a moment to be the long-awaited harbinger of fame. But Thompson could never quite capitalize on his opportunities. He still records occasionally, but, as the title of a recent song he cut—"The Boy from Tupelo"—suggests, he has never quite found a satisfactory answer to the question, Why Elvis and not me?

Warren Smith

Unlike Billy Riley or Hayden Thompson, Warren Smith did manage to see the hits he considered no less than his birthright—although they would come only after he had left Sun and would be fewer than he might have hoped. Smith had a voice that was pure country, without vocal contrivance or mimickry. He had the looks and the will to succeed, and he certainly seemed to be in the right place at the right time. Yet he managed only one fleeting hit on Sun and no more than a few years in the spotlight after he left the label.

Warren Smith was born in Humphreys County, Mississippi, near Yazoo City, and he gave February 7, 1933, as his birth date, although hospital records would indicate that he lopped a year off his age. His parents, Ioda and Willie Warren Smith, divorced when he was young, and he was brought up by his grandparents near the town of Louise, where they farmed and operated a small country store. After a spell as a machinist, he went into the Air Force in 1950. By the time of his discharge, he was fairly determined to make a career out of music. It certainly represented a more attractive option than most of the others open to a poor white Mississippi boy with little formal education. With music on his mind, Smith headed for the bright lights of Memphis and the brighter lights of West Memphis, Arkansas.

Soon after he arrived, Smith went to the Cotton Club. Stan Kesler, who was playing in a band led nominally by Clyde Leoppard, remembers Smith's arrival: "Warren came in and auditioned for us. I saw a lot of potential and brought him over to Sam Phillips together with the rest of the Snearly Ranch Boys. Sam thought he was real good too, and asked me to work up some material. I'd already written 'I'd Rather Be Safe Than Sorry' when Sam called and said that Johnny Cash had brought in 'Rock 'n' Roll Ruby.' We went over and recorded with Warren, and it was supposed to be a co-op deal because we'd discovered him and supported him."

By the time Smith and the Snearly Ranch Boys wrapped up "Rock 'n' Roll

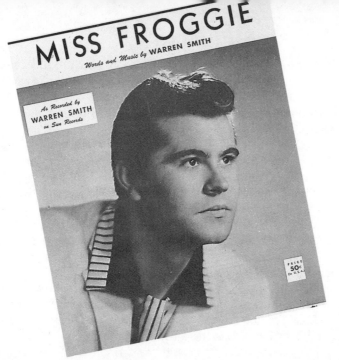

Ruby," it was obvious that Phillips had, as *Billboard* put it, "another contender in the Rock 'n' Roll sweepstakes."

In February 1956, though, it was still far from clear whether rock 'n' roll was a passing fad, and Phillips hedged his bet by coupling "Ruby" with a stone country flip side, "I'd Rather Be Safe Than Sorry." He may well have thought that he might be able to breach two markets—and he certainly recognized that he would have himself a fine new country singer if rock 'n' roll blew over. "Ruby" hit the Memphis charts on May 1, and was sitting at number 1 by May 26. A plethora of cover versions hit the market, including one by Lawrence Welk and another by a black group called the Saints.

On August 15, 1956, Smith went to Sun to pick up his first royalty statement. Even though "Rock 'n' Roll Ruby" had not charted nationally, it had sold 68,277 copies up to June 30 and was still going strong. Sun owed Smith over sixteen hundred dollars in royalties. Not even Elvis Presley, Johnny Cash, or Carl Perkins had done as well with their first record. Smith thought his place in the pantheon of rock 'n' roll greats was already assured.

There was either an implicit or explicit agreement that Smith would share his royalties with the Snearly Ranch Boys and that they would become his band. Smith reneged upon the deal shortly after "Rock 'n' Roll Ruby" broke. Stan Kesler recollects, "When Warren arrived in Memphis we didn't really need him, because we had singers and pickers, but Clyde gave him a little work and put him up in a boardinghouse—paid his rent and food for about six months. Then, after 'Rock 'n' Roll Ruby' hit, Warren just informed us that he was putting his own band together. With hindsight, I can see that the co-op deal we anticipated between Warren and us would never have worked, but there was a lot of bad feeling about it at the time."

Smith lost no time in recruiting his own band, which included guitarist Al Hopson (a friend since their school days in Mississippi), bassist Marcus Van Story (whom he had met while he was still working with the Snearly Ranch Boys), and drummer Jimmie Lott, who had played on Elvis Presley's first session with drums at the tail end of 1954.

While Smith was assembling his new band, he returned to the studio to record a follow-up to "Rock 'n' Roll Ruby." Once again, he coupled a hillbilly song with a rock 'n' roll novelty. "Black Jack David" was based on an English folk ballad, although Smith cheerfully attributed it to himself. Charles Underwood, then a student at Memphis State University, contributed "Ubangi Stomp," a song that teetered on the edge of racism and assigned a common dialect to Africans and American Indians ("heap big jam session"). The coupling was released on September 24, 1956. It had sold only a disappointing thirty-eight thousand copies by year end.

The momentum of his career sagging a little, Smith returned to Memphis early in 1957 to work on his third single. Roy Orbison contributed a song called "So Long I'm Gone" that, in Smith's hands, effortlessly crossed between country and pop. But it was the flipside, "Miss Froggie," that has won the enduring love of rockabilly fans, partly as a result of Al Hopson's dazzling guitar breaks. With lines like "She oughta been a go-rilla, boy, she sure is wild," the song was hardly calculated to win awards for profundity, but as Phillips would be the first to say, it was sound and the feel that were important, and he caught Hopson's lightning in a bottle. For his part, Smith barely strained or coarsened his voice. There was no contrivance in his style; the energy flowed from the song rather than being imposed upon it.

"So Long I'm Gone" made a fleeting appearance in the Hot 100, but had the misfortune to start breaking at the same time as "Whole Lotta Shakin' Going On." Phillips began placing all of his eggs in one basket, focusing his attention on Jerry Lee Lewis—and ended up alienating not only Carl Perkins

Left to right:
Will Hopson, Al Hopson,
Jimmie Lott, and
Warren Smith—
behind bars

(Escott)

but Warren Smith as well.

Lewis's success galled Smith. Not only was a monster unleashing itself from the bottom of the bill, but a monster ego was unleashing itself too. Smith had no shortage of pride himself, and the two were destined to clash. Smith smashed Lewis's records wherever he found them, but that act couldn't assuage the jealousy he felt when he heard those records, rather than his own, every half hour on the car radio. "Warren was an egotist—the biggest egotist I've ever met," says Lott. "A caring man and a good man, but an egotist. Warren wanted recognition. He painted WARREN SMITH—THE ROCK 'N' ROLL RUBY MAN on the back of his car—a seven- or eight-thousand-dollar Cadillac sedan."

Among the songs that Smith heard on his car radio was Slim Harpo's "Got Love If You Want It." Harpo's song was a mellow, medium-tempo blues, but when Smith made it into his fourth single, it became another celebration of joyous, primal rockabilly. Coupled with a country ballad from Al Hopson, "I Fell in Love," there was no reason that the record should not have been a hit—except perhaps that it was issued in the same month as "Great Balls of Fire."

According to Sun's royalty statements, the record had only sold a shade over seven thousand copies by the following June. Smith was disgusted, and his band began to lose the faith. Marcus Van Story dropped out, to be replaced by Al Hopson's brother, Will. Jimmie Lott also packed his bags and headed back to Memphis. Smith began working with the Hopson brothers, picking up drummers from town to town. When he returned to the studio in January 1959 after a long hiatus, he was paired with the Billy Riley band to work up his final single.

With the short-lived fad for primitive rockabilly consigned to the past, Smith's thoughts began turning toward crossover country music. Johnny Cash, Jim Reeves, Don Gibson, and others had uncovered an immense potential there for national success. Smith, certain he could cover their territory, isolated a song from Don Gibson's first album, "Sweet Sweet Girl," for his swan song on Sun.

Once again, Smith had the profound disappointment of watching a single die of neglect after *Billboard* had called it "ultra commercial," speculating that "Smith'll have the top money making coupling of his career." On the day that *Billboard* published its review, Sun prepared a royalty statement showing that Smith was unrecouped to the tune of $634.00. At roughly the same time, Smith's three-year term with Sun was up. A change was due.

Smith and his family moved to California, where he cut three singles for the new Warner Brothers label. But not until he aligned himself with the newly formed country division of Liberty Records in 1960 did Warren Smith find both a style with which he could sell records and a company willing to make a sustained commitment to him. Between 1960 and 1964 he scored a series of hits in the country charts that were refreshingly free of the choruses and overproduction that were beginning to plague Nashville.

Surprisingly, Sam Phillips did not reach back into the vaults after Smith started scoring consistently with Liberty. He had mixed feelings about his protégé: "He was probably the best pure singer for country music I've ever heard," he remembers. "He had a pure country voice and an innate feel for a country ballad. With that music he was as good as anyone I've heard before or since. 'So Long I'm Gone' was just a wonderful country record.

"Warren had a lot of emotional problems, though. I don't think he ever got on dope or anything, but he was the kind of character that needed to be loved a lot. He needed recognition more than the average person. . . . A lot of people didn't like Warren, and he perceived that. And if they didn't, in essence it was his fault in a lot of cases. He was a difficult personality, but just interesting enough that I liked him a whole lot."

Phillips was apparently unaware of Smith's problems with prescription drugs, a dependency that would come to hamper his career in the years ahead. But Warren's contemporaries agree that Phillips' assessment of his psyche is accurate. Unfortunately for Smith, his affiliation with Sun never resulted in the kind of success he had envisioned for himself. His rancor subsided for a while when it seemed as though the country music world was falling into his lap, but it eventually resurfaced as Smith pondered the inexplicable loss of success.

Warren Smith entered a sad personal and professional downslide. There were a few more short-lived label affiliations, a jail term for stealing drugs, and a succession of mundane day jobs. When the rockabilly revival craze hit Europe in the late '70s, Smith was called upon to tour overseas and record again in the rockabilly style, but he couldn't harness the reflected glory from his Sun years to build a new career. He died in Longview, Texas, on January 30, 1980, of a heart attack.

Sonny Burgess

When singers such as Warren Smith forsook rockabilly, they usually reverted back to their first love—country music. Sonny Burgess was the exception. His first love was rhythm and blues. He had a true R&B voice, like a tenor sax in full cry—short on subtlety and delicate shadings, but a magnificent rock 'n' roll instrument. Burgess' vocals were complemented by his guitar playing: rough, intense, and blues-drenched. Based in Newport, Arkansas, Burgess formed one of the hottest working bands in the mid-South. Rarely venturing to Memphis, he nevertheless cut several sessions for Sun over a four-year period.

As with Riley and Warren Smith, success often seemed very close for Burgess. Yet when the equation produced the wrong answer, Burgess accepted the verdict of the marketplace with good grace and returned to a salesman's job in Newport. His musical career was a paradox: his Sun records suggest a life lived constantly on the edge—nights spent playing gin mills, followed by drunken chases down dirt roads, firing off bottle rockets, and throwing up on the neighbor's car at dawn. In person, Burgess was, and is, an almost painfully shy and self-effacing family man. He's still prone to make the occasional comment hinting at more turbulent waters, but Burgess hasn't lived the life one

(Burgess/Showtime)

Sonny Burgess and the Pacers in one of their many incarnations

Johnny Ray Hubbard and Jack Nance on stage with Sonny Burgess
(Burgess/Showtime)

(Burgess/Showtime)

might anticipate from his lyrics: "Out to the dance hall, cut a little rug / We're runnin' like wildfire and hittin' that jug . . ."

Born near Newport on May 28, 1931, Albert "Sonny" Burgess grew up, like so many of his contemporaries, listening to the Grand Ole Opry and playing in a local country band. He started playing on a semiprofessional basis as front man for a group called the Moonlighters in 1954. After working as a support act for Elvis Presley in 1955, the Moonlighters edged closer to R&B. They auditioned at Sun, but Phillips wanted a fuller sound. Merging his band with another led by Jack Nance, Burgess assembled a new group, rechristened the Pacers, that would back him on most of his sessions at Sun.

On May 2, 1956, they drove to Memphis and auditioned at Sun. Impressed, Phillips cut their debut single that afternoon. "We Wanna Boogie" and "Red Headed Woman" stand among the rawest recordings released during the first flowering of rock 'n' roll. The lyrics were almost unintelligible and the accompaniment teetered on the edge of atonality, giving the record an atmosphere of total abandon. It sounded as though the studio floor should have been littered with liquor bottles, although Burgess maintains that they were stone-cold sober, even nervous. Despite being almost totally unmarketable according to established precepts, "We Wanna Boogie" reportedly sold over ninety thousand copies, and charted in some unlikely places—such as Boston.

Burgess believed that his second record, an original called "Ain't Got a Thing," would break through for him. Coming after the near chaos of "We Wanna Boogie," "Ain't Got a Thing" was surprisingly melodic and featured a nicely worked-up modulation during the break. The lyrics fell right into the tradition of anarchic, sharp-talking humor that was a part of R&B that Burgess loved:

I got a car ain't got no gas
I got a check but it won't cash
I got a woman ain't got no class.

Yet the record, released in January 1957, died on the vine. Burgess was disappointed, but there was worse in store. For his third single, Burgess revived the old jazz hokum novelty "My Bucket's Got a Hole in It" that Hank Williams had made his own in 1949. Burgess's record was further proof that he was among the closest white approximations of black R&B on the market—and so, in a swift kick of irony, he suffered the fate of the R&B singer: he was covered by a white pop act, Ricky Nelson. Burgess didn't even have the consolation of having written the song, thereby seeing some composer royalties from Nelson's version.

By this point, the Pacers were disillusioned. The unmarried members, drummer Russ Smith and guitarist Joe Lewis, were let go; Jack Nance left in 1958. Smith joined Jerry Lee Lewis's touring combo, while Lewis and Nance joined Conway Twitty's band (Nance would later co-write "It's Only Make Believe" with Twitty). Burgess tried to secure a record deal on the West Coast without success, and returned to cut one last single for Phillips International before joining Nance and Lewis in Twitty's road band. By the late '60s, Burgess had come to the conclusion that he would never be able to sustain a living from the music business, and he started another career as a salesman.

The recordings Burgess has made during the thirty years since he left Sun have never captured the magic that he sparked there. He often sounds anonymous and lukewarm—two qualities that never come to mind when listening to his Sun output. Phillips knew how to capture the booming and assertive quality of Burgess's vocals, and his years recording the blues gave him a feel for the dirty tone of Burgess's guitar and the Pacers' thunderous bottom end.

Tape Is Cheap

As Sam Phillips told Malcolm Yelvington's guitarist in 1953, he was willing to listen to anybody who walked in off the street—for a few years, at least. He discovered Elvis Presley, Carl Perkins, Johnny Cash, and Jerry Lee Lewis that way. All that was required was to be in the right place, which Phillips evidently was.

Some of those who came to the little storefront studio were invited back to cut a session. They were usually backed by the nucleus of the Riley band, unless they had their own musicians. Some, such as Ed Bruce and Dickey Lee, saw a release or two before going on to carve out a career elsewhere. Others, like Conway Twitty, tried hard to secure a Sun contract, but fell short. Very few had ever recorded before; some would never record again.

"Sam was totally involved in what he was doing," recalls Edwin Howard, who worked across the street at the Memphis *Press Scimitar*. "He was very enthusiastic. He played that control board like a musical instrument and talked a lot back and forth between the control room and the studio. He'd do a take, talk about it, do another, talk about it. Over and over and over." All the while the tape was rolling. "I remember Sam telling me," says Roland Janes, "that nothing was cheaper than tape."

By 1957 Phillips had begun to delegate the task of checking out tapes and aspirants to Bill Justis and Jack Clement. In the two years that followed, Sun's recorded output would increasingly bear their stamp. Unlike Sam Phillips, they were practicing musicians, and their tastes were more sophisticated than his. Yet they sometimes recognized a raw talent for what it was worth, as Jack Clement proved one afternoon toward the end of 1956, when he was asked to audition a young man who had just arrived from Ferriday, Louisiana.

Recommended Listening

A selection of the lesser-known Sun artists, including Ray Harris, Hayden Thompson, Billy Riley, and Warren Smith, can be found on *Sun Rockabilly: The Classic Recordings* (Rounder [USA] CD/SS 37).

Malcolm Yelvington's Sun recordings can be found on *The Sun Country Box* (Bear Family [Germany] BFX 15211).

Billy Riley's recordings for Sun and Rita are available on *The Classic Recordings* (Bear Family [Germany] BCD 15444).

Hayden Thompson's Sun sessions together with those he recorded for Roland Janes are on *Fairlane Rock* (Bear Family [Germany] BFX 15263).

Warren Smith's Sun recordings are issued complete on *The Classic Sun Recordings* (Bear Family [Germany] BCD 15514).

A selection of Sonny Burgess's Sun recordings is on *We Wanna Boogie* (Rounder [USA] CD/SS 36). They are issued complete on *The Classic Sun Recordings* (Bear Family [Germany] BCD 15525).

JERRY LEE LEWIS: THE FERRIDAY WILD MAN

When musicians sit around and trade their stories of wildness, onstage and off, the conversation almost inevitably turns to Jerry Lee Lewis. In a profession founded on excess, Lewis has made his name as one of the most excessive. Tortured by an unfathomable religion and driven by an ego as big as all outdoors, he has built a legend around himself that eclipses mortal bounds. He is the self-created Killer, defying God to come and reclaim him with his feats of debauchery, defying the law and the Internal Revenue Service to take him alive, and defying every singer who fancies himself a showman to follow Jerry Lee Lewis on stage.

The legend of Jerry Lee Lewis had its humble beginnings when the young singer, barely in his twenties, stood at the door of Sun Records in November 1956, waiting for a chance to sit at the tired studio spinet and ply his wares—a chance conspicuously denied him at other studios. Sam C. Phillips would later look into the singer's eyes and see a craziness that matched his own. More than that, Phillips saw an artist who could do all the things that *he* would have done if he could have sung and played. It's difficult not to believe that Sam Phillips and Jerry Lee Lewis were destined to come together, and together they defined all that is best in rock 'n' roll.

Lewis's musical reputation rests on the strength of his Sun recordings. The Top 20 hits were only four in number; few legends in popular music have been grounded in such low gross sales. Lewis is prone to brag about the sales of "Whole Lotta Shakin' Going On," but the fact remains that not merely one but two versions of "The Banana Boat Song," together with some thirty or forty other records, outsold "Whole Lotta Shakin' " in 1957. And by the middle of the following year Jerry Lee Lewis's career in the Top 20 was over. All of which goes to show that even in popular music chart placings aren't everything. God-Given Talent, as Jerry Lee Lewis will be the first to tell you, counts for something.

It was not until the 1970s and '80s that the full picture of what Lewis recorded at Sun became clear. The rejected masters and outtakes, unearthed from Shelby Singleton's basement, revealed a wonderfully consistent body of work, every

"I got the Devil in me . . . "

take minted afresh. Even the session chatter and jive between songs was entertaining. In terms of capturing the sheer joy of performing, nothing can match Jerry Lee Lewis's recordings at Sun.

Born Ferriday, Louisiana, 1935

When Jerry Lee Lewis entered Sun Records for the first time, he was twenty-one years old. He was barely educated, twice married, once jailed, and good for nothing much other than pounding the piano—which he had been doing every day for eleven years.

The subject of Jerry Lee's musical influences has been raised countless times, and continues to be because nobody can come up with a very satisfying answer—least of all the man himself, who tends to dismiss such questions by declaring he never had any. Students of the music have suggested to Jerry that he might have been influenced by artists as diverse as country boogie pianist Merrill Moore ("never heard of him, son"), or black boogie-woogie pianist Cecil Gant ("Cecil who?"). One of the few names to elicit a glimmer of recognition is Moon Mullican, the self-proclaimed King of the Hillbilly Piano Players, but Mullican probably did no more than reaffirm Lewis's conviction that the piano had a place in country music. Mullican's music was marked by restraint—never, after all, a hallmark of Lewis's style.

Lewis's cousin, Carl McVoy, was probably his most direct early influence. McVoy's mother, Lewis's mother, and Jimmy Swaggart's mother were sisters; McVoy was older than Jerry Lee and had been to New York with his father, who ran a ministry there for a few years. He learned the primitive joys of boogie-woogie in New York and returned to Pine Bluff, Arkansas, to work in construction. One summer, Jerry Lee Lewis came to stay. "He worried the hell out of me," recalled McVoy, "wanting me to show him things on the piano. I think I was instrumental in the way his style developed, because I got attention when I played. I rolled my hands and put on a damn show. When Jerry went back to Ferriday, he played everything I knew."

And then there was Haney's Big House, a black juke joint outside Ferriday. "Me and Jimmy Lee Swaggart used to slip in there, hide behind the bar, and listen to B. B. King when he wasn't but eighteen years old," Lewis recounted to Dave Booth. "That place was full of colored folks. They'd been picking cotton all day, they had a twenty-five-cent pint of wine in their back pocket, and they was gettin' with it!" Jerry Lee Lewis and Jimmy Lee Swaggart were regular, though unwelcome, guests at Haney's, owned by their uncle Lee Calhoun. Lewis and Swaggart were later seen as opposite sides of a disordered personality—until it was revealed in February 1988 that Swaggart had been consorting with prostitutes and had, as he termed it, "a problem" with pornography. The public defrocking and humiliation that followed revealed how close, in fact, they were.

In truth, the influences close to home, like Carl McVoy and the roadhouse R&B bands who played at Haney's, were probably more important in the formation of Lewis's style than artists on the radio. Yet of the artists whom Jerry heard on the radio, he has always singled out Hank Williams, Jimmie Rodgers, and Al Jolson as "stylists"—by which he means that they, like him, could take any song and mold it into an expression of their own personality.

Later, as his legend and ego grew, Jerry Lee would become more comfortable in making the connection: "Al Jolson," he would declare, "is Number One. Jimmie Rodgers is Number Two. Number Three is Hank Williams. And Number Four is Jerry Lee Lewis." And the one who held the greatest sway over Jerry Lee during his early years must have been Hank Williams. Every Saturday night during the late '40s and early '50s, Williams sang his bleak songs of misogyny and despair on the Louisiana Hayride and the Grand Ole Opry. He sang with the terrifying intensity of one who is staring the Angel of Death full in the face. Jerry has performed Williams' material throughout his career, and it usually elicits the best from him because he knows that he is up against some stiff competition in Williams himself.

Jerry Lee's first public performance was at the Ferriday Ford dealership in June 1949. He sang "Drinkin' Wine Spo-Dee-O-Dee," a song he must have picked up at Haney's, and the sweet rapture of the applause that followed set Jerry on his personal course—initially across the river to Natchez, Mississippi, and then to Shreveport, Louisiana, to audition for a Hayride package show that was to be headlined by Slim Whitman. Jerry was turned down by the Hayride, but before he left he was invited to cut an acetate in the KWKH studios. He recorded "If I Ever Needed You" and Hank Snow's hit of the day "I Don't Hurt Any More," and returned to Ferriday in Aunt Stella's car clutching the disc.

Jerry's first acetate reveals that his musical personality was already nearly complete, though his performing skills lacked the edge that later made him truly distinctive. His vocals aren't as strong, or as immediately identifiable, as they would become; the piano playing is a little mawkish and florid, as it would often tend to be on slow numbers. But the Lewis left hand was rock solid. Like Presley's first acetate, it can be invested with as much—or as little—significance as you like. It can be seen as a portent of future greatness, or merely a confirmation of the Hayride's judgment. "I believe," says Lewis, leaning toward the former, "if I heard it today, I'd declare that boy had talent."

The audition at KWKH probably took place in 1954. In 1955 Lewis went to Nashville and made the rounds of the record companies, most of which advised him to learn the guitar. One person who gave him a job was Roy Hall, a pianist and raconteur who owned a Nashville after-hours drinking spot, the Musicians' Hideaway. After escaping a raid, Lewis went back to Ferriday and took up a steady gig across the river at a Natchez club called the Wagon Wheel. Among the souvenirs he brought from Nashville was a song that Roy Hall had sung (and, by Hall's account, co-written) called "Whole Lotta Shakin' Going On."

Lewis grew fond of Elvis Presley's early recordings, and at some point in 1956, after reading an article about Elvis in *Country Song Roundup*, he decided that his music might fall upon more receptive ears in Memphis. He and his father, Elmo Lewis, sold thirteen dozen eggs and drove north to Memphis, using the money they'd raised to book themselves into a hotel with, as Lewis remembers clearly, running water. Sam Phillips was out of town and Jack Clement was in the control room. "I was working with Roy Orbison," recalls Clement, "and Sally Wilbourn brought Jerry Lee back to me. She said, 'I've got a fella here who says he plays piano like Chet Atkins.' I thought I'd better listen to that. He started playing things like 'Wildwood Flower,' and I believe he was playing piano with his right hand and drums with his left. I finally made a tape with him because he was different. We recorded 'Seasons of My Heart,' but I told him to forget about country because it wasn't happening at that time. I took his name and told him I'd let Sam hear the tape when he got back."

Crazy Arms

Phillips was in Florida, taking his first vacation in many years, and Clement decided to cut a complete demo session on Lewis while Phillips was gone. He called in the musicians he had met during his brief stint at Fernwood Records. "Jack phoned me," Roland Janes recounted to Rob Bowman and Ross Johnson, "and said, 'Man, I got this piano player, cat from down in Louisiana. He's pretty good. I'm gonna put a few things down on him. Do you want to come in and help us out?' I said, 'Yeah, sure.' He said, 'Man, could you drop by and get [drummer J. M.] Van Eaton? Think you can get him to come out?' I said, 'Yeah, I'm pretty sure I can.' He [Van Eaton] didn't drive at the time; that's how young he was.

"During the course of the session, I got up and went to the bathroom, and Jerry started doing 'Crazy Arms.' I don't think Jack was even in the control room. He was out in the studio and just left the machine running. Billy Riley had walked in about that time and he picked up my guitar. Right on the end of the song he hit a chord. . . . I came out of the washroom about halfway through the song and picked up an old upright bass and started playing it— and I don't play upright bass. Fortunately, I wasn't close to a microphone. On that song, there are technically only two instruments, drums and piano."

The date was November 14, 1956.

When Phillips returned, Clement played him the tape. "I don't know if I'd told Jack this," Phillips told Robert Palmer, "but I had been wanting to get off this guitar scene and show that it could be done with other instruments. They put that tape on and I said, 'Where in hell did this man come from?' He played that piano with abandon. A lot of people do that,

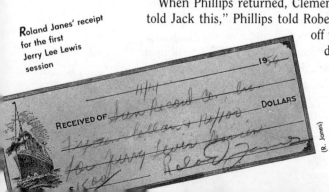

Roland Janes' receipt for the first Jerry Lee Lewis session

(R. Janes)

Jerry Lee playing back-up for Riley, late 1956

(R. Janes/Showtime)

but I could hear, between the stuff that he played and didn't play, that spiritual thing. I told Jack, 'Just get him in here as fast as you can.' "

As it happened, Clement didn't have to call Lewis. Before the end of the month Jerry Lee was back in the studio, bringing along his uncle J. W. Brown and one of the few songs Lewis ever took credit for writing. Taking Clement's advice to forget about country music, Lewis had reworked an old jug band tune—in which others heard shades of Irving Berlin—into a darkly obscure original boogie called "End of the Road."

Phillips decided to couple "End of the Road" with a song from Clement's demo session, "Crazy Arms." Originally recorded by Kenny Brown and Marilyn Kay for the small Pep label, "Crazy Arms" had been at or near the top of the country charts for months in the hands of Ray Price. Although it was late in the game, Phillips decided to test the waters with Jerry's version. It was released on December 1, 1956.

In the combination of Jerry Lee Lewis, Roland Janes, and J. M. Van Eaton, a magic formula had fallen into Sam Phillips' lap. Janes and Van Eaton happened to be friends of Clement, and Clement just happened to be running the board while Phillips was away; but Jerry couldn't have hoped for two more sympathetic accompanists. Janes, or "Roland boy" as Jerry would call out to him on sessions, read Jerry like a book, and knew better than to try and dominate his sessions; in fact, it was never in his nature to do so. J. M. Van Eaton quickly developed a rapport with Jerry comparable to that between Buddy

Holly and Jerry Allison. He had a telepathic ability to know in which direction Jerry was heading, as his subtle tempo changes and perfectly judged rolls and accents eloquently attest. Though J. W. Brown would travel with him as a bassist on the road, Jerry's solid left hand made a bass superfluous in the studio. With Roland and J.M., Jerry Lee had the core of his studio band that would bring him to the turn of the new decade.

"Crazy Arms" wasn't a hit, but it sold respectably. Lewis took work where he could find it. Jack Clement got him a gig in West Memphis substituting for the ever-unreliable Smokey Joe Baugh in the Snearly Ranch Boys; Bob Neal got him a pair of gigs in Alabama; Sam Phillips gave him a little work in the studio, backing Carl Perkins, Billy Riley, Johnny Cash, and some others. Roland Janes and Billy Riley took him out to some of the dance halls they played in Arkansas. J. W. Brown let him sleep on the couch.

On February 23, 1957, Lewis got his first crack at a big audience when he was booked onto the Big D Jamboree in Dallas. Two weeks later he was invited back. On March 31 he embarked on a tour that would last until May 5, supporting Johnny Cash, Carl Perkins, Onie Wheeler, and others who came and went as the troupe slowly made its way up into the frozen North. From the subarctic springtime in Sault St. Marie, Ontario, they trekked across the prairies, ending up in Billings, Montana.

According to Cash and Perkins, it was during the long haul that Lewis developed his stage act. Not content to remain chained to the piano stool, Lewis started clowning and expending some of the frightening energy he possessed.

Whose Barn? What Barn? Mah Barn!

Despite his touring commitments, Lewis was extraordinarily prolific in the studio during 1957 and early 1958. With Roland Janes and J. M. Van Eaton trying to follow him as best they could, Lewis would plunder his subconscious for songs, hoping to find something that would catch Phillips' ear. The variety was enormous: sentimental hillbilly weepers in waltz time, such as "I'm Throwing Rice"; contemporary country hits like "Singing the Blues"; R&B songs like "Sixty Minute Man" and "Honey Hush"; old pop favorites such as "Love Letters in the Sand"; folk songs like "Crawdad Hole"; a little gospel in the form of "Old Time Religion"; and even one giantly egotistical original, "Lewis Boogie."

Surprisingly, it is the music left in the outtake boxes that provides the definitive proof of Lewis's genius. In his hands, an impossibly wide variety of material is recast into a uniform body of work—what Robert Palmer terms an "innovative transformation of source materials." If he had written all of the songs, instead of just a few, it could not have been more consistent. Lewis was able to make almost any song into a supple vehicle for self-expression. For

In the studio with
Sam Phillips, 1957

(Escott)

that reason alone, he didn't need to write. If Sam Phillips thought a song had merit and wanted to hear it another way, Lewis could change the time signature, the tempo, the key, his phrasing—even the lyrics—at the drop of a hat.

Phillips' achievement was simply to turn on the tape machine and let his boy go, hoping to hear something he could sell from the reliquary of forgotten hits and misses in Jerry's head. One night in February 1957, Jerry recorded the song that Roy Hall had probably taught him, "Whole Lotta Shakin' Going On." Phillips initially had little faith in it, sensing that it was too suggestive. As usual, Jerry had a hard time recalling the original version and, running out of lyrics before the song was much over a minute long, he eased the band down and inserted a talking segment he had worked up on club dates, before storming back for a climactic finale, ending with a triumphant glissando.

Jerry would later record songs that were demonstrably lascivious ("Big Legged Woman" and "Meat Man," to name two). "Shakin' " has formidable energy behind it—and a suggestive tone in the talking segment—but it isn't explicitly obscene. In contrast, Bill Haley thought he had excised all the objectionable passages of "Shake, Rattle and Roll" when he rewrote out the lines, "You wear them dresses, the sun comes shining through / I can't believe all that mess belongs to you." With charming naïveté, he left the line "I'm like a one-eyed cat peeking in a seafood store"; when one considers that "seafood store" was black slang for female genitalia, it doesn't take too much imagination to figure out the identity of the one-eyed cat. Intent counts for a great deal, though, and Jerry imbued "Shakin' " with implicit sex. The record was banned in many cities.

On the single's release, Phillips had higher hopes for the other side, "It'll Be Me," a song that Jack Clement had concocted on the toilet while contemplating the possibility of reincarnation. Before recording, the line, "If you see

With Jud Phillips (Escott)

THERE'S GONNA BE A
"Whole Lot of Shakin Going On"
ON THE
STEVE ALLEN SHOW
NBC TELEVISION
Sunday Nite, July 28th
WHEN
JERRY LEE LEWIS
HITS
National Television For The First Time

See for yourself why we believe This Boy the freshest thing since Presley!

Is It A Date For A "Whole Lot Of Shakin"

a turd in your toilet bowl, baby, it'll be me and I'll be starin' at you" had become "If you find a lump in your sugar bowl"; sex may have been in, but scatology was definitely out.

Released in mid-March, the record wasn't fully promoted until Jerry returned from the tour in May, and by that time, Sam Phillips had ascertained that "Shakin' " was the side to watch. With Dewey Phillips behind it, "Shakin' " was sitting atop the local charts in Memphis, and on June 12 it entered the national country charts. Two weeks later, it entered the Hot 100 at number 70.

Sensing the explosive potential behind the singer and the song, Jud Phillips decided to take a bold chance to get Lewis off the hillbilly circuit and onto prime time. "I took him to New York," he recalled, "and presented him to Jules Green, who was managing Steve Allen, and Henry Frankel, who was talent coordinator for NBC. I took a real gamble to see whether a mass audience would accept this man. Our distributors made sure that every retail outlet in the United States had copies of 'Shakin' '; that represented a lot of merchandise that could have been returned."

On Sunday, July 28, 1957, Ferriday's pride and joy appeared on the Steve Allen Show, one slot behind Ed Sullivan in the ratings, Like Elvis's television appearances, Jerry's spots on the Allen show are landmarks in the history of rock 'n' roll. He pounded the piano, eyes fixed above with messianic intensity. When it came time to sing, he glared at the camera with a wild-eyed fury. "Whose barn? What barn? *Mah* barn!" At the top of the last chorus, he kicked the piano stool back across the stage, only to see Steve Allen send it flying back past him. Set in the context of the jugglers, ventriloquists, and singing-sister acts that were the staples of television variety in those days, Jerry's performance was nothing short of demonic.

Lewis's appearance on the Allen show gave "Shakin'" the shot in the arm it needed. Before the show, it had started to lose momentum, pegging out in the lower reaches of the Top 30. It eventually rose to the number 1 slot on the country and R&B charts, though it was excluded from the top position on the pop charts by Debbie Reynolds's "Tammy."

Nashville promoter Oscar Davis was brought in to do for Lewis what Colonel Parker had done for Presley. In fact, Davis had even worked as a front man for Parker. Jud Phillips was also a key figure in getting Lewis off the ground. He had rejoined Sun at some point in late 1956 or early 1957; after falling out with Sam again in 1958, he remained in Lewis's camp until the late '70s in an ill-defined role based primarily on the fact that he was one of the few able to match Lewis drink for drink. His flamboyance, cheery hustle, and willingness to pick up the bar tab and take care of the right people made him a born promoter, something his brother never was.

Jamboree

In August 1957, immediately after the appearance on the Steve Allen show, Jerry Lee Lewis was signed as a late addition to the movie *Jamboree*, which was to star Fats Domino and Carl Perkins. Originally, Alan Freed was to have hosted the movie, but he dropped out in a dispute over publishing royalties that almost certainly took longer to resolve than it took to script and film the movie. He was replaced by a clutch of DJs from across the country, and even a few from Canada and overseas to ensure the widest possible circulation. The basic premise was to cram as much music as possible into ninety minutes, and in that at least the producers succeeded.

Jerry had inherited a song from Perkins called "Great Balls of Fire." The idea had come from a black New York writer, Jack Hammer, who had sold the title to the movie's musical director, Otis Blackwell, in exchange for 50 percent of the composer credit. Lewis labored for two days on "Great Balls of Fire." Phillips knew how important it was to find a strong follow-up to a hit record: the complete failure of Carl Perkins' follow-ups to "Blue Suede Shoes" and the relative failure of Johnny Cash's immediate

*L*yric sheet pinned to the piano during the recording of "Great Balls of Fire"

GREAT BALLS OF FIRE

YOU SHAKE MY NERVES AND YOU RATTLE MY BRAIN
TOO MUCH LOVE DRIVES A MAN INSANE
YOU BROKE MY WILL
BUT WHAT A THRILL
GOODNESS GRACIOUS GREAT BALLS OF FIRE

I LAUGHED AT LOVE 'CAUSE I THOUGHT IT WAS FUNNY
YOU CAME ALONG AND MOVED ME HONEY
I CHANGED MY MIND
THIS LOVE IS FINE
GOODNESS GRACIOUS GREAT BALLS OF FIRE

KISS ME BABY MMMMM IT FEELS GOOD
HOLD ME BABY
I WANT TO LOVE YOU LIKE A LOVER SHOULD
YOU'RE FINE. SO KIND.
I WANT TO TELL THE WORLD THAT YOU'RE MINE, MINE, MINE

I CHEW MY NAILS AND I TWIDDLE MY THUMBS
I'M REAL NERVOUS CAUSE IT SURE IS FUN
OOH BABY
YOU DRIVE ME CRAZY
GOODNESS GRACIOUS GREAT BALLS OF FIRE

By: Otis Blackwell
Jack Hammer

(R. Janes)

follow-ups to "I Walk the Line" convinced Phillips that he must choose the material carefully and hone it to perfection. Despite Lewis's predilection for doing no more than two or three takes, the outtake boxes show that he spent days refining every nuance of "Great Balls of Fire."

It was essentially a duet between Jerry Lee Lewis and J. M. Van Eaton. The barely controlled slapback echo almost ranks as a third instrument, it gives such depth and presence to the recording. Phillips had obviously counseled against finesse during the solo, for Jerry starts with four glissandi before hammering away at the same note for six consecutive bars. When the finished product was released on November 15, 1957, there was nothing more that Phillips or Lewis could have done during the production to ensure its success.

Jamboree was also released in November, and the pay-off was swift and overwhelming. By December "Great Balls of Fire" was sitting atop most national charts. With Presley halfway into the Army, Lewis was just about the hottest phenomenon in pop music. During that same Christmas season, though so different from the one that had preceded it, Jerry also sowed the seeds of his own destruction. As the year drew to a close, he sneaked off to Hernando, Mississippi, with a marriage license in his glove compartment; he was on his way to marry his thirteen-year-old cousin, Myra Gale Brown, daughter of J. W. Brown. It was not even common knowledge to Jerry's family for a while, but within six months it would put a ten-year roadblock in his career.

Cut by the
Bitter and Poisoned Hail

1958 began with a full date book. There was to be an Alan Freed tour, a Phillip Morris tour, and a tour of Australia and even England later in the year. Before Jerry started on the promotional whirl, though, he was brought back into the studio to find a new hit. Each of the co-writers of "Great Balls of Fire" had submitted songs for consideration: Jack Hammer had sent down a Chuck Berry-esque celebration of teenage life called "Milkshake Mademoiselle" that substituted clichés for Berry's mordant wit, and Otis Blackwell had sent down another song based on an exclamation—"Breathless."

Although Jerry cut a few fine takes of Hammer's song, it was "Breathless" that was worked up for release. The song was a calculated shot at the pubescent market, with Jerry's breathy delivery of the title as its hook. Released in February, 1958, "Breathless" moved up the charts with the help of a ploy devised by Jud Phillips and Dick Clark. Beechnut chewing gum had sponsored the networking of Dick Clark's "Bandstand" show, but initial response was unfavorable until Jud and Dick Clark figured out how to kill two birds with one stone with a cross-promotion deal. Jerry sang "Breathless" on "The Dick Clark Show" (the Saturday equivalent of "Bandstand") on March 8, and Clark invited the kids to send in 50¢ together with five Beechnut chewing gum wrappers, to receive a "free" autographed copy of "Breathless."

The response was overwhelming. Sun's new promotion person, Barbara Barnes, ordered a rubber autograph stamp, and everyone in Sun's tiny

From "High School Confidential," 1958

operation—including session musicians and lesser artists—were put to work autographing and mailing thousands of copies of "Breathless." Clark received half of the proceeds from the sale of the thirty-eight thousand records shipped by Phillips during the promotion, which Phillips calculated at $2,746. Lewis was persuaded to forgo artist royalties, and Phillips decided to forgo publishing royalties on the flip side—Jerry's cavalier reworking of Roy Orbison's "Go! Go! Go!," now doing business as "Down the Line."

The Alan Freed tour commenced at Freed's old stomping ground, the Brooklyn Paramount Theater, on March 28. The tour swung out through Ohio, up into southern Ontario, then back through Michigan and Missouri before doubling back through the Midwest and Canada, finally playing the Newark Armory on May 10. By this point, Jerry had become the consummate showman, able to dominate a performance from a more or less seated position. His long hair tossed back and forth like a mane, he hammered the piano keys with hands like pistons. The ferocious energy was startling and sensational. We'll probably never know whether he actually set his piano afire after being told that Chuck Berry was topping the bill. Whether he did or not, the story is in character—which is probably why it has passed into Lewis mythology.

Before the Freed tour started, Jerry had filmed a spot in another abysmal movie. Albert Zugsmith, who would later give the world *The Teacher Was a Sexpot*, had created a quickie exploitation movie around the teenage drug problem. Called *High School Confidential*, it starred that old habituée of the casting couch, Mamie Van Doren. Part of the movie was rendered in "bop talk," the mere remembrance of which can make one shudder years after having

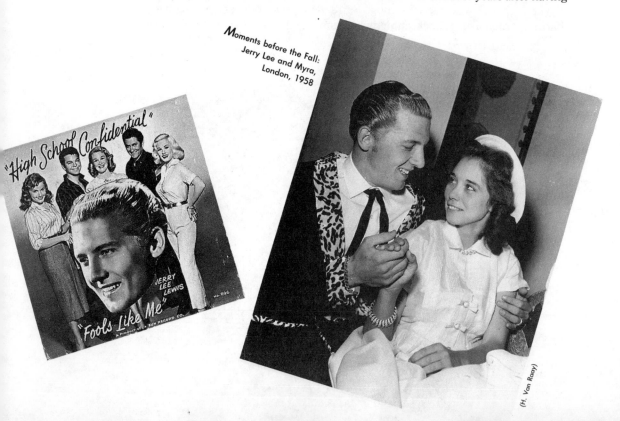

Moments before the Fall: Jerry Lee and Myra, London, 1958

(H. Van Rooy)

seen it. The sole redeeming element was the sight of Jerry Lee Lewis, his road drummer Russ Smith, and his uncle and father-in-law, J. W. Brown, hammering out the title song from the back of a flatbed truck.

Jerry had rushed back to Memphis to record the final version of the song during a break in the Freed tour. "High School Confidential" had been concocted by MGM artist Ron Hargrove, although Oscar Davis had cut Lewis in for 50 percent of the composer credit. A similar ploy was used on the flip side, when Jack Clement cut himself in for 50 percent of Pee Wee Maddux's "Fools Like Me." Rather than try a pop ballad, which Jerry knew he could not handle, Phillips and Clement preferred to offer a country ballad with a pop flavor. The country flip sides also maintained Jerry's credibility in the country market— a consideration that would stand him in good stead when, ten years later, he would begin to declare rather loudly that he had always been a country artist.

On May 23, two weeks after the riot-plagued Freed tour ended, Jerry Lee Lewis, his sister, Frankie, and his wife, Myra, arrived in England to begin a short promotional tour. The opening was in Edmonton, a suburb of London. A member of the press picked up a chance remark from one of Jerry's entourage about his wife being rather young. As Jerry and Myra went shopping the following day, members of the press who followed him became suspicious, and asked exactly *how* young. Jerry's answer, that Myra was fourteen (which was two months short of the truth) "and might look young and be young but is growed," provoked a howl of outrage from the British press. Hounding a rock 'n' roll singer who sported a red-lined black jacket trimmed with ocelot fur was welcome relief for Fleet Street journalists jaded by their diet of lying politicians and embezzling clergy. Within days Jerry, a new target for their big guns, was being greeted with howls of derision at his concerts.

An investigation was launched to determine how Lewis and his underage bride came to be allowed into the country. It was found that the immigration officer had shown a degree of compassion that was otherwise absent from Lewis's treatment in England. It "seemed to be an unusually young age for a married woman," said the report of the immigration officer, "but since both parties came from the southeastern part of the United States, where the legal age for marriage is lower than in other parts of the world, no action on my part seemed to be called for."

The promoter, J. Arthur Rank, took Jerry off the tour and replaced him with a local teenager, Terry Wayne, too young to have committed any indiscretions. The scandal even raised the collective eyebrow of the British House of Commons. Sir Frank Medlicott asked if the Home Secretary were not aware that "we have more than enough rock 'n' roll entertainers of our own without importing them from overseas." Home Secretary Iain Macleod replied that it was indeed a "thoroughly unpleasant case which had been ended by . . . the disappearance of the man."

Scanning the morning papers as he left England under a cloud, Jerry remarked, "Who is this DeGaulle? He seems to have gone over bigger'n us."

The Dark Ages

Jerry and his entourage had expected to arrive back in the United States to find that the disclosure of Myra's age—and the more recent news that Jerry's divorce from his previous wife had not been finalized when he married Myra —would have no effect on his burgeoning career.

They were wrong.

The first to disown Lewis was Dick Clark, who almost tripped over himself in his hasty cancellation of Jerry's bookings. Alan Freed defended Lewis, saying that jazz musicians and the Hollywood crowd were far worse. "Jerry's a country boy," added Freed, "and Tennessee boys get married quite young." It was courageous of Freed to defend Lewis, although his defense missed the point —it wasn't *Jerry's* age that shocked people. Elvis Presley, who within a few years would be cohabiting with an underage woman himself, offered a limp-wristed defense, saying only that "if he loves her, I guess it's all right."

By the middle of June, Jerry Lee had been blacklisted from the newly emerging Top 40 format. Without exposure, his records went back from the stores to the distributors, and from the distributors back to Sun. Sam Phillips was understandably dismayed. "It was a stupid damn thing. I think Jerry's innocence back then, and his trying to be open and friendly and engaging with the press, backfired. They scalped him. It turned out to be a very ghastly and deadly thing. So many people wanted to point a finger of scorn at rockers and say, 'We told you so; rockers are no good.' "

Trying desperately to save the situation, Sun adopted two tactics. The first was to satirize the issue with a novelty record concocted by Jack Clement. Titled "The Return of Jerry Lee," it used clips from Jerry's records interspersed with questions, in the manner of Buchanan and Goodman's "Flying Saucer" records. For example, to the reporter's question, "What did Queen Elizabeth say about you?" Jerry called out "Goodness gracious, great balls of fire!" That alone ensured that the record would not be released in England. At the same time, Sam Phillips and his press officer, Barbara Barnes, were composing a fully penitent and pious letter, published later in the month in the trade papers. "I sincerely want to be worthy of the decent admiration of all the people who admired what talent (if any) I had," said the letter, in perhaps the most uncharacteristic utterance ever to have Jerry Lee Lewis's name appended to it.

Oscar Davis made matters worse by booking Jerry into the Café de Paris in New York as a belated and futile stab at respectability. Almost nobody showed up, and the booking was canceled by mutual agreement after two nights. Jerry returned to Memphis to lick his wounds. His first album was shipped at the height of the storm, together with three EPs drawn from it; but Phillips held off releasing another single for two months in the hope that the furor would die away.

A new arrival at Sun, Charlie Rich, had been promised before the scandal

BREAK-UP

Billboard
Pop Spotlight Winner
C&W Spotlight

Cash Box
Pop Disk of the Week
C&W Bullseye

by
JERRY LEE LEWIS

b/w I'll Make It All Up to You

SUN 303

SUN RECORD CO.   SUN   MEMPHIS

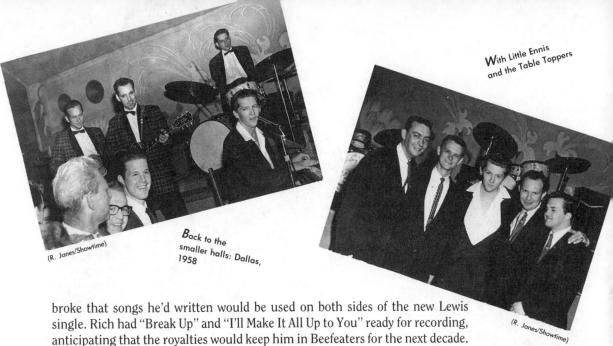

With Little Ennis
and the Table Toppers

(R. Janes/Showtime)

*B*ack to the smaller halls: Dallas, 1958

(R. Janes/Showtime)

broke that songs he'd written would be used on both sides of the new Lewis single. Rich had "Break Up" and "I'll Make It All Up to You" ready for recording, anticipating that the royalties would keep him in Beefeaters for the next decade. But it was not to be: the single climbed uncertainly up to number 50, then died quickly away. The news was doubly bad for Phillips, since Johnny Cash, his other major artist, had quit the company just as the storm broke. Jud Phillips also left Sun to start Judd Records in August 1958, although he took over Lewis's management from Oscar Davis early in 1959.

The effect of the scandal on Lewis's record sales was devastating. The virtual airplay blackout ensured that records already out in the marketplace would come back by the truckload, and that new ones would be hard to move. After "Break Up" fell stillborn from the presses, Jud Phillips tried to spark some action on the next single, a revival of Moon Mullican's "I'll Sail My Ship Alone," by offering the first 100,000 at the royalty-free price of 16¢, but there were few takers.

Jerry's personal appearances were still successful, although without the hit records he could not command his accustomed fees. As Jerry himself said later, "From $10,000 a night to $250 a night is a hell of a disappointment." He retreated back to the South, where his personal appearances were still riotously successful. A report of a show in Sheffield, Alabama, at the end of June 1958 noted that the hall was full, with 450 turned away: "There was a crowd as if the President was down to re-dedicate Muscle Shoals," said reporter Henry Mitchell. "Lewis began sedately at the piano, needing only a brace of candles to pass himself off as Liberace, but this calm rapidly vanished. His feet were the first sign, whisking back and forth like runaway pendulums. Soon they were on the keyboard, then on the music rack, and all the while a great noise came from the piano as his hands pounded with the tirelessness of an electric switch. By this point, Lewis could have kicked old ladies without changing the applause in the slightest. It is my considered opinion that Lewis has as strong an attraction for the leaders of tomorrow as ever."

Hot on the
comeback trail,
June 1959

(R. Janes/Showtime)

Roland Janes says that Lewis never showed that he had been hurt by the scandal. "He's a very deep person," said Janes, who had come to know Lewis from days and nights spent together on the road. "He could be hurting and never let it show. I don't think he ever quite understood why it happened. He's such an honest person, and he didn't think he'd done anything that was unacceptable to anyone. He didn't think the public would be concerned about what he did if it didn't relate to his music, which was a total miscalculation on his part. The truth is that you've got the world, and you've got Jerry Lee Lewis. He'll do things his way regardless of what anyone thinks. He felt betrayed, though, and he had every right to, but he held his head up and didn't cry."

Janes stayed on the road with Lewis until 1959. "I think things were starting to look up for Jerry when I left—certainly in terms of bookings. However, Billy Riley and I [had] decided to start our own record label, and I'd just got married. I wanted to do something in music other than work on the road. It was very painful to leave Jerry, though, because I loved him like a brother."

Janes continued to play with Lewis in the studio, as they struggled to find something that would tempt programmers to end their blacklist. But Jerry rarely wrote his own material, and music publishers were no longer sending him their hottest new prospects. This forced Jerry back to his roots; there was a heavier concentration of revamped older material in the years that followed his downfall.

Sun's new promotion manager, Cecil Scaife, tried to talk Lewis into adopting a new image. Scaife's account of the conversation shows how marginally Lewis grasped any concepts other than those he had already developed on his own.

"At that time," recalls Scaife, "Jerry had his hair peroxided blond and it was extraordinarily long. That, and his thirteen-year-old bride, was the image that the cartoonists caricatured. She would be holding a teddy bear in her hand.

"I had a very serious talk with Jerry about his image. We went to the restaurant next door to the studio and sat down in a booth. Jerry had one of his pickers with him. He always had someone with him. You could rarely get him one-on-one. I told him what I thought we should do, in as much detail as I thought he could absorb in one sitting. I wanted to get him out of typical rock 'n' roll regalia. Ivy League was in. I wanted him to get a crewcut. I wanted to hold a press conference where Jerry would announce that he was somewhat remorseful. He would take on an adult image.

"We discussed it for over an hour. Jerry was very polite and listened. He would nod every once in a while, but he kept looking at his watch. Finally, he shook it like it wasn't working and he looked at his buddy across the table and said, 'What time is it?' The guy said, 'It's five before one.' Jerry said, 'Oh! The double feature at the Strand starts in five minutes. It's *Return of the Werewolf* and *The Bride of Frankenstein Meets Godzilla*. Then he jumped up and left the table. That was the last time we discussed Jerry's image."

Scaife and Phillips came up with the idea of releasing a pseudonymous instrumental by Jerry under the name "The Hawk," on Sun's sister label, Phillips International. But the result, a half-hearted version of the big-band standard "In the Mood," another rendition of which by Ernie Freeman was then in the charts, was as commercially stillborn as Lewis's other singles released in 1959 and 1960. As if he hadn't enough problems, he was also involved in a dispute with the American Federation of Musicians, which barred him from playing in the United States until he paid his union dues. Jerry sidestepped the ban by taking up residence at the Coq d'Or club in Toronto in January 1961 until his attorney engineered a settlement of the ten-thousand-dollar debt, allowing him once again to entertain whatever fellow Americans were willing to hear him.

On February 9, 1961, Lewis breezed into Sam Phillips' new studio in Nashville and laid down its inaugural session. The last song recorded that night was a revival of the 1959 Ray Charles classic "What'd I Say." Phillips had such confidence in it that he released it three weeks after the session. *Billboard* said, "Lewis's pumping piano work is tops and vocal matches it. This can go." And it did.

On April 3 Jerry Lee Lewis re-entered the Hot 100 for the first time in three years. By the middle of May, "What'd I Say" had reached number 30, where it pegged out. It wasn't 1958 and "Great Balls of Fire" all over again, but the response was strong enough that a feeling of new life came over Sun's approach to Jerry Lee Lewis. In the next few years, Jerry's records took on a soulful cast. It may be that they would have anyway, as Jerry's own ear had led him to Ray Charles in the first place, but the list of releases Sam Phillips put out

on Jerry in the months that followed showed just how hard he was working to color his boy as an R&B–based artist. The follow-ups included a gesture toward the Twist craze, "I've Been Twistin' " (actually a revamped version of Junior Parker's 1953 Sun hit "Feelin' Good"); an early cover of Barrett Strong's "Money," a song the Beatles would take a few years later; and a version of Chuck Berry's "Sweet Little Sixteen" that actually grazed the Hot 100—the last record on the original Sun label to do so.

Phillips even shipped another album, *Jerry Lee's Greatest*, in the wake of "What'd I Say," but the absence of new material—few of the songs were original, and some had been recorded as far back as 1957—made the whole project feel a little uneven. As chart success fleeted from his grasp again, Jerry began to look toward the expiration of his Sun contract and the prospect of an aggressive new approach to his recording career.

Can't Seem to Say Goodbye

In May 1962—almost four years to the day since he had been chased out— Jerry made a triumphant return to England. In April 1963 he came back again. The 1962 tour had been a financial disaster, partly because of the uncertainty over Lewis's reception and partly because some of the fees had been garnisheed by the Rank Organisation, recouping their front money from 1958. But the '63 tour and all subsequent tours were relative goldmines. Lewis's tours of Europe in the '60s became an annual rite of faith renewal for the diehard lovers of vintage music. They may well have been important to Lewis as well in the years before 1968, when the applause at home was faint.

Lewis's contract was due to expire on September 6, 1963. In April Lewis allied himself with a Memphis businessman, Frank Casone; determined to sign Lewis with another company, Casone wanted to translate Jerry's success on the road into record sales, something that Sun, with their diminishing commitment to the business, seemed unable to do.

As Jerry's termination date drew near, Casone opened negotiations with Mercury, Liberty, Columbia, and RCA. Phillips, sensing the inevitable, recorded sessions with Jerry Lee's sister, Linda Gail, and even his father in an attempt to keep Jerry within the fold. He even planned a third album, which, like Linda Gail's single, was not released after the news broke that Jerry planned to sign with Mercury.

On August 28, 1963, Jerry Lee Lewis went into the Sun studio for the last time as a contracted artist. Arranger Vinnie Trauth had contracted a string section and vocal group to back Jerry and his band. In honor of the occasion, Roland Janes forsook the producer's chair at his own studio, and became a backing musician once more. Scotty Moore led the pickers on the studio floor. Together, they recorded four songs: "Carry Me Back to Old Virginia," "Invitation to Your Party," "I Can't Seem to Say Goodbye," and "One Minute Past Eternity."

"Carry Me Back to Old Virginia," a minstrel song that had originally contained such endearing lines as "dat's where de darkey's heart am longed to go," was chosen as his last single on the old Sun label; it was released two years later, in March 1965. The full significance of that final session, and the other songs recorded that day, would not become apparent for another six years.

In July 1969 Shelby Singleton, who as a Mercury employee in 1963 had taken the initiative to sign Jerry away from Sun, purchased the Sun catalog from Phillips. A year before, Lewis had just begun a winning streak in the country market that would last well into the next decade. When Singleton listened to the tapes he had purchased from Sun, he must have thought it was his birthday: those three unreleased songs from that final session were a blueprint for Jerry's country success on Mercury. Singleton had "Invitation to Your Party" on the market before the ink was dry on his deal with Phillips. It eventually rose to the number 6 slot on the country charts.

The End of the Road

It is not for his final Sun session that Jerry Lee Lewis will be judged, however. His earlier sides, especially those made between 1956 and 1960, stand as one of the most impressive bodies of recordings to emerge from that turbulent era—maybe *the* most impressive.

The simple truth is that Lewis could never have made those recordings for a major label. Phillips' willingness to keep the tape running while Lewis plundered his memory was crucial to Jerry's development as an artist and performer. "Whole Lotta Shakin' " was the product of one of those rambling sessions, as were dozens of other half-remembered and reconstructed tunes from his vast repertoire. Other studios would schedule a standard three-hour session and have four songs ready to record, but Phillips knew his artist: "Jerry is an informal person," he has said, "and the conditions had to be right. You had to have a good song, of course, but atmosphere is nearly everything else. Jerry had to know that the people around him, the people responsible for the session, understood him. He had such spontaneity. With great artists, almost 50 percent of something good they might do happens because of an almost instant reaction to what is taking place around them."

Lewis's early recordings at Sun also exemplified the virtue of simplicity. No one else would have dared risk recording Lewis with such a spartan backing, but from the records it's clear that any additional instruments would have been superfluous. As Hank Davis has written, Phillips' technique in recording Lewis was crucial: "The fullness is produced by essentially two instruments— piano and drums. Part of the magic of the opening two bars of 'Whole Lotta Shakin'' is the reverb on Jerry Lee's piano. . . . The driving, pounding sound of that record came from miking the piano just right and feeding the sound back upon itself at just the right rate to fatten it up. By the time the drums

(Escott)

Left to right:
Sam, Jerry Lee, and
Jerry Wexler and Ahmet Ertegun
of Atlantic Records

(Escott)

join in and Jerry Lee begins to sing, the record is throbbing with its own hypnotic life."

Lewis was also a born entertainer. He was plying his trade in the studio to an audience of three or four, but the enthusiasm communicated itself vividly on record. "Even when we were going over material," recalls Cecil Scaife, "Jerry would play to you as if you were an audience of ten thousand people. He would sit there and entertain you." Roland Janes echoes those thoughts: "People are always trying to compare musicians, but I can't find anyone to compare with Jerry. What you hear him doing on records is only a small percentage of what he's capable of doing. I don't think even he knows how great he is. He can take a solo with either hand, and sing a song five different ways, every one of them great. I remember when we worked the package shows—Jerry would sit backstage after the show at the piano and all the big stars would gather around him and watch. Chuck Berry, Buddy Holly, the Everly Brothers, and so on. Jerry would be leading the chorus and everyone would be having a ball."

Recommended Listening

The most comprehensive anthology of Lewis's career on Sun is *Jerry Lee Lewis: Classic, 1956–1963*, 8 CDs and booklet (Bear Family [Germany] BCD 15420).

Rhino (USA) has reissued the two original Sun albums as CDs: *Jerry Lee Lewis* (R21K 70656) and *Greatest* (R21K 70657), as well as an album of rarities, *Rare Tracks* (R21S 70899), and an album of *18 Original Sun Golden Hits* (R21S 70255).

Two additional LPs of Sun recordings include rare titles: *Keep Your Hands Off of It!* (Zu-Zazz [UK] Z 2003) and *Don't Drop It* (Zu-Zazz [UK] Z 2004).

Image cultivation:
Charlie Rich, 1960

the webbs

(The Webbs/Escott)

Chapter Twelve

LONELIER WEEKENDS: CHARLIE RICH AND CARL MANN

The last three hits of any substance on Sun Records were by Jerry Lee Lewis, Carl Mann, and Charlie Rich. Lewis's revival of "What'd I Say" gave him a fleeting reprise of the acclaim he had won and lost so quickly. Carl Mann's "Mona Lisa" was a surprise left-field hit from an artist in whom Sam Phillips had little faith. And Charlie Rich's first hit, "Lonely Weekends," was the product of a man torn in half a dozen musical directions, but it was nonetheless one of the late-blooming classics of the era.

Mona Lisa

Just southwest of Huntingdon, Tennessee, an unmarked dirt road leads to a logging camp. Carl Mann was born on that road, and returned there after a bizarre odyssey that brought him near the top of the charts and to the ocean playgrounds of the rich and famous. He was playing local radio stations when he was thirteen and had his first hit when he was sixteen, but by the time he was nineteen the party had ended and Mann had taken the bottle for a friend.

Sun's promotion manager, Cecil Scaife, took the initiative to sign Mann: "We had invited this guy in from Jackson, but his car blew up on him, so we just had the backing group: Carl Mann, Eddie Bush, and W. S. Holland. Carl did a beat arrangement of 'Mona Lisa.' He was playing it on the piano and faking a lot of it. I turned the machine on and I remember thinking. 'This ol' boy has the potential of cutting a hit if we can get it right.'

"I couldn't wait for Sam to hear 'Mona Lisa,' but he wasn't interested in it. Weeks and months went by, and then Conway Twitty was on his way into town and called to see if I had any material in our publishing catalogs for him to record. He was coming off 'It's Only Make Believe,' and I had helped get that song off the ground because we had been old friends from Helena. I played Conway the arrangement of 'Mona Lisa' and he got excited. I said, 'You can borrow the arrangement if you put it out on an LP. I still have hopes of putting it out as a single.' Conway put it out on an LP and then MGM pulled an EP from the album and 'Mona Lisa' started getting a lot of play in the Midwest.

Carl Mann

"I took the charts to Sam and said, 'We're losing a hit,' but Sam said, 'We don't put out mediocre product.' There was a DJ convention coming up in Miami and I said, 'Sam, unless you tell me *not* to put out "Mona Lisa," I'm gonna put it out and do a promo number in Miami that everyone will remember.' So I put it out, and hired a model to stand in the hotel lobby with a sash saying 'Ask Me About "Mona Lisa,"' handing out promo copies. I was telling everyone that we had the original, even though Conway's version had come out first. It was Dick Biondi, who was a top-rated DJ in Buffalo, who broke the record for us. He laid on it till it started to cut loose."

Mann's revival of "Mona Lisa," a Nat King Cole hit from 1951, may not have had the visceral quality that Phillips cherished, but it benefits from an unusual contrast. Mann delivers his vocal straight as an arrow with good range and clear diction; against that vocal is juxtaposed the eccentric guitar of Eddie Bush. Many talented pickers had set up their amps in the old Sun studio and, in his way, Bush was as good as any of them. His fills and solos were harmonically and technically advanced, and he allied sheer technique with a brilliant musical imagination.

"Mona Lisa" took off, eventually peaking at number 25 on the *Billboard* charts. Whisked from Huntingdon into a promotional vortex, Mann was booked into New York, and then onto the 1959 Summer Dance Party tour. The Winter Dance Party earlier that year had claimed the lives of Buddy Holly, Ritchie Valens, and the Big Bopper. As Mann, Skip and Flip, Jo Ann Campbell, and the rest of the performers followed in the footsteps of the earlier tour, they took grim notice of Holly's autograph scratched onto changing room walls.

Phillips' delight was compounded by the outrage he encountered from the publisher of the song, who tried to deny Sun a mechanical license after they'd heard Mann's unorthodox rendition. Phillips had now been a thorn in the side of the industry—a role he relished—for almost a decade.

Celebrating the success of "Mona Lisa": Carl Mann with Sun promotional assistant Barbara Barnes, and Cecil Scaife, in the Sun studio, July 1959

Sticking true to the formula of rocking up a standard, Mann lighted upon another Nat King Cole hit, "Pretend," for a follow-up, but it pegged out halfway up the Hot 100. That should have served notice to Mann and Phillips that the formula had run its course; instead, "Pretend" was followed by "Some Enchanted Evening," "South of the Border," and "The Wayward Wind," each selling progressively fewer copies. Ironically, both Charlie Rich and Eddie Bush were contributing some strong material to Mann's repertoire (including "I'm Coming Home," which Elvis Presley later copied note-for-note), but their songs were relegated to B sides and album tracks. The combination of Mann and Bush might have had staying power, but their potential was foiled by Phillips' insistence upon revamping standards.

Carl Mann was only seventeen when his career began its downward slide, but that was hardly the worst of his problems: unable to handle the rigors of heavy touring, he had become an alcoholic. After his band broke up, Mann toured briefly with Carl Perkins, neither able to find that elusive second hit. Finally Mann returned whence he came, to Huntingdon; he kept his hand in, playing a few night spots, but they were a far cry from the venues he had worked during the summer of 1959 when the kids had stood and cheered for another encore of "Mona Lisa." His last Phillips International single, shipped in June 1962, coupled the strangely appropriate ode to illicit liquor "Mountain Dew" with yet another oldie, "When I Grow Too Old to Dream." It sold a shade over one thousand copies.

Mann was drafted in 1964 and sent to Germany for his tour of duty. After his return he tried to pick up the pieces of his recording career, and cut some sides for Monument Records; but by that point his alcoholism had rendered him unable to promote his career. He married in 1968 and started the painful process of weaning himself off the bottle. A liaison with ABC-Dot in 1970 produced five singles in the contemporary country mold, none of which was that second major hit.

"There's hardly a week goes by that I don't wish at some point that I'd stayed with it," said Mann in 1987. "I'd probably have done been gone though. I needed to change the way I was going with the booze, but it's hard to get off it when you're on the road." A more recent conversion to Christianity has further removed Mann from the desire to perform.

If Mann ever needed to reflect upon the value of home and security, the example of Eddie Bush, who continued to drink and drift, certainly offered food for thought. Bush was last seen in the early '80s in the record store that Shelby Singleton (owner of the Sun catalog since 1969) operated in Nashville. Fortified by the bottle, Bush announced to the patrons that he was the greatest guitarist who had ever come to Nashville. Those who took any notice probably thought that they were listening to a drunk living out a delusion. Don Powell, manning the store that day for Singleton, knew better; he had toured once with Mann and Bush, and knew that Bush really *was* one of the best. Powell's attempts at conversation about the old days faltered, as Bush tried to bum some cash.

No Headstone on My Grave:
The Enigma of Charlie Rich

Sam Phillips has always been eager to celebrate the artists he recorded at Sun, but rarely have his generous evaluations of their talent been so well justified as in the case of Charlie Rich. "I don't think I ever recorded anyone who was better as a singer, writer, and player than Charlie Rich," he has said, and indeed Rich's talent was unique among Sun artists. "It is all so effortless," Phillips marvels even today, "the way he moves from rock to country to blues to jazz."

Rich was the most musically eclectic of all the artists who recorded at Sun, a distinction that was both a blessing and a curse. In Rich, Phillips had an artist who could turn in a blues-drenched version of "Don't Put No Headstone on My Grave" in one breath, and in the next offer something as crassly commercial as "Popcorn Polly." He could bring a little joy to the drunks at the Sharecropper Club with his gin-soaked ballads, and yet be out on a package show the following week peddling "Lonely Weekends" to the teens and preteens. Sun never quite knew what to do with Rich; in the studio, Phillips let him play what he wanted, hoping to find something he could release when he listened to the playbacks the following day.

Rich was born in Forrest City, Arkansas, on December 14, 1934. His family soon moved to Crawfordsville and then Colt, and it was on a farm near Colt that Charlie Rich grew up. He will be the first to tell you that his family never had to scrape: "I've never lived in poverty except when I was very young during the Depression, and most country folks were poor then. From the age of seven things were all right." Rich's uncle Jack later became a key property developer in eastern Arkansas, and built many of the shopping malls and housing developments in West Memphis. Jack Rich also held substantial land holdings around Forrest City and was a major stockholder in the Bank of West Memphis. Hardly the family background of which blues singers are born—and a sharp contrast with Billy Riley, living with his family under an Army tent a few miles away.

With an early fascination for music, Rich learned some basic blues piano riffs from a black tenant farmer, C. J. Allen. At the same time, he learned rudimentary composition from his parents. Uncle Jack gave Rich money to enroll at Arkansas State College on a football scholarship, but an injury sent him off to the University of Arkansas as a music major. He quit after one semester because he failed the compulsory English course, and because he had no car to visit the girl who had entered his life.

Margaret Ann Greene, a year younger than Rich, would follow—and sometimes lead—him through his best songs and worst times. They had met one December day, when Margaret Ann's father asked permission to cut a Christmas tree from the Rich property. As they cut the tree, Charlie rode by on a horse, with a guitar on his back in Gene Autry style. They began dating, and soon resolved to stay together. After Rich quit school, he entered the Air Force.

(Escott)

Charlie Rich:
the first publicity
photo, 1957

While he was stationed in Enid, Oklahoma, he married Margaret Ann, on May 25, 1952. Uncle Jack had given them enough money for a honeymoon in Memphis. They stayed at the Peabody Hotel and spent their forty-five dollars in savings on records. If they had been married a year earlier, Sam Phillips might have been engineering the sound as Charlie and Margaret Ann danced under the stars that night in the Peabody's rooftop ballroom.

Rich and Margaret Ann lived well in Enid. They played in a little group on the weekends called the Velvetones, modeling themselves on the hipper-than-thou vocalese of Lambert, Hendricks, and Ross. With their ancillary income, they made more money than most officers. Despite the fact that some of Rich's most ardent admirers see his leanings toward supper club music as an aberration forced upon him by unsympathetic producers, there is every indication that it was a major component of his musical persona from the beginning.

Uncle Jack re-entered the picture after Rich returned to civilian life, lending him enough money to buy a five-hundred-acre farm near Forrest City. Rich grew cotton and soybeans. The first year was good, and Rich repaid much of Jack's loan. The second year was so-so, and it rained so heavily during the third year that Rich never even got his crops into the ground. All the while he was farming, Rich was heading over to Memphis on weekends to play music.

Margaret Ann placed their little Webcor tape deck next to Rich's piano, and they took some of his songs to Bill Justis, musical director at Sun Records. "I thought from the start he had a real good talent," remembered Justis. "The only problem was that he was an exceptional musician and wasn't entirely commercial. I recall taking him into the stockroom at Sun Records and giving him a whole bunch of [records that had been returned]. I told him to take them home and come back when he'd got that bad."

At first Rich reached too low in his attempt to write for the rock 'n' roll market; songs like "Rock 'n' Roll Party" and "Donna Lee" were unworthy of him or anyone else. But he soon found a good commercial groove, and Justis persuaded Phillips to place him on a draw against future earnings as a staff writer at Sun Records. He also played session piano, replacing the lately departed Jimmy Wilson. In 1958 he was given what he thought would be his big break: two of his tunes, "Break Up" and "I'll Make It All Up to You," were chosen as the two sides of the upcoming Jerry Lee Lewis single. But when Lewis fell from grace in England, Charlie Rich's vision of the big paycheck went out the window.

With the departure of Cash and the ruination of Jerry Lee Lewis, Rich finally began to think seriously about cutting his own record. He was happier playing session piano, writing songs, and playing at local clubs, but grim economic reality was staring him in the face. On August 17, 1958, two months after Lewis returned from England, Rich settled down to record his debut single. "Philadelphia Baby" was designed to catch the ear of Dick Clark, who networked American Bandstand out of Philadelphia. Sales must have been encouraging, for in February Rich was back in the studio to cut a follow-up.

In October 1959, just as Phillips was preparing to close the old Union Avenue studio, Rich went in with Roland Janes, saxophonist Martin Willis, and J. M. Van Eaton and recorded a tune he called "Lonely Weekends." Phillips gave the tape to Charles Underwood, who took it over to the new studio and overdubbed it for release with a chorus, some echo-laden rim shots, and more echo thrown onto the finished master for good luck. The resulting cut was issued in January 1960. Van Eaton's double-timed lick on the bass drum and Rich's assertive Presleyesque voice made the record irresistible.

"Lonely Weekends" became Charlie Rich's first hit, and he was swept out of the clubs and into the promotional whirlwind. "He could make a front man like me a little nervous," recalls Cecil Scaife. "Charlie was a good-looking boy, and on promotional trips people often mistook him for Elvis Presley. He had *that* look . . . but he was so shy. I remember on one trip to New York we were scheduled to be on the Dick Clark Show. Charlie was a nervous wreck, perspiring something awful. I said, 'Charlie, all you gotta do is sit there and lip-sync it. The mike's dead.' After he'd sung 'Lonely Weekends,' Dick Clark tried

Hardly the typical teen idol—Rich at home with Margaret Ann and the kids

(Escott)

(Escott)

*S*toking the
star-making machinery:
with Rodney Jones in
Chicago

to interview him and Charlie just clammed up. Dick would ask a question and
then have to answer it. I thought that would be the end of us on Dick Clark."

Rich was an unlikely teen idol—his hair streaked with premature gray, his
record collection heavy with jazz, his home shared with his wife and three
kids. Rich detested the traveling and the one-night stands: "I was traveling
quite a bit with all the pop stars of that time, but that only allowed me to sing
'Lonely Weekends' and maybe two other songs. I certainly wasn't progressing
anywhere, so I went back to the clubs and barrooms." In fact, the success of
"Lonely Weekends" brought the first serious strain to his marriage. Margaret
Ann left him, and, when she went to find him a few days later, he was holed
up in the YMCA, the floor strewn with empty gin bottles. With no money to
pay the bill, they sneaked out. The good times were obviously not all they were
cracked up to be.

Although Rich continued to record fine music at Sun, he seemed to have
expended his commercial potential on "Lonely Weekends." On several occasions
during his career, Rich has shot himself in the foot by choosing weak follow-
ups; "Gonna Be Waitin'," which followed "Lonely Weekends," was unexcep-
tional. The music that Rich made for Phillips was as multifaceted as his diverse
musical tastes. But the teenagers who had responded to the echoes of Elvis in
"Lonely Weekends" were unlikely to respond to the profoundly adult sentiments
of a record like "Sittin' and Thinkin'," which opened with the announcement,
"I got loaded last night on a bottle of gin . . ."

If there was a recording that embodied Rich's musical values, it
was surely "Who Will the Next Fool Be." It was not strictly a
pop, country, or R&B record, but it borrowed from all three
idioms. Using the piano as an extension of his vocal lines,
Rich molded a performance that was agonized and intense.
Many performers have tried to recapture the magic that
Rich drew from within himself on that February evening in
Nashville when he first recorded the song, but it stands as
a truly definitive performance. After the session, the
master was embalmed with a vocal chorus; when it
was finally stripped and the original cut reissued
twenty-five years later, an intensity that had been
partially hidden all that time was finally revealed.

(Escott)

Indeed, Rich was the consummate white blues artist, because he made so few conscious attempts at black vocal mannerisms. He sang the blues his way, and when he coarsened his voice for effect, it had a heightened emotional impact. That was demonstrated vividly on a demo of "Don't Put No Headstone on My Grave," a song that moved Sam Phillips to say, "Hell, even I could sing that song and make it a hit." Rich *shrieked* the first word of the title on his publishing demo; at other moments during the song he was moody, almost inaudible. The blues brought out Rich's mastery of vocal dynamics and tightrope tension.

The song became an underground classic, although never a hit—despite Phillips' obvious faith in it. The first commercial version was by Little Esther Phillips. Rich himself recorded an overblown version for Epic, but it was Jerry Lee Lewis who came closest to making a hit out of the song, cutting it at his London sessions in 1973. Jerry missed the point by a mile, singing "I *want* the world to know / Here lies the fool who loved you so," instead of "I *don't want* the world to know . . ." But it was all in keeping with his braggadocio style, as was his closing pronouncement: "I don't want a headstone on my grave . . . I want a monument . . ."

Sam Phillips signed Rich to one of his standard three-year contracts after the success of "Lonely Weekends." Rich acquired a new manager, Seymour Rosenberg, a Memphis attorney who also played a little jazz trumpet under the name of Sy Rose. Rosenberg was anxious to place Rich with a company that paid higher royalties and had a stronger commitment to the record business than Sun. When his contract came up for renewal in March 1963, Rosenberg signed Rich to the reactivated Groove division of RCA. Phillips filed a suit against Rich, claiming that the singer had verbally agreed to re-sign with Sun or give Phillips the chance to match any other offer he might secure. After a month of bickering, Phillips finally reconciled himself to the inevitable and let Rich depart.

Sam Phillips' contribution to the complexion of Rich's music had been to introduce him to the world of commercial rock 'n' roll and country music, which set the stage for his moment in the spotlight ten years later. "At first I didn't dig country," recalled Rich to *Fanfare* magazine in 1975. "As a matter of fact, we put it down because we wanted to be jazz pickers. I had to make a drastic change at Sun Records and I didn't really appreciate country music until I went there. Now I like to mix them up—put some jazz licks in country and some country licks into a heavy driving jazz piece."

Rich's career continued on its roller-coaster ride after he left Sun. The liaison with Groove initially produced a hit with "Big Boss Man," but ended two years later with Rich's career back in the doldrums. Rosenberg then placed Rich with the Smash division of Mercury for one year and another hit ("Mohair Sam") before moving on yet again to Hi Records. One year later Rich signed with the Epic division of CBS/Columbia under the tutelage of Billy Sherrill, who had engineered Rich's recordings for Phillips in Nashville between 1961 and 1962.

After a few minor hits, Rich finally hit paydirt with "Behind Closed Doors" in 1973. In many ways, Sherrill was the most astute A&R manager with whom Rich worked. He channeled the singer's talents into one direction instead of letting him ramble aimlessly, and placed him with a good promotion man who got him out of the nightclubs. Smooth, silky vocals had been a part of Rich's musical vocabulary since the earliest days; Sherrill's contribution was to emphasize them at the expense of all else. The results were artistically arid, but commercially successful; Rich's Epic recordings found the Holy Grail of Crossover that populates every country producer's dreams. Much was lost along the way, including Rich's piano, which was never heard on an Epic recording after "Behind Closed Doors."

But Charlie Rich found massive success no easier to handle than playing low-life bars for unresponsive drunks. Probably the worst period of his life was the fall of 1975, a time when the records and tour dates were bringing in five thousand dollars a day. In October, the steadfast Margaret Ann briefly filed for divorce; the following month, presenting the Country Music Association award for Entertainer of the Year, Rich set fire to the envelope that announced that John Denver had won. Many thought he was acting under the heavy burden of drink; a hasty press release attributed it to an allergic reaction to painkillers. Though some of Rich's admirers would rate this among his finest moments, what it ultimately suggested was how woefully out of place Charlie Rich was among the glitterati.

By the end of the '70s, Rich's records were back in the ninety-nine-cent bins, but his insurance was in the bank. Rosenberg's investments on Rich's behalf weren't beyond question, but the most prescient was in the Wendy's hamburger chain. Rich cashed in his chips and, as his musical fortunes waned, was able to retire with grace into a Memphis suburb. Only recently has he thought about a return to recording. One of his dream projects—and perhaps the one least likely to come to fruition—is a jazz album to be produced by Sam Phillips.

No one would want to deny Rich the $2 million he made in 1975, but it is unfortunate that he will go into the history books for performances that reveal so little of the man and his gifts. Whether Rich's Sun recordings are his best depends on the perspective that one brings to his work. In Sam Phillips, Rich found a producer who appreciated his talent and was willing to showcase it with only one eye on *Billboard*. Phillips was also willing to let Rich indulge his yearning to experiment. It was that latitude for experimentation that brought forth "Who Will the Next Fool Be" and "Don't Put No Headstone on My Grave"—which many regard as more enduring than his better-known hits.

Recommended Listening

A complete retrospective of Carl Mann's career can be found on *The Complete Carl Mann* (Bear Family [Germany] BCD 15274).

The undubbed version of Charlie Rich's "Who Will the Next Fool Be," together with the demo of "Don't Put No Headstone on My Grave," and other Sun-era recordings, are on *Don't Put No Headstone on My Grave*. (Zu-Zazz [UK] Z 2002).

INTO THE '60s

Although few could have perceived it at the time, July 1958 was a watershed in the history of Sun Records. Jerry Lee Lewis had returned from England with his career in tatters; Johnny Cash was just completing his divorce from the label. A few weeks later, Jud Phillips left to start his eponymous Judd label.

Despite the bad news, Sam Phillips pushed forward. Foremost in his mind was his concern over the recording conditions at 706 Union Avenue: his studio was creeping into obsolescence. The floor, while larger than many have supposed, was too small to accommodate the increasingly large groups Sun was recording. The control room was too small to install the crucial new multitrack recorders. And the office area, where Sam rambled around as always among other people's desks, was too cramped to house even his skeleton staff. By 1958 he knew he would have to take his recording operations into new quarters—even if his own, very good, instincts warned him against it.

Phillips also wanted to diversify into custom recording (hiring out studio time), and developing Phillips International into an album label with diverse brands of music. All of this, requiring more space, more personnel, and updated technology, was impossible at 706 Union Avenue.

639 Madison

In the summer of 1958 Phillips bought a property on Madison Avenue in Memphis, just a few city blocks from the old studio. At various points in its history, 639 Madison had housed a Midas Muffler shop and Hart's Bakery. Phillips gutted the interior and installed two modern recording studios on the ground floor. On the second floor he laid out the new A&R and promotion offices, and set aside a vault for tape storage. On the third floor, adjacent to the accounting and publishing offices, Phillips finally gave himself his own office—complete with jukebox and nearby wet bar, ensuring that he was surrounded by a few of his favorite things. The final touches were administered

639 Madison Avenue:
Before and after

Punching in a selection on the en-suite jukebox: Sam Phillips in his new office, 1960

(Escott)

by Decor by Denise, who favored early space age motifs: door handles were housed in miniature sputniks, and the offices soon took on the look of a late '50s Buick.

Although it had been in use, on and off, since January 1960, the new studio was launched in a promotional whirl on September 17. The complex was everything that 706 Union was not: spacious, state-of-the-art, and soulless.

Phillips added to his staff at the new location. By this point, Phillips had separated from his wife, Becky, and was living with Sally Wilbourn, who had joined Sun in late 1955. She moved with him as office manager, as did promotion person Barbara Barnes (who left later in 1960, sensing the game was over, to pursue a career in academia). Scotty Moore was brought over from Fernwood Records in June 1960 and named studio manager and chief cutting engineer; Charles Underwood, composer of "Ubangi Stomp," was hired as A&R manager and assistant engineer. Moore and Underwood largely filled the holes created by the departure of Bill Justis and Jack Clement; together they joined Bill Fitzgerald and Cecil Scaife, who had been hired shortly before the new studio was finished.

Bill Fitzgerald had been an early partner in Duke Records before it had been acquired by Don Robey. Fitzgerald then concentrated on building the Music Sales distributorship in Memphis. After nine years in distribution, he took on the ill-defined role of general manager at Sun in August 1959, staying until the bitter end.

Cecil Scaife was born in Helena, Arkansas, and had originally planned to parlay his looks into a career in movies. He went to Hollywood as a protégé of Paramount Pictures, staying a few months before returning to the South bereft of his illusions about the movie business. Scaife joined Hi Records as promotion manager, becoming their first full-time employee; Sam Phillips was

(Escott)

Cecil Scaife pours a tall cool one for Bill Fitzgerald, 1960 . . .

(Escott)

. . . meanwhile downstairs, Charles Underwood directs the pickers.

impressed with his work in getting Carl McVoy off the ground, and phoned him in the wee hours one morning offering him the job of promotion manager that Jud Phillips had just vacated. After dinner the following night, Scaife accepted.

Studio A

The main studio on Madison Avenue was roughly twice the size of the old studio floor on Union Avenue, and the console in the control room was arranged in a futuristic V design. It housed a four-track recorder and two single-track machines. Scotty Moore would later bring in a three-track recorder so that he could be compatible with the studios in Nashville. Moore and Phillips also installed two state-of-the-art Neumann cutting lathes so that they could cut their own masters, although the lathes never became fully operational.

Scotty Moore at his Neumann lathe, 1960

(Escott)

The difficulties began to mount even before the tapes started rolling. The studio architect was drafted, leaving others to pick up the pieces. "We had problems from day one," says Cecil Scaife. "For a start, the roof leaked because of all the flat surfaces. Every time it rained I'd have to go over there with buckets and mops. It delayed the opening for six months."

That was nothing compared to the real problem with the building—untamed acoustics. "The room wasn't tuned properly," asserts Scaife. "I took some Nashville guys over there to record, and they walked out. The sound was too hot. Too alive." Phillips' instincts as an audio engineer, which had served him so well at the old studio, deserted him on Madison Avenue. The tightly focused slapback echo at the old studio had been replaced by a cavernous hollow sound, as the audio signals leaped around the huge floor and off the corrugated ceiling. To combat the problem, Phillips ordered baffles that could be recessed into the wall when not in use; but they turned out to be more decorative than functional.

The problems ran even deeper than technical and design flaws. The funkiness of the old studio had been replaced by a high-tech environment. "It was awful hard to create there," recalls Scaife. "706 Union had a terrific atmosphere. A creative atmosphere. There was a naturalness about it. You felt *up* when you walked in. The new studio had a sterile atmosphere—it was like a doctor's office."

Phillips himself seems to have been ambivalent about the new facility. In his first flush of enthusiasm, he told Edwin Howard, "Woodshed recordings have had it. You've got to have latitude today—all the electronic devices, built-in high and low frequency equalization and attenuation, echoes, channel splitting and metering on everything." But it's doubtful that Phillips ever truly learned to love the new technology.

Phillips' oldest son, Knox, watched his father at work in the new studio. A single-track machine was run in tandem with the multitrack so that everything could be recorded twice. Phillips would premix through the board to the single-track machine—as he had at the old studio—leaving no latitude for rebalancing. The four-track tapes could be used for stereo mixdowns and overdubbing, if necessary. Invariably, though, it was what he captured on the single-track that Phillips regarded as *the* cut. "His concern was to get it on the floor and capture it on the single-track," explained Knox. "He believed that if the feeling wasn't there on the floor *right then*, there wasn't any point in doctoring it up later."

317 *Seventh Avenue North*

Shortly after opening the new studio on Madison Avenue, Phillips decided to branch out with a studio in Nashville. After years of refusing to rent out his studio to anyone, Phillips made a complete turnabout, deciding to enter the custom recording business in a grandiose way. The success of Bradley's Barn

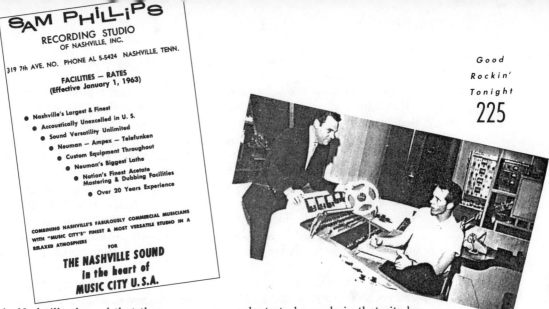

Kelso Herston and
a young Billy Sherrill
in the Nashville
studio, 1961

in Nashville showed that there was money aplenty to be made in that city by catering to the smaller labels and the overflow business from the larger studios. "I thought Nashville could be a good center not only for country music but for the range of music we were recording," recalled Phillips. "I was also trying to bring a new kind of influence into the business there."

Phillips had leased office space in the old Cumberland Lodge building in Nashville for his publishing companies, which were run locally by Kelso Herston. In the same building, Billy Sherrill and Bill Cooner had built a small studio, which was on the point of going bankrupt. Herston told Phillips that it was available, and Phillips came to look it over. Newly conscious of the importance of room ambience after the disappointments back in Memphis, Phillips was impressed with the Seventh Avenue studio. Its high ceiling and wooden floors and walls gave a warm, focused sound. After attending a session, Phillips decided to buy it and hired Billy Sherrill as his engineer. The multitrack installation was by Ray Butts, who had earlier built the Echoplex amplifier that had enabled Scotty Moore to re-create the studio reverb on stage.

After the previews at the end of 1960, the studio finally opened in February 1961. Jerry Lee Lewis breezed into town for the inaugural session and cut "What'd I Say," the hit that took him back into the charts after four years in the commercial wilderness. Two days later, Charlie Rich came to Nashville and recorded "Who Will the Next Fool Be"; the portents were excellent.

"Billy Sherrill had a good basic feel for what I wanted," recalled Phillips. "On top of that, he was a really excellent musician." Sherrill's evolving production philosophy was worlds away from Phillips', though: "He had a feeling for the way things were changing, and a tendency to arrange things more than would have been my way." After joining Epic Records, Sherrill completely foreswore his roots in R&B and developed the most overwrought production style in Nashville. His success became the benchmark by which producers were measured. Phillips must be given credit for seeing Sherrill's talent; however, the string and chorus-laden productions that Sherrill favored were the antithesis of Phillips' musical values—indeed, the antithesis of what many regard as country music.

The Cumberland Lodge building was not in the heart of what is now considered the Music Row area of Nashville, but at that time, the old Masonic building was itself the heart of the music business. "Mercury Records, the Wilburn Brothers, Tree Publishing, and some other publishers were there," recalls Cecil Scaife. "I remember the Wilburns brought Loretta Lynn there when she first came to Nashville. She practiced walking in high heels on the marble floors outside our office. We did a lot of demo work for publishers, and a lot of custom work for other labels." Phillips' best customer in Nashville was Bill Beasley and Allen Bubis's Hit Records operation, which churned out imitations of current hits to sell in dime stores at thirty-nine cents. When Scaife quit Sun in March 1963 it was to take a position as sales manager for Hit Records.

Phillips sold the studio in February 1964 after a plague of minor problems and one galling annoyance: the Nashville musicians were accustomed to working on the American Federation of Musicians guidelines, which called for four songs from a three-hour session, with overtime pay for any runovers. Phillips tried to bring in his own musicians from Memphis, but encountered some resistance. The bottom line, according to Phillips, was that he was unable to supervise the studio to his satisfaction. "I was never able to make myself have the confidence in other people. I knew they were talented people, and Billy Sherrill proved that, but it just didn't come out the way it could have. We tried to bring in something of a new concept there, but I just didn't stay with it personally long enough to usher it in fully. And there was just so much opposition from the people in Nashville."

Phillips offered the studio to Cecil Scaife, who had left Sun by that point, but Scaife passed. Fred Foster of Monument Records eventually bought the facility; he had cut some of Roy Orbison's biggest hits there. "I don't think Sam really wanted to sell," recalled Foster. "He loved to negotiate and he wanted a big negotiating scene—and that's what we had. It lasted three days and two nights. I was a zombie by the time we closed the deal. Then, shortly after we bought the studio, National Life, who owned the building, tore it down, so we had to move everything."

ANNOUNCING
A
NEW WORLD
OF
ENTERTAINMENT

Phillips International

During the 1960s, as Sam Phillips struggled to maintain his company's toehold in the marketplace, his original vision of Sun Records seemed suddenly to lose its focus. It was a period marked by attempts at diversification, and as Phillips cast his net more broadly, the inevitable result was the loss of the classic Sun Sound. Phillips' various managers and producers made random stabs at a bewildering variety of musical styles; consequently, his own personal stamp faded from the Sun catalog.

Feeling that the Sun label was too closely identified with rock 'n' roll to support a wider range of music, Phillips had launched a second label, Phillips International, in 1957. The label's stationery boasted offices in New York, Hollywood, and Memphis, and the label design itself had a more uptown image than Sun. "Many of the earlier releases will be rock 'n' roll," gushed the promo copy accompanying the launch. "Future plans call for a wide variety of music including standard pop and jazz." The new label also enabled Phillips to test a second set of distributors in major markets.

The first batch of releases included "Raunchy," which augured well—although, as it happened, Phillips International would start on the highest note it ever hit. Charlie Rich and Carl Mann ensured that the label began the new decade with a strong profile but, from that point, hits were elusive.

After the move to the new studio, Phillips used his new label to make a tentative gesture toward the long-play market, which he despised. There were eight LPs on Phillips International. Predictably, three of those were by Bill Justis, Carl Mann, and Charlie Rich. The balance was an eclectic mix: Phillips signed a one-shot deal with big band leader Chuck Foster, whose broadcasts from the Hotel Peabody he had engineered in leaner times; there was cocktail piano from Graham Forbes, back country blues from Frank Frost, lukewarm country gospel from Eddie Bond, and contemporary R&B from Frank Ballard.

The venture suffered from Phillips' lack of deep commitment. Other companies, such as Liberty Records, had carved out a sector of the marketplace for their albums. Phillips' tentative gestures betrayed his fundamental lack of faith in long-players, and his unwillingness to bankroll their higher production costs. He undertook neither the advertising nor the promotion that would have signified a sustained commitment toward creating an identity for Phillips International as an album label.

The label eventually folded in 1963 after a series of discussions with Philips BV, the Dutch electrical giant that had bought Mercury Records. They had launched their own imprint in North America in 1962, and saw Phillips International as a potential source of confusion.

The Old Payola Roll Blues

The decline that affected Phillips' labels through the early '60s had even deeper causes than his diminishing interest or the audio characteristics of the new studio. The character of the entire industry was changing.

Sun had swept to prominence with some of the most starkly underproduced music ever recorded. "Blue Suede Shoes," "I Walk the Line," and "Whole Lotta Shakin' Going On" featured just three or four instruments and a vocalist, but such productions were swiftly going out of vogue. If Phillips had followed his nose back toward rhythm and blues, he would have been well placed to capitalize upon the soul music boom a few years later. Instead, he and his staff followed the trend toward a fuller pop sound. As a result, a Sun record produced in the early '60s was less likely to be distinguishable from the fifty or one hundred other records released during the same week.

Other factors hastened the retrenchment. The wide-ranging payola investigations under way in the late '50s effected subtle but important changes within the industry. Payola (the payment of money or other incentives in exchange for radio play) had started with song pluggers before World War II, and after the war it became a feature of the R&B business. It was not until the R&B record labels began to get national exposure, using the same promotional methods they had perfected in leaner times, that the protests started.

In 1959 the Federal Communications Commission started investigating payola. Phillips was called on to explain his dealings with Dick Clark on the "Breathless" promotion, but otherwise emerged unscathed. Parsimony had brought forth its reward. Other companies, such as Chess, made detailed disclosures of their payments to disc jockeys. The protracted saga was played out as the FCC hearings made their way across the country. Leonard Chess from Chess Records and Jerry Wexler from Atlantic were among those compelled to confess and recant. A few careers were shattered, most notably that of Alan Freed. In the end, payola went underground for a few years, but the more insidious result was that the music business became more conservative.

In the move back to safer ground, the major labels reasserted their power, and there was a general atmosphere of caution. Six of the Top 10 records from June 1957 had been on independent labels; by June 1960 just three carried that distinction.

By the early '60s, Sun was part of the musical establishment. Like the rest of the industry, they were concentrating on good-looking boys with a white-bread sound. What Sam Phillips had been able to do in the mid-'50s, with Elvis Presley, Jerry Lee Lewis, Johnny Cash, and all the others was carve out a sector of the market no one had known to exist. The artists that Sun signed during the '60s were competing in the same sector of the market as the major labels, but without the majors' promotional clout. In the mid-'50s the majors were playing catch-up to Phillips; by the early '60s, he was trying to catch up to them.

Long Shots and Outside Chances

As Sun and Phillips International scaled down their activities during the '60s, few artists—besides the old standbys, Charlie Rich, Carl Mann, Jerry Lee Lewis, and the long-departed Johnny Cash—showed enough staying power to see more than one release. For the first time, Phillips signed artists who had already seen a hit elsewhere. A typical case was Luther Perkins' brother, Tommy, who, as Thomas Wayne, had recorded his only hit, "Tragedy," for Scotty Moore at Fernwood Records. After he failed to follow it up, he came to Sun for one single, but failed to rekindle the magic.

Much the same pattern was repeated with Harold Dorman. A native of Sledge, Mississippi, Dorman had come to Memphis in 1955 and auditioned at Sun in 1957. Both his songs and his performances were undistinguished, but Roland Janes heard something he liked in the singer, and when he and Billy Riley started Rita Records in the fall of 1959 they brought a much-improved Dorman into the studio. With Jack Clement at the board, they cut "Mountain of Love," which became a one-off hit comparable to "Tragedy" the previous spring.

Like Thomas Wayne, Dorman was unable to sustain the momentum, and Rita Records soon folded. Dorman hurried back to Sun, where he recorded three singles, none of which reignited his career. He then turned to songwriting and submitted one of his songs, "Mississippi Cotton Picking Delta Town," to Charley Pride, another native of Sledge who had also auditioned at Sun in the late '50s. It became one of Pride's biggest hits and encouraged him to revive "Mountain of Love" in 1981.

Sun had also begun to trade off its past glories for the first time. They dusted off Roy Orbison's "Devil Doll" after he had found his true musical voice at Monument, and resurrected Smokey Joe's 1955 oddball recording of "Signifying Monkey" after Sam the Sham revived it. Phillips even recorded Elvis Presley's last pre-Army girlfriend, Anita Wood, in a beleaguered attempt to get a little mileage from the Presley connection. All were stillborn ventures. Arguably, all deserved to be.

While newer labels such as Stax and Berry Gordy's Motown were brewing up original musical recipes—just as Phillips himself had in the 1950s—Sun seemed able only to make futile gestures toward the mainstream. Nowhere was the contrast more ironic than in the recordings of a local teenager, Tony Rossini, who recorded five singles for the label between 1960 and 1963. These were arid pop records of no distinction, which would hardly be a surprise were it not for the fact that the backing groups included some of the finest musicians in Memphis. Besides Scotty Moore, Ace Cannon, and Roland Janes, the sessionmen included Steve Cropper, Booker T. Jones, and Al Jackson, who would later form the nucleus of the Stax house band and record on their own as Booker T. and the MGs. Somehow these crack players came together to produce some of the least memorable music to emerge under the Sun imprint. Rossini later moved to California, where he showed his true colors and became a lounge act.

The sad truth was that disc jockeys no longer rushed to open the little package of singles postmarked from Memphis and bearing the distinctive gold mailing label. In its attempt to sustain a national profile, Sun was becoming a local label again.

(Escott)

Thomas Wayne

Dane Stinit   (Escott)

With another glance backward, Sun tried to hang onto Johnny Cash's audience by experimenting with a singer who modeled his style on Cash's. Dane Stinit (real name Stinnett) was a Kentuckian who had transplanted himself to Gary, Indiana. On a trip back home in 1965 he was discovered at a party and was brought to the Sun studio by local promoter Bettye Berger to produce an album of Cash covers.

As it happened, Phillips walked in the studio during the session, took over the controls, and was impressed enough to sign the singer to Sun. In January 1966 Phillips brought him back into the studio to cut a single that marginally updated the Cash sound. "Don't Knock What You Don't Understand" was released in May, and sold well enough for Stinit to be invited back during his next vacation to record another shot.

The second session, which took place in November, yielded a tune called "That Muddy Old River (Near Memphis, Tennessee)." It was to be the last time that Sam Phillips took the controls as president of Sun Records. Stinnett (as he returned to calling himself) never recorded again, although he continued to play to homesick Southerners in the land of the wind chill factor.

Return to the Roots

But, of course, Sam Phillips' first love had always been the music he founded his studio to record: rhythm and blues. Few came closer to the music Phillips loved than Frank Frost. Phillips' words about Frost say a great deal about his own musical values as the sixties moved on: "I saw a place for Frank Frost, even though [he] was the most bluesy thing I had recorded in years. By the '60s there were more radio stations that could expose the blues to a white audience than there had been earlier. Rock music had gone in other directions, but I felt that there was a chance of going against the odds and producing solid down-home blues that would still get played and bought."

A native of Lula, Mississippi, Frost came to Phillips' studio in April 1962 and, over the course of three marathon sessions, cut some of the last truly great blues recordings to emerge from Memphis. He was hardly an innovator, but his music was still nourished from within his own community rather than by white college audiences, which gave it a cutting edge that blues recordings increasingly lacked. As Phillips recalls, "John R. [a DJ] on WLAC in Nashville, told me that the Frank Frost album was the best record he had ever heard—and John R. was a big name." Yet, John R.'s endorsement notwithstanding, the Frost album was a sales disaster.

Sun also tried a number of experiments with two local white performers, Billy Adams and Bill Yates, whose records probably sold well in Memphis but who, as Phillips knew, were never national contenders. Adams was a drummer who had played with Carl Perkins and Jerry Lee Lewis, among others, before taking up residency at Hernando's Hideaway in Memphis. He recorded prolifically at Sun, usually in the company of the more riveting pianist Bill Yates. Together and separately, they saw seven singles issued on Sun between 1964 and 1966. Yet their sound too harked back to the past, at a time when the Memphis music industry was changing its tune.

Cadillac Man

Sun's true last gasp was provided by a bizarre aggregation called the Jesters. The leader of the group was guitarist Teddy Paige (real name Edward LaPaglia). Paige, a credible blues guitarist, was joined by Sam Phillips' younger son, Jerry, on rhythm guitar. Jerry Phillips had been making one hundred dollars a night when he was eleven or twelve working in midget wrestling tournaments in Arkansas. Billing himself as "DeLane Phillips—The World's Most Perfectly Formed Midget," he retired prematurely after a member of the audience tried to stab him. Retreating to safer ground, he took up the guitar.

(J. Dickinson)

*J*im Dickinson with
Jerry Phillips

*T*he Jesters, *left to right:*
Jerry Phillips, Sam Phillips,
Eddie Robertson, Billy Wulfers,
and Teddy Paige

(J. Dickinson)

The lead vocalist, Tommy Minga, had written a Chuck Berry sound-alike tune called "Cadillac Man," and the Jesters auditioned it for Knox Phillips. "I just wanted something really strange because I had been raised on Jerry Lee Lewis and drunken Charlie Rich sessions," says Knox. The Jesters recorded "Cadillac Man" with Minga, but Paige considered the results to be unsatisfactory. He called in Jim Dickinson, who was under contract to Bill Justis, to play piano and try the vocal part. Dickinson handled the role to perfection. Knox experimented with feed-in from one microphone to another so that when he increased the level on the piano mike during the solo, the drum level also increased with an eerie echo that Dickinson characterized as "pure Africa."

The Jesters soon broke up. Paige helped Shelby Singleton catalog the Sun blues tapes and played session guitar for Knox Phillips and Singleton, before moving to Ireland. Jerry Phillips joined the family business. Minga, in common with the other members of the band, dropped out of the music scene.

Dickinson felt that "Cadillac Man," which owed more to 1961 than 1966, was doomed from the outset. With good national promotion, it might have stood a chance. In any event, with justice it should have been the last Sun record: Its rowdy, anarchic energy would have made an appropriate closing gesture.

The End

By the time Sun neared the end of its course, Memphis was making its mark on the music business once again. Stax, Hi, and Goldwax Records were the new foci of activity, the new bearers of the "Memphis Sound" banner. Sun played a minor role as a custom studio, but when Knox Phillips tried to capitalize on the new wave of black music emerging from the city, the results were mixed. One of his signings, the Climates, fronted the stellar rhythm section of Reggie Young, Mike Leech, Tommy Cogbill, and Gene Chrisman, but never rose above mediocrity. The final Sun record, issued with little fanfare in January 1968, was by a group dubbed Load of Mischief. One side featured riffs copped from the Stax catalog and the other from Motown. It was a lamentable finale.

Sam Phillips has admitted that Sun Records perished because of his diminishing commitment to the record business. "The basic reason that Sun did not become a major label," he has said, "was that I preferred to invest my time in other things. I didn't want to hook up with a major corporation because I knew I couldn't do the job the way I wanted to do it as part of a big company—even though I had several offers.

"In the '60s, things were changing rapidly and drastically as far as distribution was concerned. Most top-selling artists were lured away from the small companies during the latter part of the '50s, and a number of the indie labels themselves were bought out. I could see what was coming and I wanted no part of it. It is not my way to work for somebody."

*S*am Phillips with his
sons Knox and Jerry shortly
before the sale
of Sun Records

Phillips also saw that the days when you could get some cuts on tape, mastered, pressed, and promoted for a few hundred dollars were long gone. Modern sessions called for more musicians, most of whom demanded union scale. In fact, every facet of the industry, from the technical to the promotional, was becoming more expensive.

In the changing climate, albums were a necessity, and singles were increasingly seen as trailers or loss leaders for LPs. Phillips never truly believed in the album market; in fact, Shelby Singleton issued more albums of Sun product in the first year after he bought the catalog than Phillips had issued in fifteen years. Some have seen Phillips' lack of interest in the album market as evidence of his parsimony, but for him it was a much more complex issue: "Albums weren't selling that much, but beyond that, I was always very cautious about not putting out a lot of product on my artists simply to ensure a certain level of income. I think that opportunity has always been abused by the major record companies. You only have to look at some of the crap they put out on Elvis Presley, with no regard for the man's great abilities."

If the record business is a lottery, Sam Phillips accomplished one of the most difficult feats a gambler can: he had the good fortune to win the big money, and the good sense to reinvest his winnings broadly, instead of risking them all on the chance of an even bigger payback. As Sun Records wound down, he bought radio stations, Holiday Inn stock (he was one of the first investors in the chain), properties with mineral rights, and so on. Though it's easy to lament his eventual departure from the recording industry, it's clear that financially he made the right choice. Knox explains his father's thinking: "Sam wasn't going to gamble his money promoting records any more. He had seen some of his friends go broke, such as the people who ran Vee-Jay, and he became very conservative. We still had some records that sold well on a regional level, but there wasn't a commitment of spirit."

Postscript:
Holiday Inn Records

The first Holiday Inn opened on Summer Avenue in Memphis during August 1952. The founder of the Holiday Inn chain, Kemmons Wilson, was a maverick figure like Phillips and by the mid-'60s he had begun to contemplate a new publicity project for the chain: "Kemmons and I had some conversations," recalled Phillips, "and he was very much interested in expanding the Holiday Inn operation. They were beginning to put bands into piano bars in Holiday Inns all across the country and he had the idea of setting up a label that could promote those bands. They had also just bought the Trailways bus line and Kemmons thought he could sell records in racks at the bus terminals to all the people passing through and killing time."

Sam Phillips was named president of Holiday Inn Records on March 8, 1968, some two months after the last Sun record was issued. Jud Phillips was named national sales and promotion manager and Knox Phillips was one of the in-house producers. But Sam soon bowed out, citing an overabundance of vice presidents as the principal reason. The infusion of Holiday Inn's capital could not compensate for the fact that no talent had been infused, and the venture was folded.

Recommended Listening

Harold Dorman's Rita recordings have been reissued on *Mountain of Love* (Bear Family [Germany] BFX 15262).

Dane Stinit's Sun sessions are available in their entirety on *Original Sun Recordings* (Bear Family [Germany] BFX 15337).

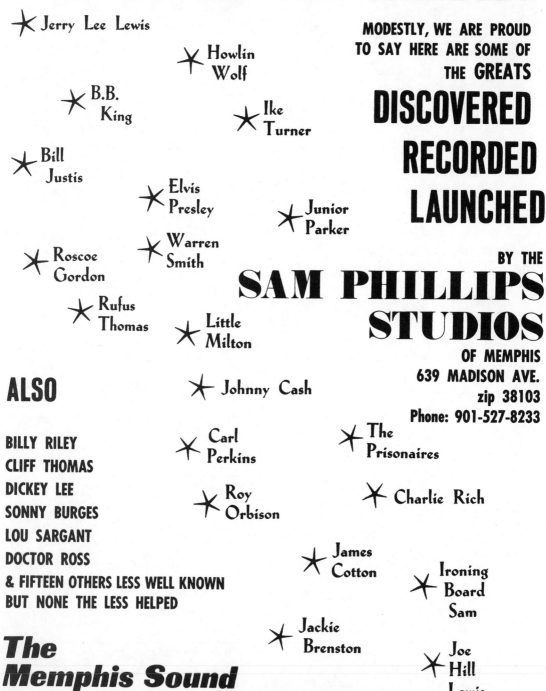

the MEMPHIS SOUND

★ Jerry Lee Lewis

★ Howlin Wolf

★ B.B. King

★ Ike Turner

★ Bill Justis

★ Elvis Presley

★ Junior Parker

★ Roscoe Gordon

★ Warren Smith

★ Rufus Thomas

★ Little Milton

MODESTLY, WE ARE PROUD
TO SAY HERE ARE SOME OF
THE GREATS

DISCOVERED

RECORDED

LAUNCHED

BY THE

SAM PHILLIPS

STUDIOS

OF MEMPHIS
639 MADISON AVE.
zip 38103
Phone: 901-527-8233

ALSO

★ Johnny Cash

BILLY RILEY
CLIFF THOMAS
DICKEY LEE
SONNY BURGES
LOU SARGANT
DOCTOR ROSS
& FIFTEEN OTHERS LESS WELL KNOWN
BUT NONE THE LESS HELPED

★ Carl Perkins

★ The Prisonaires

★ Roy Orbison

★ Charlie Rich

★ James Cotton

★ Ironing Board Sam

★ Jackie Brenston

★ Joe Hill Lewis

The Memphis Sound heard 'Round the World

Sun In The Age Of Plenty

By *1967* an entirely new kind of music had come to dominate the nation; among its many strains was a new brand of Memphis music, descended from the black gospel music that Phillips had always *meant* to record. Many of the musicians who congregated daily at Stax, Hi, American, Sonic, or Sounds of Memphis had passed through Sun on their way; some of the new studio bosses, such as Stan Kesler, Roland Janes, Quinton Claunch, and Ray Harris, had started their careers at Sun. Even a few of the hit records of the day, like Sam the Sham's "Woolly Bully," were cut at the Sun studio; but the Sun label itself was firmly consigned to the past.

The Sun catalog sat in abeyance for a year. Since the mid '60s Phillips had received offers for the label—most persistently from CBS/Columbia, which was anxious to get the Cash masters out of circulation. Phillips had considered a deal with Mercury Records in 1962, in which Sun would act as a production company for Mercury. The founder and president of Mercury, Irving Green, came to see Phillips, and new releases were suspended for a few months, but the negotiations fell through. Jerry Wexler at Atlantic Records pursued a similar deal to the one that brought Stax into the Atlantic fold, but again, nothing was finalized.

After Sun ceased releasing new product, Phillips started considering offers for the catalog. Jud Phillips, acting in his role as Jerry Lee Lewis's business manager, approached his brother with the idea of purchasing all of the Lewis masters after Lewis revived his career in the country market, but Sam refused to commit just one portion of the catalog.

By 1969 Phillips had found his buyer: a shrewd Louisiana businessman and record executive named Shelby Singleton.

Sun International

With the obligatory Cadillac parked out back, an address book chock full of household names, and a thin cigar between his lips, Shelby Singleton looks like the prototypical record czar. Born in Waskom, Texas, twenty miles from

(B. Millar)

A late-'60s promotional flyer for the Phillips studios. The word "Sun" is conspicuously absent

Signing away the
kingdom: Sam Phillips and
Shelby Singleton,
July 1, 1969

(Sun Ent. Corp.)

Shreveport, Louisiana, in 1931, Singleton became involved in the comings and goings of the Louisiana Hayride after his first wife, Margie, became a featured performer. Margie recorded for Starday Records in Beaumont, Texas, and after Starday entered into a short and unhappy marriage with Mercury Records in 1957, Singleton came on board as a field promo man for Mercury-Starday.

When the Mercury-Starday pact dissolved in 1958, Singleton stayed with Mercury as a field promo rep, moving to Nashville to head up their country music operation in January 1961. Keeping his ear close to the ground, he was able to pick up masters such as Bruce Channel's "Hey Baby" and Matt Lucas's "I'm Movin' On" from small independent southern labels ("I'm Movin' On" was leased from Sun sessionman Roland Janes). Singleton also had success when he produced his own masters. By late 1961 he was heading the Mercury A&R department in New York, inheriting such artists as Clyde McPhatter (for whom he found "Lover Please"), Brook Benton, and Dinah Washington. In 1966 Singleton decided to trade upon his distinguished track record and launch his own company.

After some initial success in the R&B market, Singleton branched into country music and struck platinum immediately with Jeannie C. Riley's "Harper Valley PTA." For a while, Singleton's empire grew in quantum leaps and embraced a dozen labels; but it was probably the profit from the Riley record that gave him the resources he needed to approach Sam Phillips, whom he had originally approached on behalf of Mercury. "The only way I could buy the company," he recalls, "was to promise that everything would come out on Sun. That was the key factor."

The exact terms of the deal by which Sun Records was sold in July 1969 were not made public. Phillips appears to have retained a percentage of the newly formed Sun International Corporation, and 100 percent of his music publishing interests (which would, of course, benefit enormously from any reissue program). He would also retain the studio, and his sons, Knox and Jerry, would act as independent producers for Sun International.

Singleton brought a truck to the door of the Madison Avenue studio and loaded out all of the Sun masters and outtakes after a preliminary effort had been made at cataloging them. Understandably, Singleton was most interested in the Johnny Cash and Jerry Lee Lewis masters: Cash had just started his own television series, and Jerry Lee had emerged from a decade in the wilderness with a career reborn in country music. Furthermore, Roy Orbison was still a big draw, and Charlie Rich had seen a few minor hits that presaged his enormous success a few years later.

Singleton had albums by all of those artists on the market before the ink was dry on the contract. He also recycled much of the same repertoire to a budget company, Pickwick Records. He took a good listen to the last Jerry Lee Lewis session for Sun, and found three potential top 10 country singles in the three unissued masters. In fact, those singles took Sun Records back into the charts before the year was out.

But Sun International was designed to be more than a vehicle for recycling vintage repertoire. Knox and Jerry Phillips supplied new masters by Jerry Dyke, the Gentrys, and others, and Singleton also placed some of his signings on the label. The first was none other than Billy Lee Riley, who had kept more or less abreast of the music scene since his days at Sun. His first Sun International single was recorded in Memphis with a backing group led by Jim Dickinson and the Dixie Flyers. "Kay" was the bitter lament of a taxi driver whose ex-girlfriend had become a singer and could be heard on the radio every fifteen minutes. It moved Sam Phillips to pronounce it "the best record Riley ever made." Riley's version was probably too close to rock 'n' roll for the country market, and too close to country music for the rock market, so he lost the hit to John Wesley Ryles. But in its way "Kay" *was* as good as anything Riley had ever done.

At the same time, Singleton tried launching a black music label called Midnight Sun with product from Memphis. But the first and only artist was Cliff Jackson, who recorded two singles before the venture was folded. The relationship between Singleton and the Phillips family soured not long into the new decade. At roughly the same time, Singleton's bubble burst: he had overextended himself, and he trimmed down his operation, concentrating on recycling what he had, both in terms of repertoire and non-Sun publishing copyrights.

(Escott)

*B*illy Riley returns
to Sun, 1969: the
weirdness continues

Who Was That Masked Man?

Despite the slower pace, Singleton continued to release product on the Sun label into the 1970s. The human jukebox, rockabilly Sleepy LaBeef, was one of the keepers of the flame who found himself on Sun, albeit twenty years after he might have wished. Nevertheless, he made some recordings that were essentially true to the Phillips credo.

Less creditable to many ears were the recordings of Jimmy Ellis, who recorded under the pseudonym Orion Eckley Darnell (some have placed the emphasis on the "ecch"). Ellis appeared on stage in a bejeweled mask, performing a soulless impersonation of Fat Elvis; he scored some minor country hits between 1979 and 1982, but his following was largely confined to those who refused to believe that Elvis Presley had actually expired on his bathroom floor in August 1977. Orion's ultimate problem for anyone other than Elvis necrophiliacs was that his style began and ended with affectation. The best Sun artists had a unique slant on their music, in which exaggeration was secondary; Orion offered nothing but secondhand mannerisms.

But the real life of Sun was in the earlier recordings, and Singleton's European licensees kept the vintage Sun product flowing. "The way the material has been handled, it truly amazes me that it hasn't been killed," said Phillips in 1981. "It was not my way to repackage every damn thing every other week or month, because the recordings had too much meaning for the people who were buying the product. In the long run, though, I don't think the reissues have cheapened the image as much as I feared they would."

On the contrary—the constant flow of Sun reissues has contributed to the beatification of Sam Phillips. His massive achievement is on public display in those recordings, and it shows him in an almost unerringly favorable light. The outtakes, chatter, and jive captured on the Sun tapes, as well as the issued masters, reveal his role as the one man who understood, and drew the best from, some of the greatest artists in American music.

After the sale to Singleton, Sam Phillips retained only a marginal involvement in the record business. He nursed his investment portfolio, and maintained a hands-on approach to managing his radio stations. He expressed an interest in producing Bob Dylan, and had a fleeting involvement in Knox and Jerry Phillips' production of John Prine for Asylum Records in 1978; otherwise, he has steadfastly refused any temptation he might have had to resume record production. "He had a creative flow, [but] never tried to get it back," says Jim Dickinson. "Knox and I did a lot of work once to get him a B. B. King session. We didn't check with him first, and, when we asked him, he said 'No.' Knox said, 'You can't just say no. Why not?' Sam said, 'You can't go to Picasso and ask him to paint a little picture.' That may sound presumptuous, but that's the way he saw it. Everything in recording is input and output, and when you lose that signal flow, you never get it back."

Although Phillips has periodically expressed an interest in offloading the studio on Madison Avenue, his sons have persuaded him to retain it as a custom recording house. Despite the recent addition of a 24-track recorder, it looks much like it did in 1960. More surprising, the original Sun studio on Union Avenue also looks just about like it did in 1950. The property was bought and refurbished with Phillips' help, to become both a museum and a custom studio. The Irish superstars U2 are among the musicians who have come to set up their amps in the spot where Sam Phillips first drew the magic from young Elvis; in 1990, Jerry Lee Lewis returned to record two cuts for the soundtrack of Warren Beatty's *Dick Tracy*.

*S*un alumni greet
Sam Phillips on his
elevation to sainthood:
Phillips with B. B. King,
Charlie Rich, and
Jerry Lee Lewis

(MSU, Photo Services)

Consistently Better Records...

To Shelby Singleton, Sun Records is very much an ongoing entity. Trading
on the cachet attached to the trademark, he renamed his enterprise the Sun
Entertainment Corporation, and floated it on the Vancouver Stock Exchange
in 1987 with a view to reentering the production and manufacturing end of
the business. To many others, though, Sun Records ended in 1969; to musical
purists, it ended a decade before that, when the old studio was closed.

The indisputable fact is that the reputation of Sun Records is founded upon
a series of recordings made between 1952 and 1959 in Sam Phillips' little
storefront studio. When Phillips settled down to sketch out his corporate
letterhead in 1952, he positioned his rooster crowing at the dawn's early rays.
To the right of the rooster he placed his first attempt at a corporate slogan,
"Up Above Them All With Records That Sell," which represented more wishful
thinking than achievement. Beneath the address ran the second slogan, "Consistently Better Records for Higher Profits." They weren't elegant words, but
they defined both Phillips' trademark and his credo.

Under his direction, Sun was true to the slogans on that letterhead. It was no mere coincidence that Elvis Presley, Jerry Lee Lewis, Johnny Cash, and so many others gave their finest performances in the Sun studio. The excitement they generated, along with Phillips' almost messianic ability to bring out the rawest emotion in their art, qualifies the man as probably the first modern record producer, and possibly the greatest. It also ensures that his legacy is among the most important in popular music.

APPENDIX A: SOURCES

In writing this book, we have inevitably drawn upon some secondary as well as original sources. Wherever possible, we have tried to keep track of these, but the listing below will inevitably bear some omissions. Most of the information, though, was derived from original interview material, which is largely unattributed in the text. In view of the mythology surrounding some of the Sun artists—some of it perpetuated by the artists themselves and some by their followers—we have tried to double-check most of what has passed for established wisdom.

Some general reference materials included:

History and Encyclopedia of Country, Western and Gospel Music by Linnell Gentry (2nd revised edition) (Nashville, Tenn.: Clairmont Corp., 1969).

Joel Whitburn's Top Pop Singles, 1955–1986 (Menomonee Falls, Wisc.: Record Research, 1986).

Joel Whitburn's Top R&B Singles, 1942–1988 (Menomonee Falls, Wisc.: Record Research, 1988).

Joel Whitburn's Top Country Singles, 1944–1988 (Menomonee Falls, Wisc.: Record Research, 1988).

The files of *Billboard* (1950–1969), *Cashbox* (1950–1969), and *Country Music Reporter* (later *Music Reporter*) (1956–1966).

The clippings file of the Showtime (Toronto) Archive, including press releases, UPI reports, contemporary news clippings, and other material.

What follows is a detailed list of printed source material, organized on a chapter-by-chapter basis.

Chapter One

The Dee-Jays by Arnold Passman (New York: Macmillan, 1971) provides essential background on the major forces in the postwar music industry.

Country Music USA by Bill C. Malone (Austin, Tex.: University of Texas Press, 1968) offers background on the country music industry.

Sam Phillips interviewed by Martin Hawkins, Hank Davis, and Colin Escott.

Background on Hoyt Wooten and WREC from "WREC Sold for $6 Million" by Robert Johnson, Memphis *Press Scimitar*, November 3, 1958.

Chapter Two

An unpublished analysis of Phillips' studio configuration by Bruce Leslie, PRO Recorders. Additional information from Bill Cantrell.

B. B. King interviewed by David Booth (unpublished).

Liner notes to Joe Hill Louis, *The One Man Band* (Muskadine 101) by Steve LaVere.

Sam Phillips interviewed by Hank Davis and Colin Escott; by Robert Palmer in *Memphis*, Vol. 3, No. 9, and in *Deep Blues* (New York: Viking Press, 1981).

Rosco Gordon interviewed by Hank Davis, *Living Blues* #49.

"Rocket Becomes Flying Disc, Spins Toward Record Glory" by Lydel Sims, Memphis *Commercial Appeal*, March 28, 1951.

'Tell 'em Phillips Sent'cha' by Randy Haspel, *Memphis* magazine, June 1978.

Chapter Three

Sam Phillips interviewed by Martin Hawkins, Colin Escott, and Hank Davis. Also the interview by Robert Palmer published in *Memphis*, Vol. 3, No. 9.

"Duke Records: The Early Years" by Roger Weeden and George A. Moonoogian, *Whiskey, Women, And . . .* No. 14, contains additional background on Duke Records and its sale to Peacock.

Walter Horton, Rufus Thomas, and Little Milton interviewed by David Booth (unpublished).

"Warden Uses Prisonaires as Example of Humane Policy," *Ebony*, November 1953.

"Prison Singers May Find Success With Record They Made in Memphis" by Clark Porteous, Memphis *Press Scimitar*, July 15, 1953.

"Just Walkin' in the Rain Showers Convict With $$$," UPI report, November 10, 1956.

Sun Spot information courtesy of Dave Sax.

"Little Milton: The Living Blues Interview" by Lynn Summers and Bob Scheir, *Living Blues*, No. 18.

"Auburn Hare Trades in Ol' Guitar for Harp With Golden Strings," *The Mirror*: Stillwater State Penitentiary, Vol. 93, No. 5.

Chapter Four

"Jack Sallee: Writes Hit in Ten Minutes," Memphis *Press Scimitar*, March 17, 1955.

Peter Guralnick, liner notes to *The Complete Sun Sessions* (RCA 6414).

Dewey Phillips interviewed by Stanley Booth in "A Hound Dog, To The Manor Born,"
reprinted in *The Age of Rock*, ed. by Jonathan Eisen (New York: Vintage Books,
1969).
Elvis Presley interviewed in *The Charlotte Observer*, reprinted in *Long Lonesome
Highway* by Ger Rijff (Amsterdam: Tutti Frutti Productions, 1985).
Interviews with Sam Phillips by Charles Raiteri excerpted in liner notes to Dewey
Phillips' *Red Hot and Blue* (Zu-Zazz Z 2012); and by Robert Palmer in *Memphis*
magazine, Vol. 3, No. 9.
Presley's Opry appearances detailed in "Muscle Behind the Music: The Life and Times
of Jim Denny, Part 3," *Journal of Country Music*, XI.3.
Bill Randle interview in *Memphis Lonesome* by Ger Rijff (Amsterdam: Tutti-Frutti
Productions, 1988).

Chapter Five

Johnny Cash and Marshall Grant interviewed by David Booth (unpublished).
Sam Phillips interviewed by Martin Hawkins, Colin Escott, and Hank Davis.
Information on Gordon Jenkins' *Crescent City Blues* courtesy of Allen Rush and Al
Cooley.
"Johnny Cash: American" by Bill Flanagan, *Musician*, May 1988.
"Johnny Cash Tells the Stories Behind His Songs" by Ed Salamon, *Country Music*,
July/August 1980.
"John R. Cash: I Will Rock & Roll With You (If I Have To)" by Peter Guralnick,
Country Music, July/August 1980.
"Ballad of a Teenage Queen" by Johnny Cash, *Cashbox*, June 14, 1980.

Chapter Six

"Harmonica Frank: Sun's Hall of Fame" by Steve LaVere, *Rockville International*,
June-July 1974; liner notes to Puritan 3001 by Steve LaVere.
"Hardrock Gunter: The Mysterious Pig-Iron Man" by Nick Tosches, in *Unsung Heroes
of Rock 'n' Roll* (New York: Charles Scribner's Sons, 1984).
"Charlie Feathers: Last of the Rockabillies" by Peter Guralnick, in *Lost Highway*
(Boston: David R. Godine, 1979).
"The Miller Sisters" by Hank Davis in "The Sun Country Years" booklet, Bear Family
Records, Bremen, West Germany, 1986.

Chapter Seven

Carl Perkins interviewed by David Booth and Don Bird (unpublished).
Disciple in Blue Suede Shoes by Carl Perkins with Ron Rendleman (Grand Rapids,
Mich.: Zondervan Publishing, 1978).
"The Very Large Legend of Carl Perkins" by Lenny Kaye, *Guitar World*, July 1982.
"Carl Perkins: Born to Rock" by Dave Sholin, *Gavin Report*, July 4, 1986.

Chapter Eight

"A Candid Conversation With Roy Orbison" by Jeff Tamarkin, *Goldmine*, October 1979.

"Twenty-Five Years Behind the Shades" by Penny Reel, *New Musical Express*, December 20, 1980.

"The Face Interview" by Nick Kent, *The Face*, January 1989.

Roy Orbison interviewed by David Booth (unpublished).

Information on Je-Wel/Petty recordings courtesy of John Beecher, Bill Inglot, and Allen Rush.

Chapter Nine

"He's Made $2 Million on Disks—Without a Desk" by Edwin Howard, Memphis *Press Scimitar*, 1959.

"Howard Tells How Forty-Leven Times Was Recorded" by Edwin Howard, Memphis *Press Scimitar*, 1959.

"Platter Sales Route Strewn With Roadblocks: How Forty-Leven Times Fared" by Edwin Howard, Memphis *Press Scimitar*, 1959.

"Bill Riley, Roland James (sic) Produce, Lease Records" by Edwin Howard. Memphis *Press Scimitar*, September 8, 1959.

"Bandleader Justis Sets Up Record Company in Memphis" by Edwin Howard, Memphis *Press Scimitar*, April 20, 1959.

"Golden Notes Played by Sid Manker, Local Musician" by William A. Bruning, Memphis *Commercial Appeal*, September 27, 1959.

"Guitarist Sid Manker Tells Why It's Hell To Be a Drug Addict" by Joseph Sweat, Memphis *Press Scimitar*, January 1, 1960.

"Co-Composer of 'Raunchy' Must Serve Time" by Elton Whisenhunt, Memphis *Press Scimitar*, April 29, 1960.

Billy Riley interviewed by Bill Millar, 1973 (unpublished).

"Let's All Help the Cowboy Sing the Blues" by Peter Guralnick in *Lost Highway* (Boston: David R. Godine, 1979).

"J. M. Van Eaton: Rockabilly Rhythm" by Rob Bowman and Ross Johnson, *Modern Drummer*, Vol. 11, No. 5.

"Roland Janes: Behind the Scenes at Sun" by Rob Bowman and Ross Johnson, *Journal of Country Music*, Vol. 10, No. 3.

"Stan Kesler: The Flip Side of the Sun Sound" by Rob Bowman and Ross Johnson, *Journal of Country Music*, Vol. 12, No. 3, and Vol. 13, No. 1.

Chapter Ten

Billy Riley interviewed by Bill Millar, 1973 (unpublished); Liner notes to *Billy Riley: The Classic Recordings* by Rob Bowman and Ross Johnson, Bear Family. BCD 15444.

"Warren Smith" by Adam Komorowski, *New Kommotion*, No. 22.

"Sonny Burgess" booklet by Adam Komorowski, New Kommotion Publications, 1984.

Chapter Eleven

Lewis has attracted four attempts at a biography. None is entirely satisfactory; as a
compelling read, *Hellfire* by Nick Tosches (New York: Dell, 1982) is best. *Great
Balls of Fire* by Myra Gale Lewis with Murray Silver (New York: Quill, 1982) is
also good—better than one might expect, bearing in mind that it was used as the
basis for the execrable bio-pic of the same name.

Jerry Lee Lewis interviewed by David Booth, issued as a bonus record with *Jerry Lee
Lewis: The Killer, 1963–1968,* Bear Family Records, BFX 15210.

"Roland Janes: Behind the Scenes at Sun" by Rob Bowman and Ross Johnson, *Journal
of Country Music,* Vol. 10, No. 3.

"J. M. Van Eaton: Rockabilly Rhythm" by Rob Bowman and Ross Johnson, *Modern
Drummer,* Vol. 11, No. 5.

Sam Phillips interviewed by Robert Palmer, *Memphis* magazine, Vol. 3, No. 9.

"Fans Still Love Jerry Lee," by Henry Mitchell, Memphis *Commercial Appeal,* June
27, 1958.

"Jerry Lee Lewis: The Sun Sound" by Hank Davis in SUNBOX 102.

Chapter Twelve

"The Silver Fox at Bay" by Peter Guralnick, *Country Music,* June 1976.

"Charlie Rich: It's Been a Long Hard Climb," *Melody Maker,* December 28, 1974.

"Portrait of a Late Bloomer" by Peter McCabe, *Country Music,* June 1974.

"Charlie Rich Supplement," *Billboard,* September 14, 1974.

"Good Evening" column by Robert Johnson, Memphis *Press Scimitar,* May 17, 1963.

"Charley (sic) Rich Sues Phillips," Memphis *Press Scimitar,* June 13, 1963.

"Sam Phillips Says Rich Will Dismiss Lawsuit," Memphis *Press Scimitar,* June 14,
1963.

Chapter Thirteen

"Plush Phillips Studios Open Tomorrow," by Edwin Howard, Memphis *Press Scimitar,*
September 16, 1960.

"Phillips Opens Swank Studios," by Charlie Lamb, *Music Reporter,* September 26,
1960.

"Mood Lighting Is Artist Aid at Phillips Nashville Studio," by Charlie Lamb, *Music
Reporter,* June 12, 1961.

Discographical Note:

Information relating to Sun Records sessions is contained in *Sun Records: The Dis-
cography* (Vollersode, West Germany: Bear Family Books, 1987). Available from:
Showtime Music, 191 Concord Ave., Toronto, Ont., Canada M6H 2P2.

APPENDIX B: SUN RECORDS AND AFFILIATED LABELS NUMERICAL LISTINGS

Note 1: Song and artist descriptions occasionally varied according to where and when the record was pressed. Spellings reflect initial pressings, and may not be consistent with names and titles as given in the text.

Note 2: Labels are sequenced in the order in which they were launched.

Record No. / Artist	Titles	Release Date
1. 'The Phillips'		
9001 JOE HILL LOUIS **9002**	Gotta Let You Go / Boogie in the Park	Aug. 1950
NOTE: Single had different numbers on A and B sides.		
2. Sun Records: Part 1: Singles		
174 JACKIE BOY AND LITTLE WALTER	Blues in My Condition / Sellin' My Whiskey	
NOTE: Sun 174 unissued.		

175	JOHNNY LONDON—Alto Wizard	Drivin' Slow / Flat Tire	Apr. 1952
176	WALTER BRADFORD and the Big City Four	Dreary Nights / Nuthin' But the Blues	Apr. 1952
177	GAY GARTH HANDY JACKSON	Got My Application Baby / Trouble (Will Bring You Down)	Jan. 1953
178	JOE HILL LOUIS	We All Gotta Go Sometime / She May Be Yours (But She Comes to See Me Sometime)	Jan. 1953
179	WILLIE NIX (The Memphis Blues Boy)	Baker Shop Boogie / Seems Like a Million Years	Jan. 1953
180	JIMMY and WALTER	Easy / Before Long	Mar. 1953
181	RUFUS "Hound Dog" THOMAS Jr.	Bear Cat (The Answer to "Hound Dog") / Walkin' in the Rain	Mar. 1953
182	DUSTY BROOKS and His Tones	Heaven or Fire / Tears and Wine	Mar. 1953
183	D. A. HUNT	Lonesome Ol' Jail / Greyhound Blues	June 1953
184	BIG MEMPHIS MARAINEY— Onzie Horne Combo	Call Me Anything But Call Me / Baby No! No!	June 1953
185	JIMMY DeBERRY	Take a Little Chance / Time Has Made a Change	June 1953
186	THE PRISONAIRES	Baby Please / Just Walkin' in the Rain	July 1953
187	LITTLE JUNIOR'S BLUE FLAMES	Feelin' Good / Fussin' and Fightin' (Blues)	July 8, 1953
188	RUFUS THOMAS Junior	Tiger Man (King of the Jungle) / Save That Money	July 8, 1953
189	THE PRISONAIRES— Confined to Tennessee State Penitentiary, Nashville	My God Is Real / Softly and Tenderly	July 8, 1953
190	RIPLEY COTTON CHOPPERS	Blues Waltz / Silver Bells	Sept. 1953
191	THE PRISONAIRES— Confined to Tennessee State Penitentiary, Nashville	A Prisoner's Prayer / I Know	Nov. 1, 1953

192	LITTLE JUNIOR'S BLUE FLAMES	Mystery Train / Love My Baby	Nov. 1, 1953
193	DOCTOR ROSS	Come Back Baby / Chicago Breakdown	Dec. 24, 1953
194	LITTLE MILTON	Beggin' My Baby / Somebody Told Me	Dec. 24, 1953
195	BILLY "The Kid" EMERSON	No Teasing Around / If Lovin' Is Believing	Feb. 20, 1954
196	HOT SHOT LOVE	Wolf Call Boogie / Harmonica Jam	Feb. 20, 1954
197	EARL PETERSON— Michigan's Singing Cowboy	Boogie Blues / In the Dark	Feb. 20, 1954
198	HOWARD SERATT	Troublesome Waters / I Must Be Saved	Feb. 20, 1954
199	JAMES COTTON	My Baby / Straighten Up Baby	Apr. 15, 1954
200	LITTLE MILTON	If You Love Me / Alone and Blue	Apr. 15, 1954
201	HARDROCK GUNTER	Gonna Dance All Night / Fallen Angel	May 1, 1954
202	DOUG POINDEXTER— Starlite Wranglers	No She Cares No More for Me / My Kind of Carryin' On	May 1, 1954
203	BILLY "The Kid" EMERSON	I'm Not Going Home / The Woodchuck	May 1, 1954
204	RAYMOND HILL	Bourbon Street Jump / The Snuggle	May 1, 1954
205	HARMONICA FRANK	The Great Medical Menagerist / Rockin' Chair Daddy	July 1, 1954
206	JAMES COTTON	Cotton Crop Blues / Hold Me in Your Hands	July 1, 1954
207	PRISONAIRES	There Is Love in You / What'll You Do Next	July 1, 1954
208	BUDDY CUNNINGHAM Cliff Parman's Orchestra	Right Or Wrong / Why Do I Cry	July 15, 1954
209	ELVIS PRESLEY— Scotty and Bill	That's All Right / Blue Moon of Kentucky	July 19, 1954
210	ELVIS PRESLEY— Scotty and Bill	Good Rockin' Tonight / I Don't Care If the Sun Don't Shine	Sept. 22, 1954

211	MALCOLM YELVINGTON—Star Rhythm Boys	Drinkin' Wine Spo-Dee-O-Dee / Just Rollin' Along	Nov. 10, 1954
212	DOCTOR ROSS	The Boogie Disease / Jukebox Boogie	Nov. 10, 1954
213	THE JONES BROTHERS	Look to Jesus / Every Night	Jan. 8, 1955
214	BILLY "The Kid" EMERSON	Move Baby, Love / When It Rains It Pours	Jan. 8, 1955
215	ELVIS PRESLEY—Scotty and Bill	Milkcow Blues Boogie / You're a Heartbreaker	Jan. 8, 1955
216	SLIM RHODES	Don't Believe (Vocal: Brad Suggs) / Uncertain Love (Vocal: Dusty & Dot)	Apr. 1, 1955
217	ELVIS PRESLEY—Scotty and Bill	I'm Left, You're Right, She's Gone / Baby Let's Play House	Apr. 25, 1955
218	SAMMY LEWIS–WILLIE JOHNSON COMBO	I Feel So Worried / So Long Baby Goodbye	Apr. 25, 1955
219	BILLY "The Kid" EMERSON	Red Hot / No Greater Love	June 21, 1955
220	LITTLE MILTON	Homesick for My Baby / Lookin' for My Baby	June 21, 1955
221	JOHNNY CASH—Tennessee Two	Cry! Cry! Cry! / Hey! Porter	June 21, 1955
222	FIVE TINOS	Don't Do That / Sittin' by the Window	June 21, 1955
223	ELVIS PRESLEY—Scotty and Bill	Mystery Train / I Forgot to Remember to Forget	Aug. 1, 1955
224	CARL PERKINS	Let the Jukebox Keep on Playing / Gone! Gone! Gone!	Aug. 1, 1955
225	SLIM RHODES	The House of Sin (Vocal: Dusty and Dot) / Are You Ashamed of Me? (Vocal: Brad Suggs)	Aug. 1, 1955
226	EDDIE SNOW	Ain't That Right / Bring Your Love Back Home to Me	Aug. 1, 1955
227	ROSCO GORDON	Just Love Me Baby / Weeping Blues	Sept. 1955
228	SMOKEY JOE	The Signifying Monkey / Listen to Me Baby	Sept. 15, 1955

229	MAGGIE SUE WIMBERLY	Daydreams Come True / How Long	Dec. 1955
230	THE MILLER SISTERS	There's No Right Way to Do Me Wrong / You Can Tell Me	Jan. 15, 1956
231	CHARLIE FEATHERS	Defrost Your Heart / Wedding Gown of White	Dec. 1955
232	JOHNNY CASH—Tennessee Two	So Doggone Lonesome / Folsom Prison Blues	Dec. 15, 1955
233	BILLY "The Kid" EMERSON	Little Fine Healthy Thing / Something for Nothing	Jan. 15, 1956
234	CARL PERKINS	Blue Suede Shoes / Honey, Don't!	Dec. 1955
235	CARL PERKINS	Sure to Fall / Tennessee	

NOTE: Sun 235 unissued. May have been scheduled as Carl and Jay Perkins

236	JIMMY HAGGETT	No More / They Call Our Love a Sin	Dec. 1955
237	ROSCO GORDON	The Chicken (Dance With You) / Love for You, Baby	Dec. 1955
238	SLIM RHODES	Gonna Romp and Stomp (Vocal: Dusty and Dot) / Bad Girl (Vocal: Brad Suggs)	Apr. 1956
239	WARREN SMITH	Rock and Roll Ruby / I'd Rather Be Safe Than Sorry	Apr. 1956
240	JACK EARLS and The Jimbos	Slow Down / A Fool for Loving You	Apr. 1956
241	JOHNNY CASH—Tennessee Two	Get Rhythm / I Walk the Line	Apr. 1956
242	ROY ORBISON—Teen Kings	Ooby Dooby / Go! Go! Go!	May 1956
243	CARL PERKINS	Boppin' the Blues / All Mama's Children	May 1956
244	JEAN CHAPEL	Welcome to the Club / I Won't Be Rockin' Tonight	June 1956
245	BILLY RILEY	Trouble Bound / Rock With Me Baby	May 1956
246	MALCOLM YELVINGTON	Rockin' With My Baby / It's Me Baby	Aug. 3, 1956

247	SONNY BURGESS	Red Headed Woman / We Wanna Boogie	Aug. 3, 1956
248	THE RHYTHM ROCKERS	Fiddle Bop (Voc: Buddy Durham) / Jukebox Help Me Find My Baby (Voc: Hardrock Gunter)	Aug. 3, 1956
249	CARL PERKINS	I'm Sorry I'm Not Sorry / Dixie Fried	Aug. 3, 1956
250	WARREN SMITH	Black Jack David / Ubangi Stomp	Sept. 24, 1956
251	ROY ORBISON—Teen Kings	You're My Baby / Rockhouse	Sept. 24, 1956
252	KENNETH PARCHMAN NOTE: Sun 252 unissued.	Love Crazy Baby / I Feel Like Rockin'	
253	BARBARA PITMAN	I Need a Man / No Matter Who's To Blame	Sept. 24, 1956
254	RAY HARRIS	Where'd You Stay Last Night / Come on Little Mama	Sept. 24, 1956
255	THE MILLER SISTERS	Ten Cats Down / Finders Keepers	Aug. 3, 1956
256	SLIM RHODES	Take and Give (Voc: Sandy Brooks) / Do What I Do (Voc: Sandy Brooks)	Nov. 21, 1956
257	ROSCO GORDON	Cheese and Crackers / Shoobie Oobie	Nov. 21, 1956
258	JOHNNY CASH— Tennessee Two	Train of Love / There You Go	Nov. 21, 1956
259	JERRY LEE LEWIS	Crazy Arms / End of the Road	Dec. 1, 1956
260	BILLY RILEY— and His Little Green Men	Flying Saucer Rock and Roll / I Want You Baby	Jan. 23, 1957
261	CARL PERKINS	Matchbox / Your True Love	Jan. 23, 1957
262	ERNIE CHAFFIN	Feelin' Low / Lonesome for My Baby	Jan. 23, 1957
263	SONNY BURGESS	Ain't Got a Thing / Restless	Jan. 24, 1957
264	GLENN HONEYCUTT	I'll Be Around / I'll Wait Forever	Jan. 24, 1957
265	ROY ORBISON— and The Roses	Sweet and Easy to Love / Devil Doll	Jan. 24, 1957

266	JOHNNY CASH— Tennessee Two	Don't Make Me Go / Next in Line	Mar. 15, 1957
267	JERRY LEE LEWIS	It'll Be Me / Whole Lot of Shakin' Going On	Mar. 15, 1957
268	WARREN SMITH	So Long I'm Gone / Miss Froggie	Apr. 15, 1957
269	WADE and DICK— The College Kids	Bop, Bop Baby / Don't Need Your Lovin' Baby	Apr. 15, 1957
270	JIMMY WILLIAMS	Please Don't Cry Over Me / That Depends on You	Sept. 14, 1957
271	RUDI RICHARDSON	Fools Hall of Fame / Why Should I Cry	Apr. 15, 1957
272	RAY HARRIS	Greenback Dollar, Watch and Chain / Foolish Heart	June 1957
273	MACK SELF	Every Day / Easy to Love	June 1957
274	CARL PERKINS	Forever Yours / That's Right	Aug. 15, 1957
275	ERNIE CHAFFIN	I'm Lonesome / Laughin' and Jokin'	Aug. 15, 1957
276	EDWIN BRUCE	Rock Boppin' Baby / More Than Yesterday	Aug. 15, 1957
277	BILLY RILEY— and His Little Green Men	Red Hot / Pearly Lee	Sept. 14, 1957
278	TOMMY BLAKE— Rhythm Rebels	Lordy Hoody / Flat Foot Sam	Sept. 14, 1957
279	JOHNNY CASH— and the Tennessee Two	Home of the Blues / Give My Love to Rose	Sept. 14, 1957
280	DICKEY LEE and The Collegiates	Memories Never Grow Old / Good Lovin'	Oct. 12, 1957
281	JERRY LEE LEWIS and His Pumping Piano	Great Balls of Fire / You Win Again	Nov. 3, 1957
282	DICK PENNER	Your Honey Love / Cindy Lou	Nov. 3, 1957
283	JOHNNY CASH— and the Tennessee Two	Ballad of a Teenage Queen / Big River	Dec. 1957
284	ROY ORBISON	Chicken Hearted / I Like Love	Dec. 1957
285	SONNY BURGESS	My Bucket's Got a Hole in It / Sweet Misery	Dec. 1957

286	WARREN SMITH	Got Love If You Want It / I Fell in Love	Dec. 1957
287	CARL PERKINS—The Rockin' Guitar Man	Glad All Over / Lend Me Your Comb (Vocal: Carl and Jay)	Dec. 1957
288	JERRY LEE LEWIS and His Pumping Piano	Down the Line / Breathless	Feb. 1958
289	BILLY RILEY— and His Little Green Men	Baby Please Don't Go / Wouldn't You Know	Feb. 1958
290	RUDY GRAYZELL	Judy / I Think of You	Apr. 9, 1958
291	JACK CLEMENT	Ten Years / Your Lover Boy	Apr. 9, 1958
292	EDWIN BRUCE	Sweet Woman / Part of My Life	Apr. 9, 1958
293	THE SUN RAYS	Love Is a Stranger / The Lonely Hours	Apr. 9, 1958
294	MAGEL PRIESMAN	I Feel So Blue / Memories of You	Apr. 9, 1958
295	JOHNNY CASH—and The Tennessee Two	Guess Things Happen That Way / Come in Stranger	Apr. 9, 1958
296	JERRY LEE LEWIS and His Pumping Piano	High School Confidential / Fools Like Me	Apr. 9, 1958
297	DICKEY LEE and the Collegiates	Fool, Fool, Fool / Dreamy Nights	Apr. 9, 1958
298	RAY SMITH	So Young / Right Behind You Baby	Apr. 9, 1958
299	GENE SIMMONS	Drinkin' Wine / I Done Told You	Apr. 9, 1958
300	TOMMY BLAKE	Sweetie Pie / I Dig You Baby	June 1958
301	Narration by GEORGE and LOUIS / JERRY LEE LEWIS	The Return of Jerry Lee / Lewis Boogie	June 1958
302	JOHNNY CASH—and the Tennessee Two	The Ways of a Woman in Love / You're the Nearest Thing to Heaven	May 1958
303	JERRY LEE LEWIS and His Pumping Piano	Break Up / I'll Make It All Up to You	Aug. 10, 1958
304	SONNY BURGESS	Itchy / Thunderbird	Aug. 10, 1958
305	ROSCO GORDON	Sally Jo / Torro	Sept. 20, 1958

306	JIMMY ISLE	I've Been Waiting / Diamond Ring	Oct. 25, 1958
307	ERNIE CHAFFIN	(Nothing Can Change) My Love for You / Born to Lose	Oct. 15, 1958
308	RAY SMITH	Why, Why, Why / You Made a Hit	Oct. 25, 1958
309	JOHNNY CASH—and the Tennessee Two	I Just Thought You'd Like to Know / It's Just About Time	Nov. 12, 1958
310	VERNON TAYLOR	Breeze / Today is a Blue Day	Nov. 12, 1958
311	JACK CLEMENT	The Black Haired Man / Wrong	Nov. 20, 1958
312	JERRY LEE LEWIS and His Pumping Piano	It Hurt Me So / I'll Sail My Ship Alone	Nov. 20, 1958
313	BILLY RILEY	No Name Girl / Down by the Riverside	Feb. 1, 1959
314	WARREN SMITH	Goodbye Mr. Love / Sweet Sweet Girl	Feb. 15, 1959
315	ONIE WHEELER	Jump Right Out of This Jukebox / Tell 'em Off	Feb. 15, 1959
316	JOHNNY CASH—and The Tennessee Two	Thanks a Lot / Luther Played the Boogie	Feb. 15, 1959
317	JERRY LEE LEWIS and His Pumping Piano	Lovin' Up a Storm / Big Blon' Baby	Feb. 15, 1959
318	JIMMY ISLE	Time Will Tell / Without a Love	Mar. 23, 1959
319	RAY SMITH	Sail Away / Rockin' Bandit	Mar. 23, 1959
320	ERNIE CHAFFIN	Don't Ever Leave Me / Miracle of You	Apr. 27, 1959
321	JOHNNY CASH—and The Tennessee Two	Katy Too / I Forgot to Remember to Forget	June 2, 1959
322	BILL RILEY	One More Time / Got the Water Boilin' Baby	June 2, 1959
323	ALTON AND JIMMY	Have Faith in My Love / No More Cryin' the Blues	June 2, 1959
324	JERRY LEE LEWIS and His Pumping Piano	Let's Talk About Us / The Ballad of Billy Jo	June 15, 1959
325	VERNON TAYLOR	Sweet and Easy to Love / Mystery Train	July 16, 1959

326	JERRY McGILL and the Topcoats	I Wanna Make Sweet Love / Lovestruck	Aug. 11, 1959
327	JOHNNY POWERS	With Your Love With Your Kiss / Be Mine, All Mine	Sept. 15, 1959
328	SHERRY CRANE	Willie, Willie / Winnie the Parakeet	Aug. 11, 1959
329	WILL MERCER	You're Just My Kind / The Ballad of St. Marks	Sept. 15, 1959
330	JERRY LEE LEWIS and His Pumping Piano	Little Queenie / I Could Never Be Ashamed of You	Sept. 15, 1959
331	JOHNNY CASH—and The Tennessee Two	You Tell Me / Goodbye Little Darlin'	Sept. 15, 1959
332	JIMMY ISLE	What a Life / Together	Sept. 15, 1959
333	RAY B. ANTHONY	Alice Blue Gown / St. Louis Blues	Oct. 25, 1959
334	JOHNNY CASH—Tennessee Two and the Gene Lowery Singers	Straight as in Love / I Love You Because	Dec. 31, 1959
335	TRACY PENDARVIS and the Swampers	A Thousand Guitars / Is It Too Late?	Jan. 1960
336	MACK OWEN	Walkin' and Talkin' / Somebody Just Like You	Jan. 1960
337	JERRY LEE LEWIS and His Pumping Piano	Old Black Joe (With the Gene Lowery Singers) / Baby Baby Bye Bye	Mar. 1960
338	PAUL RICHY With the Gene Lowery Singers	The Legend of the Big Steeple / Broken Hearted Willie	Mar. 8, 1960
339	RAYBURN ANTHONY	Whose Gonna Shoe Your Pretty Little Feet (With the Gene Lowery Singers) / There's No Tomorrow	Mar. 30, 1960
340	BILL JOHNSON With the Gene Lowery Singers	Bobaloo / Bad Times Ahead	Mar. 30, 1960
341	SONNY WILSON With the Gene Lowery Singers	The Great Pretender / I'm Gonna Take a Walk	Aug. 1, 1960
342	BOBBIE JEAN—Ernie Barton Orchestra	Cheaters Never Win / You Burned the Bridges	July 7, 1960
343	JOHNNY CASH—and the Tennessee Two	The Story of a Broken Heart / Down The Street to 301	July 14, 1960

344	JERRY LEWIS and His Pumping Piano	John Henry / Hang Up My Rock and Roll Shoes	Aug. 1, 1960
345	TRACY PENDARVIS	Southbound Line / Is It Me	Aug. 15, 1960
346	BILL STRENGTH With the Gene Lowery Singers	Senorita / Guess I'd Better Go	Sept. 12, 1960
347	JOHNNY CASH—and the Tennessee Two	Port of Lonely Hearts / Mean Eyed Cat	Oct. 1960
348	LANCE ROBERTS With the Gene Lowery Singers	The Good Guy Always Wins / The Time Is Right	Oct. 1960
349	TONY ROSSINI	I Gotta Know (Where I Stand) / Is It Too Late (With the Gene Lowery Singers)	Nov. 14, 1960
350	THE ROCKIN' STOCKINGS NOTE: Also issued as Sun 1960.	Yulesville USA / Rockin' Old Lang Syne	Nov. 14, 1960
351	IRA JAY II	You Don't Love Me / More Than Anything	Nov. 14, 1960
352	JERRY LEE LEWIS	When I Get Paid / Love's Made a Fool of Me	Nov. 14, 1960
353	ROY ORBISON NOTE: Reissue of Sun 265.	Sweet and Easy to Love / Devil Doll	Nov. 25, 1960
354	BOBBY SHERIDAN	Sad News (and the Gene Lowery Singers) / Red Man	Dec. 10, 1960
355	JOHNNY CASH—and the Tennessee Two	Oh, Lonesome Me (With the Gene Lowery Singers) / Life Goes On	Dec. 10, 1960
356	JERRY LEE LEWIS and His Pumpin' Piano	What'd I Say / Livin' Lovin' Wreck	Feb. 27, 1961
357	Unissued		
358	GEORGE KLEIN	U. T. Party Part I / U. T. Party Part II	Mar. 10, 1961
359	TRACY PENDARVIS	Belle of the Suwanee / Eternally	Apr. 25, 1961
360	WADE CAGLE and the Escorts	Groovey Train / Highland Rock	Apr. 25, 1961
361	ANITA WOOD	I'll Wait Forever / I Can't Show How I Feel	June 25, 1961
362	HAROLD DORMAN	I'll Stick by You / There They Go	May 21, 1961
363	JOHNNY CASH—and the Tennessee Two	Sugartime / My Treasure(r)	May 21, 1961

364	JERRY LEE LEWIS and His Pumping Piano	Cold, Cold Heart / It Won't Happen With Me	May 26, 1961
365	SHIRLEY SISK	I Forgot to Remember to Forget / Other Side	Aug. 1961
366	TONY ROSSINI	Well I Ask Ya / Darlena	Aug. 1961
367	JERRY LEE LEWIS and His Pumping Piano	Save the Last Dance for Me / As Long as I Live	Sept. 1, 1961
368	DON HOSEA	Since I Met You / U Huh Unh	Oct. 9, 1961
369	BOBBY WOOD NOTE: Sun 369 probably unissued.	Human Emotions / Everybody's Searchin'	Oct. 9, 1961
370	HAROLD DORMAN	Uncle Jonah's Place / Just One Step	Nov. 7, 1961
371	JERRY LEE LEWIS and His Pumping Piano	Bonnie B. / Money	Nov. 21, 1961
372	RAY SMITH	Travelin' Salesman / I Won't Miss You ('til You Go)	Nov. 21, 1961
373	RAYBURN ANTHONY	How Well I Know / Big Dream	Jan. 19, 1962
374	JERRY LEE LEWIS and His Pumping Piano	I've Been Twistin' / Ramblin' Rose	Jan. 19, 1962
375	RAY SMITH	Candy Doll / Hey, Boss Man	Feb. 9, 1962
376	JOHNNY CASH—and The Tennessee Two	Blue Train / Born to Lose	Apr. 27, 1962
377	HAROLD DORMAN	In the Beginning / Wait 'til Saturday Night	Apr. 4, 1962
378	TONY ROSSINI	(Meet Me) After School / Just Around the Corner	Apr. 4, 1962
379	JERRY LEE LEWIS and His Pumping Piano	Sweet Little Sixteen / How's My Ex Treating You	July 7, 1962
380	TONY ROSSINI and The Chippers	You Make It Sound So Easy / New Girl in Town	July 10, 1962
381	THE FOUR UPSETTERS	Midnight Soiree / Crazy Arms	Nov. 5, 1962
382	JERRY LEE LEWIS	Good Golly Miss Molly / I Can't Trust Me (In Your Arms)	Nov. 5, 1962
383	NOTE: Assigned to Johnny Cash but unissued.		

384	JERRY LEE LEWIS and His Pumping Piano	Teenage Letter / Seasons of My Heart (With Linda Gail Lewis)	Apr. 1963
385	LINDA GAIL LEWIS NOTE: Sun 385 unissued.	Nothin' Shakin' (But the Leaves on the Trees) / Sittin' and Thinking	
386	THE FOUR UPSETTERS	Surfin' Calliope / Wabash Cannonball	July 15, 1963
387	TONY ROSSINI	Nobody / Moved to Kansas City	July 15, 1963
388	THE TEENANGELS NOTE: Sun 388 only issued as promos.	Ain't Gonna Let You (Break My Heart) / Tell Me My Love	
389	BILLY ADAMS	Betty and Dupree / Got My Mojo Workin'	Jan. 1, 1964
390	BILL YATES and His T-Birds	Don't Step on My Dog / Stop, Wait and Listen	May 1, 1964
391	BILLY ADAMS—Duet: Billy Adams and Jesse Carter	Trouble in Mind / Lookin' for Mary Ann	May 1, 1964
392	JOHNNY CASH—and the Tennessee Two	Wide Open Road / Belshazar	May 1, 1964
393	SMOKEY JOE	The Signifying Money / Listen to Me Baby	May 1, 1964
394	BILLY ADAMS	Reconsider Baby / Ruby Jane	Sept. 1964
395	RANDY and the Radiants	Peek-a-Boo / Mountain High	Jan. 1965
396	JERRY LEE LEWIS	Carry Me Back to Old Virginia / I Know What It Means	Mar. 15, 1965
397	GORGEOUS BILL	Carleen / Too Late to Right My Wrong	Mar. 15, 1965
398	RANDY and the Radiants	My Way of Thinking / Truth From My Eyes	Nov. 25, 1965
399	BILL YATES	Big Big World / I Dropped My M&Ms	Feb. 1, 1966
400	THE JESTERS	Cadillac Man / My Babe	Feb. 1, 1966
401	BILLY ADAMS	Open the Door Richard / Rock Me Baby	Feb. 1, 1966

402	DANE STINIT	Don't Knock What You Don't Understand / Always on the Go	May 1966
403	DAVID HOUSTON NOTE: Reissue of Phillips International 3583	Sherry's Lips / Miss Brown	Oct. 10, 1966
404	THE CLIMATES	No You for Me / Breakin' Up Again	Feb. 1967
405	DANE STINIT	That Muddy Ole River (Near Memphis Tennessee) / Sweet Country Girl	Feb. 1967
406	BROTHER JAMES ANDERSON NOTE: Issued as "Gospel Series"	I'm Gonna Move in the Room With the Lord / I'm Tired, My Soul Needs Resting	Feb. 1967
407	LOAD OF MISCHIEF	Back in My Arms Again / I'm a Lover	Jan. 1968

3. Sun Records Part 2—EP Listing
EPA series

101	JOHNNY CASH	
102	JOHNNY CASH	
103	JOHNNY CASH	

NOTE: 101–103 advertised as available in October 1957 but probably not issued.

104	JERRY LEE LEWIS	(Tentative compilation)
105	JERRY LEE LEWIS	(Tentative compilation)
106	JERRY LEE LEWIS	(Tentative compilation)

NOTE: 104–106 not issued.

107	JERRY LEE LEWIS	The Great Ball of Fire
108	JERRY LEE LEWIS	Jerry Lee Lewis
109	JERRY LEE LEWIS	Jerry Lee Lewis
110	JERRY LEE LEWIS	Jerry Lee Lewis
111	JOHNNY CASH	Sings Hank Williams
112	JOHNNY CASH	Johnny Cash
113	JOHNNY CASH	I Walk the Line
114	JOHNNY CASH	His Top Hits
115	CARL PERKINS	Blue Suede Shoes

116 JOHNNY CASH	Home of the Blues	
117 JOHNNY CASH	So Doggone Lonesome	

4. Sun Records Part 3—LP Listing
LP / SLP series

1220 JOHNNY CASH — With His Hot and Blue Guitar

1225 CARL PERKINS — Dance Album of..

NOTE: Reissued with different jacket as 'Teenbeat'

1230 JERRY LEE LEWIS — Jerry Lee Lewis

1235 JOHNNY CASH — Sings the Songs That Made Him Famous

1240 JOHNNY CASH — Greatest

1245 JOHNNY CASH — Sings Hank Williams and Other Favorite Tunes

1250 VARIOUS ARTISTS — Million Sellers

NOTE: Reissued with different jacket as *Sun's Gold Hits, Volume 1*

1255 JOHNNY CASH — Now Here's . . .

1260 ROY ORBISON — At the Rockhouse

1265 JERRY LEE LEWIS — Jerry Lee's Greatest

1270 JOHNNY CASH — All Aboard the Blue Train

1275 JOHNNY CASH — Original Sun Sound

5. The Flip Label—Singles Listing

501 CARL PERKINS — Movie Magg / Turn Around

502 BILL TAYLOR—Clyde Leoppard's Snearly Ranch Boys — Lonely Sweetheart

BILL TAYLOR and SMOKEY JO Clyde Leoppard's Snearly Ranch Boys — Split Personality

503 CHARLIE FEATHERS — I've Been Deceived / Peepin' Eyes

504 THE MILLER SISTERS — Someday You Will Pay / You Didn't Think I Would

NOTE: Flip 503 and 504 also issued as Sun 503 and 504 after legal action from the Flip label in Los Angeles. Sun 227, 228, 231, and 237 also issued on Flip Records as Flip 227 etc.

3516 BUDDY BLAKE — You Pass Me By / Please Convince Me

3517 HAYDEN THOMPSON — Love My Baby / One Broken Heart

3518 BARBARA PITTMAN — Two Young Fools in Love / I'm Getting Better All the Time

3519 BILL JUSTIS and His Orchestra — Raunchy / Midnight Man

3520 JOHNNY CARROLL — That's The Way I Love / I'll Wait

3521 CLIFF THOMAS, ED and BARBARA — Treat Me Right / I'm on the Way Home

3522 BILL JUSTIS and His Orchestra — College Man / The Stranger (Vocal by the Spinners)

3523 WAYNE POWERS — My Love Song / Point of View

3524 BILL PINKY and The Turks Bill Justis Orchestra — After the Hop / Sally's Got a Sister

3525 BILL JUSTIS and His Orchestra — Wild Rice / Scroungie

3526 CARL McVOY — You Are My Sunshine / Tootsie

3527 BARBARA PITTMAN With the Bill Justis Orchestra — Everlasting Love / Cold, Cold Heart

3528 ERNIE BARTON — Stairway to Nowhere / Raining the Blues

3529 BILL JUSTIS ORCHESTRA — Cattywampus / Summer Holiday

3530 LEE MITCHELL—The Curley Money Trio — The Frog / A Little Bird Told Me

3531 CLIFF THOMAS, ED and BARBARA — Sorry I Lied / Leave It to Me

3532 CHARLIE RICH — Whirlwind / Philadelphia Baby

3533 MICKEY MILAN With the Bill Justis Orchestra — Somehow Without You (with the Montclairs) / The Picture (with Chorus)

3534 KEN COOK — Crazy Baby / I Was a Fool

3535 BILL JUSTIS and His Orchestra — Bop Train / String of Pearls-Cha Hot Cha

3536 CLEMENT TRAVELERS — The Minstrel Show / Three Little Guitars

3537 JIMMY DEMOPOULOS — Hopeless Love / If I Had My Way

3538 CLIFF THOMAS — All Your Love / Tide Wind

3539	CARL MANN	Mona Lisa / Foolish One
3540	EDWIN HOWARD	Forty 'leven Times / More Pretty Girls Than One
3541	ERNIE BARTON	Open the Door Richard / Shut Your Mouth
3542	CHARLIE RICH	Rebound / Big Man
3543	BOBBIE and the Boys	To Tell the Truth / Silly Blues
3544	BILL JUSTIS and His Orchestra	Flea Circus / Cloud Nine
3545	BRAD SUGGS	706 Union / Low Outside
3546	CARL MANN	Rockin' Love / Pretend
3547	MEMPHIS BELLS	The Midnite Whistle / Snow Job
3548	MACK SELF	Willie Brown / Mad at You
3549	BRAD SUGGS Orchestra and Chorus	I Walk the Line / Oo-wee
3550	CARL MANN	Some Enchanted Evening / I Can't Forget (and the Gene Lowery Chorus)
3551	SONNY BURGESS	A Kiss Goodnite / Sadie's Back in Town
3552	CHARLIE RICH	Lonely Weekends (The Gene Lowery Chorus) / Everything I Do Is Wrong
3553	BARBARA PITTMAN With the Gene Lowery Singers	The Eleventh Commandment / Handsome Man
3554	BRAD SUGGS	Cloudy / Partly Cloudy
3555	CARL MANN	South of the Border (With the Gene Lowery Singers) / I'm Coming Home
3556	DON HINTON	Jo-Ann (With the Gene Lowery Singers) / Honey Bee
3557	JEB STUART With the Gene Lowery Singers	Sunny Side of the Street / Take a Chance
3558	EDDIE BUSH	Baby I Don't Care / Vanished
3559	THE HAWK	I Get the Blues When it Rains / In the Mood
3560	CHARLIE RICH With the Gene Lowery Singers	Schooldays / Gonna Be Waiting
3561	DANNY STEWART	Somewhere Along the Line / I'll Change My Ways

3562 CHARLIE RICH	On My Knees / Stay
3563 BRAD SUGGS	My Gypsy / Sam's Tune
3564 CARL MANN	Wayward Wind / Born to Be Bad
3565 JIMMY LOUIS	Gone and Left Me Blues / Your Fool
3566 CHARLIE RICH	Who Will the Next Fool Be / Caught in the Middle
3567 JEB STUART	Dream / Coming Down With the Blues
3568 NELSON RAY	You're Everything / You've Come Home
3569 CARL MANN	If I Could Change You / I Ain't Got No Home
3570 JEAN DEE	My Greatest Hurt / Nothing Down (99 Years to Pay)
3571 BRAD SUGGS	Elephant Walk / Catching Up
3572 CHARLIE RICH	Just a Little Bit Sweet / It's Too Late
3573 MIKKI WILCOX	I Know What It Means / Willing and Waiting
3574 FREDDIE NORTH	Don't Make Me Cry / Someday She'll Come Along
3575 JEB STUART	Betcha Gonna Like It / Little Miss Love
3576 CHARLIE RICH	Easy Money / Midnight Blues
3577 THOMAS WAYNE	I Got it Made / The Quiet Look
3578 FRANK FROST	Crawlback / Jelly Roll King
3579 CARL MANN	When I Grow Too Old to Dream / Mountain Dew
3580 JEB STUART and the Chippers	I Ain't Never / In Love Again
3581 DAVID WILKINS	Thanks a Lot / There's Something About You
3582 CHARLIE RICH	Sittin' and Thinkin' / Finally Found Out
3583 DAVID HOUSTON	Sherry's Lips / Miss Brown
3584 CHARLIE RICH	There's Another Place I Can't Go / I Need Your Love
3585 JEANNE NEWMAN	Thanks a Lot / The Boy I Met Today
3586 THE QUINTONES	Times Sho' Gettin' Ruff / Softie

7. Phillips International Part 2—LP Listing
PILP or PLP series

1950 BILL JUSTIS and
His Orchestra

Cloud Nine (Far Out Tunes By . . .)

1955 GRAHAM FORBES and the Trio

The Martini Set

1960 CARL MANN

Like Mann!

1965 CHUCK FOSTER

At Hotel Peabody Overlooking Old
Man River

1970 CHARLIE RICH

Lonely Weekends With . . .

1975 FRANK FROST With
the Nighthawks

Hey, Boss Man!

1980 EDDIE BOND

Sings Greatest Country Gospel Hits

1985 FRANK BALLARD With
Phillip Reynolds' Band

Rhythm Blues Party

INDEX